北京市属高等学校人才强教计划项目（PHR201107151）资助

SPECIAL ENGLISH FOR BIOTECHNOLOGY

生物技术专业英语

▣ 苏东海　主编

化学工业出版社

·北京·

内容简介

本教材分为六章：生物技术基础入门、发酵工程、酶、细胞工程、基因工程、蛋白质工程。每章都包括阅读材料、词汇、练习和参考译文。入选的文章突出了最新成果和发展方向，同时也尽可能反映技术领域的基础知识，使读者在掌握了最新科技突破的同时又巩固了基本知识。为了扩大学生的专业阅读量，书后增加了阅读材料供学生和教师选用。

本书可作为生物技术、食品、生物制药等专业高职高专学生和应用型本科学生的专业英语教材或参考书。

图书在版编目（CIP）数据

生物技术专业英语/苏东海主编.—北京：化学工业出版社，2012.8（2023.10 重印）
ISBN 978-7-122-14939-8

Ⅰ.①生… Ⅱ.①苏… Ⅲ.①生物工程-英语-高等学校-教材 Ⅳ.①H31

中国版本图书馆 CIP 数据核字（2012）第 166047 号

责任编辑：李植峰　梁静丽	文字编辑：焦欣渝
责任校对：宋　夏	装帧设计：韩　飞

出版发行：化学工业出版社（北京市东城区青年湖南街 13 号　邮政编码 100011）
印　　装：涿州市般润文化传播有限公司
787mm×1092mm　1/16　印张 12　字数 331 千字　2023 年 10 月北京第 1 版第 7 次印刷

购书咨询：010-64518888　　　　　　　售后服务：010-64518899
网　　址：http://www.cip.com.cn

凡购买本书，如有缺损质量问题，本社销售中心负责调换。

定　　价：35.00 元

《生物技术专业英语》编写人员

主　　编　苏东海

副 主 编　訾韦力

编写人员（按姓名笔画排列）

王　宇（辽宁科技学院）

田　锦（北京农业职业学院）

史雅静（辽宁科技学院）

杨春华（北京科技职业学院）

李　颖（北京联合大学）

苏东海（北京电子科技职业学院）

张利民（北京科技经营管理学院）

张虎成（北京电子科技职业学院）

蒋　丹（北京联合大学）

訾韦力（北京服装学院）

前　言

生物技术的发展日新月异，取得了许多惊人的新成果，各国投入巨资，组织力量追踪和攻关，以促进这一新兴高科技的快速发展。生物技术可以解决人类所面临的诸如粮食问题、健康问题、环境问题以及能源问题，对国计民生产生巨大而深远的影响。

在科技领域，英语的重要性日益突出，生物技术领域的期刊大多要求以英语发表，重要的国际会议都以英语为工作语言，涉及生物技术类的公司所需的资料大多也是英文。专业英语是学生完成基础英语学习后的一门继续课程，通过指导学生阅读有关专业英语文献，使他们进一步提高阅读和翻译科技资料的能力，并能以英语为工具获取专业所需的信息，针对高职院校生物技术类专业英语教科书较少的现状，化学工业出版社组织了部分高职院校的老师编写了本教材。教材编写过程中坚持以下原则：有利于学生通过专业知识学英语；涉及生物技术的领域较宽，以便于学生扩大专业词汇量；课文难度略高于科普读物。入选的文章突出了最新成果和发展方向，同时也尽可能反映技术领域的基础知识，使读者在掌握了最新科技突破的同时又巩固了基本知识。对每篇文章都进行详细的注释和说明，并附有练习。我们希望本书能够帮助广大读者更好地掌握生物技术知识，提高阅读科技英语的能力。

本书共分六章，由苏东海主编，具体分工如下：第一章由訾韦力编写；第二章由苏东海和张虎成编写；第三章由杨春华编写；第四章由田锦、张利民编写；第五章由史雅静、王宇编写；第六章由蒋丹、李颖编写。为了扩大学生的专业阅读量，书后增加了阅读材料供学生和教师选用，阅读材料由訾韦力编写。中国农业大学许文涛、中国食品发酵工业研究院鲁军审阅了全书。本书可作为食品生物技术、生物制药等专业高职高专学生和应用型本科生的专业英语教材或参考书。本书得到了北京市属高等学校人才强教计划项目[PHR(IHLB)]资助。

由于编者水平有限，书中难免有许多不足之处，敬请广大读者批评指正，以便再版时补充修正。

编者
2013 年 3 月

Contents

Added Reading Material 160

参考文献 184

Chapter One

A Basic Primer on Biotechnology

Reading Material

1. Biotechnology Definition

Biotechnology can be broadly defined as "using living organisms or their products for commercial purposes". As such, biotechnology has been practiced by human society since the beginning of recorded history in such activities as baking bread/brewing alcoholic beverages or breeding food crops or domestic animals. A narrower and more specific definition of biotechnology is "the commercial application of living organisms or their products, which involves the deliberate manipulation of their DNA molecules". This definition implies a set of laboratory techniques developed within the last 20 years that have been responsible for the tremendous scientific and commercial interest in biotechnology, the founding of many new companies and universities. These laboratory techniques provide scientists with a spectacular vision of the design and function of living organisms, and provide technologists in many fields with the tools to implement exciting commercial applications.

(1) Genome

The complete set of genetic instructions for a living organism is contained in its genetic code, referred to as its genome. The genome for each organism differs by the number and size of chromosomes and the number of genes each contains. Each chromosome is composed of a single strand of deoxyribonucleic acid (DNA) and specialized protein molecules. Coding regions called genes are along the DNA strand of each chromosome. Only specific regions of each chromosome code for genes. Alternate forms of genes in each organism account for the differences between individuals. Each DNA strand is composed of similar repeating units called nucleotides. Four different nucleotide bases are present in DNA. They are adenine(A), thymine (T), cytosine (C), and guanine (G). The specific order of these bases in a gene coding region on the DNA strand specifies exact genetic instructions.

Two DNA strands are held together by bonds between the bases; these constitute base pairs. Often the size of a genome is referred to by its number of base pairs. Each time a cell divides, the full genome is replicated and each daughter cell receives an exact copy of the genetic code. Each strand of DNA directs the synthesis of a complementary strand with free nucleotides matching up with their new complementary bases on each of the strands. Strict base pairing is adhered to; A will only pair with T, and C will only pair with G. Each daughter cell receives one old and one new DNA strand.

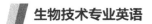

(2) Genes

The genes on each DNA strand contain the basic physical and functional units of heredity. A gene is a specific sequence of nucleotide bases, whose sequences carry the information required for constructing proteins. In turn, proteins regulate the expression of the genes and provide structural components and enzymes for biochemical reactions necessary for all living organisms. The protein-coding instructions from genes are transmitted indirectly through messenger ribonucleic acid (mRNA), a transient intermediary molecule similar to a single strand of DNA. For the information within a gene to be expressed, a complementary RNA strand is produced (by a process called transcription) from the DNA template in the nucleus. This mRNA is moved from the nucleus to the cellular cytoplasm, where it serves as the template for protein synthesis. The cell's protein-synthesizing machinery then translates the genetic code, or condons, into a string of amino acids that well constitute the protein molecule (by a process called translation) encoded by the gene. Following modification, the resulting protein can begin its function either as an enzyme, structural or regulatory protein.

Proteins are large, complex molecules made up of long chains of amino acid subunits. There are 20 different amino acids. Within a gene, each specific sequence of three DNA bases (condons) directs the cell's protein-synthesizing machinery to add a specific amino acid. For example, the base sequence ATG codes for the amino acid methionine (any biochemistry text will have a complete list of amino acids and their corresponding condons). The genetic code is thus a series of condons that specify which amino acids are required to make the specific protein a gene codes for. The genetic code is the same for all living organisms.

Not all genes are expressed in all tissues. For example, the tassel and developing ears on a corn plant (Zea mays) produce pollen and embryos that will develop into seed. The differences between these two plant parts are ultimately controlled by gene expression. The differential expression of genes is controlled by its promoter. The expression of a few genes in plants is controlled by environmental factors such as sunlight, temperature, and day length. These three factors are important in triggering flowering in many plant species.

2. Using of biotechnology

Biotechnology includes a vast array of tools used in research and modification of biological systems. These include: genetic mapping, the process of identifying the location of a gene on a chromosome and elucidating the gene sequence; molecular based disease diagnosis, identifying specific alleles (alternate forms of a gene) of a gene which cause genetic diseases; gene therapy, replacing an absent or defective gene with a working one enabling normal body function; forensic science, solving crimes and identifying human remains not previously possible; and genetic transformation, movement of a gene or group of genes from one organism to another. This process is also called genetic engineering.

(1) Genetic Transformation (genetic engineering)

Genetic transformation is the area of biotechnology that has created the greatest amount of stir and which will be the focus from this point on. Organisms with genetic material from another organism are often referred to as genetically modified organisms or GMOs. Since all crop and domesticated animal species have been genetically modified since the dawn of time, technically they are also GMOs. When referring to organisms with a gene from another species, transgenic is a more accurate description.

Many of the processes of biotechnology have been used for many years. Insulin from pigs and cows was historically used to treat diabetes and was beneficial to a many. However, there was not a consistent supply and some individuals developed adverse reactions to this type of insulin because their bodies recognized it as foreign and mounted an immune response. Human insulin produced through cloning and inserting human genes in bacteria resulted in insulin that did not cause an immune response. This was the first pharmaceutical produced through biotechnology and it has insured a consistent reliable source of human insulin.

Before a gene is transferred to another organism it must be identified, isolated and cloned. In the laboratory, the mRNA molecule from a gene being expressed can be isolated and used as a template to synthesize a complementary DNA (cDNA) strand. This isolated cDNA strand can then be cloned (duplicated) for transformation into another species. The cDNA strand can be used to locate the corresponding gene on a chromosome, or map it.

Transformation is typically accomplished by using either Agrobacterium tumefaciens or particle acceleration and the gene gun. Agrobacterium tumefaciens is a bacteria that occurs in nature. It contains a small circular piece of DNA called a Ti plasmid (Ti for tumor inducing). When this bacterium infects certain woody plant species, the Ti plasmid enters cells of the host plant. Certain regions of the Ti plasmid insert themselves into the host cell's genome. This insertion occurs in a region of the DNA strand with a specific sequence. The host cell then expresses the gene from the bacteria, which induces massive cell growth and the resultant plant tumor the bacteria is named for. Biotechnology utilizes this natural transformation process by removing the bacterial genes from the region transferred to the host genome and substituting genes of interest. Agrobacterium use for transformation is limited because it will only infect certain dicotyledonous species.

The other transformation process involves coating gold particles with genes of interest. The gold particles are shot into single cells of the plant of interest with the gene gun. This is commonly referred to as particle acceleration. In a process not fully understood, the transgene(s) are incorporated into a DNA strand of the host genome. This process is inefficient but does not have the host species limitation of Agrobacterium.

Both processes require the use of plant tissue culture. Individual cells of the plant to be transformed are cultured. These are then subjected to the transformation process. Non-transformed cells must be eliminated. This is done with selectable marker genes. In the case of the Roundup Ready gene, Roundup (glyphosate) is used directly as the selectable marker, since Roundup will kill non-transformed cells. When another trait of interest is being transformed in the crop, a selectable marker like antibiotic or herbicide resistance is used. The cells in culture are treated with the herbicide or an antibiotic. Only those cells that were transformed with the two genes will survive. Whole plants are then regenerated from the single cells that survive.

Following transformation and plant regeneration, the transgenic plants must be tested in the field to ensure that the transgene functions properly. Not all transgenic plants will express the trait or gene product properly. Once a transgenic plant that expresses the trait has been identified and is stable, then the trait can be bred using conventional plant breeding methods into cultivars with adaptation to the environmental conditions where the crop is produced.

(2) Specific applications of genetic engineering

Specific applications of genetic engineering are abundant and increasing rapidly in number.

Genetic engineering is being used in the production of pharmaceuticals, gene therapy, and the development of transgenic plants and animals.

① Pharmaceuticals

Human drugs such as insulin for diabetics, growth hormone for individuals with pituitary dwarfism, and tissue plasminogen activator for heart attack victims, as well as animal drugs like the growth hormones, bovine or porcine somatotropin, are being produced by the fermentation of transgenic bacteria that have received the appropriate human, cow, or pig gene.

② Gene Therapy

The first clinical gene therapy is underway to correct an enzyme deficiency called ADA in children. Bone marrow cells are removed, defective DNA in bone marrow cells is supplemented with a copy of normal DNA, and the repaired cells are then returned to the patient's body.

③ Transgenic Plants

Transgenic plants that are more tolerant of herbicides, resistant to insect or viral pests, or express modified versions of fruit or flowers have been grown and tested in outdoor test plots since 1987. The genes for these traits have been delivered to the plants from other unrelated plants, bacteria, or viruses by genetic engineering techniques.

④ Transgenic Animals

Presently, most transgenic animals are designed to assist researchers in the diagnosis and treatment of human diseases. Several companies have designed and are testing transgenic mammals that produce important pharmaceuticals in the animal's milk. Products such as insulin, growth hormone, and tissue plasminogen activator that are currently produced by fermentation of transgenic bacteria may soon be obtained by milking transgenic cows, sheep, or goats.

3. Using Biotechnology in Diagnostic Applications

Since each living creature is unique, each has a unique DNA recipe. Individuals within any given species, breed, or hybrid line can usually be identified by minor differences in their DNA sequences- as few as one difference in a million letters can be detected! Using the techniques of DNA fingerprinting and PCR(polymerase chain reaction) scientists can diagnose viral, bacterial, or fungal infections, distinguish between closely related individuals, or map the locations of specific genes along the vast length of the DNA molecules in the cells.

(1) Identifying Organisms

By using RFLP technology (restriction fragment length polymorphism), DNA fingerprints can be generated. Any individual organism can be uniquely identified by its DNA fingerprint. DNA Consequently, this fingerprint can be used to determine family relationships in paternity litigation, match organ donors with recipients in transplant programs, connect suspects with DNA evidence left at the scene of a crime (in the form of hair or body fluids), or serve as a pedigree for seed or livestock breeds.

(2) Identifying Genes

One important aspect of genetic engineering projects is to identify the DNA gene that controls a particular trait. In the same way that a visitor might use state, city, street, and house number to locate a friend's house, genetic engineers use genetic maps to locate genes. The genetic maps are generated by statistical analyses, PCR, RFLP, DNA sequencing. Maps are being developed for humans, mice, swine, cattle, corn, wheat, and other plants or animals with commercial or research importance.

(3) Diagnosing Infectious Diseases and Genetic Disorders

Diagnosis of infectious diseases is a profound application of new DNA technology. Tuberculosis, AIDS, papilloma virus, and many other infectious diseases, addition to the inherited disorders cystic fibrosis or sickle cell anemia, are diagnosed within hours by the PCR technique rather days or weeks by traditional methods. The greatly increased sensitivity and speed of the PCR technique, as compared with traditional methods, allows earlier intervention and treatment. PCR assays will soon be available to diagnose diseases of crops and livestock.

Glossary

1. living organism	生物体
2. brewing	*n.* 酿造
3. molecule	*n.* 分子
4. genetically modified organisms (GMOs)	转基因生物
5. genome	*n.* 基因组，染色体组
6. chromosome	*n.* 同源染色体
7. deoxyribonucleic acid	脱氧核糖核酸
8. protein	*n.* 蛋白质
9. nucleotide	*n.* 核苷酸
10. adenine(A)	*n.* 腺嘌呤
11. thymine (T)	*n.* 胸腺嘧啶
12. cytosine (C)	*n.* 胞核嘧啶，氧氢嘧啶
13. guanine (G)	*n.* 鸟嘌呤(核酸的基本成分)
14. daughter cell	*n.* 子细胞
15. enzymes	*n.* 酶类，酵素；酶（enzyme 的复数）
16. messenger ribonucleic acid (mRNA)	*n.* 信使核糖核酸
17. intermediary	*n.* 中间人；调解人；媒介物
18. template	*n.* 样板；模板；标准
19. the cellular cytoplasm	细胞质
20. condon	密码子
21. amino acids	氨基酸类
22. methionine	*n.* 蛋氨酸，甲硫氨酸
23. tassel	*n.* 穗，缨，流苏
24. pollen	*n.* 花粉
25. embryo	*n.* 〈生〉胚，胚胎
26. mapping	映射，绘制……的地图，计划
	等位基因
27. alleles	*adj.* 用于法庭的；法医的
28. forensic	*n.* 胰岛素
29. insulin	*n.* 1.〈医〉糖尿病；2. 多尿症
30. diabetes	*adj.* 制药的；配药的；卖药的
31. pharmaceutical	*n.* 药物

32. Agrobacterium tumefaciens	根癌土壤杆菌
33. plasmid	*n.* 质粒，质体
34. plant tumor	植物瘤
35. dicotyledonous	*adj.* 双子叶的
36. glyphosate	*n.* 草甘膦
37. antibiotic or herbicide	抗生素或除草剂
38. cultivar	*n.* 栽培品种
39. pituitary dwarfism	垂体性侏儒症
40. plasminogen	*n.* 血纤维蛋白溶酶原,血浆酶原
41. bovine	*adj.* 牛的，关于牛的，迟钝的，笨拙的
	n. 牛；牛科动物
42. porcine somatotropin	猪源生长激素
43. marrow	*n.* 骨髓；脊髓；髓
44. mammals	*n.* 哺乳动物
45. hybrid	*n.* 杂交生成的生物体，杂交植物(或动物)；
46. fungal	*adj.* 真菌的，由真菌引起的
47. polymorphism	*n.* 多型现象，多态性
48. paternity litigation	亲子鉴定
49. pedigree	*n.* 世系，家谱，系谱
	adj. 纯种的
50. tuberculosis	*n.* 肺结核，结核病
51. papilloma virus	*n.* 乳突淋瘤病毒，刺瘤病毒
52. cystic fibrosis	*n.* 囊性纤维化 (属遗传性胰腺病)
53. sickle cell	*n.* 镰状细胞，镰刀形红细胞
54. assays	*n.* 化验，试金，分析试验

Exercises

1. *Matching*

① living organism — (a) any of a large group of nitrogenous organic compounds that are essential constituents of living cells; consist of polymers of amino acids, essential in the diet of animals for growth and for repair of tissues

② enzyme — (b) using living organisms or their products for commercial purposes

③ genome — (c) a living thing that has (or can develop) the ability to act or function independently

④ protein — (d) the ordering of genes in a haploid set of chromosomes of a particular organism; the full DNA sequence of an organism

⑤ brewing — (e) any of several complex proteins that are produced by cells and act as catalysts in specific biochemical reactions

⑥ Biotechnology — (f) making (beer) by soaking, boiling, and fermentation

2. Fill in the blanks with the words or expressions given below, and change the form where necessary.

genome	genetic engineering	DNA fingerprinting
DNA gene	brewing	gene

① Biotechnology has been practiced by human society since the beginning of recorded history in such activities as baking bread/_____ alcoholic beverages or breeding food crops or domestic animals.

② The complete set of genetic instructions for a living organism is contained in its genetic code, referred to as its _____.

③ A _____ is a specific sequence of nucleotide bases, whose sequences carry the information required for constructing proteins.

④ _____ is being used in the production of pharmaceuticals, gene therapy, and the development of transgenic plants and animals.

⑤ Using the techniques of _____ and PCR(polymerase chain reaction) scientists can diagnose viral, bacterial, or fungal infections, distinguish between closely related individuals, or map the locations of specific genes along the vast length of the DNA molecules in the cells.

⑥ One important aspect of genetic engineering projects is to identify the _____ that controls a particular trait.

Translation

生物技术基础入门

1. 生物技术的定义

从广义上说，生物技术可以定义为"为了商业目的而对生物体及其产品进行利用的行为或手段"。从这一定义来看，可以说有历史记载以来，人类社会就在实践活动中应用了生物技术，如烤面包、酿酒、种植庄稼或饲养家禽等。从狭义上说，对生物技术更科学的定义是"通过对生物体及其产品的 DNA 分子进行操作而达到商业应用目的的行为或手段"。在这一定义中体现了近 20 年发展起来的一系列实验室技术，这些技术不仅对生物技术领域中巨大的科技及商业利益，也对许多新的公司及大学的建立起着重要的作用。这些实验室技术不仅为科学家们提供了剖析生物体构造和功能的深入视野，也在许多领域为技术人员提供了实现商业应用的手段。

（1）基因组

生物体的遗传代码中包含了一整套的遗传信息，称作基因组。各生物体的基因组因染色体数目、大小以及每条染色体所含基因数的不同而不同。每条染色体是由一个单链脱氧核糖核酸（DNA）分子和数个特异化蛋白质分子组成的。每条染色体 DNA 的编码区，称为基因。每条染色体上只有特定的区域才能编码基因。不同生物体内基因的不同造就了个体之间的差异。每条 DNA 链是由称作核苷酸的近似重复单位组成，DNA 中含有四种不同的核苷酸碱基。

它们是腺嘌呤（A）、胸腺嘧啶（T）、胞嘧啶（C）及鸟嘌呤（G）。这些核苷酸碱基在 DNA 链上基因编码区的专门序列指定了精确的遗传指令信息。

碱基之间通过键将两条 DNA 链结合起来，构成碱基对。基因组的大小通常指碱基对的数量。每次细胞分裂时，整个基因组都会进行复制，每个子细胞会收到遗传代码的精确拷贝。每条单链 DNA 链与游离核苷酸结合，引导合成新的互补链。遵守严格的配对原则。腺嘌呤只与胸腺嘧啶配对，胞嘧啶只与鸟嘌呤配对。每个子细胞获得一条旧 DNA 链和一条新 DNA 链。

（2）基因

每一条 DNA 链上的基因包含遗传的基本生理及功能单位。基因是具有特定序列的核苷酸碱基，其序列携带合成蛋白质所需的信息。反过来，蛋白质调控基因表达，提供所有生物体生化反应中所需的结构成分及酶。来自基因的蛋白质编码指令间接通过信使核糖核酸（mRNA，一种类似于单链 DNA 的中介）传递。对于基因内要表达的信息，在核内会根据 DNA 模板生成互补的 RNA 链（这一过程称为转录）。mRNA 从细胞核转入细胞质中，作为蛋白合成的模板。细胞的蛋白质合成机制把基因代码（或密码子）翻译成相应的氨基酸序列，从而精确地构建由基因编码的蛋白质分子（这一过程称为翻译）。通过修饰，生成的蛋白质即以酶、结构蛋白或调节蛋白的形式发挥功能。

蛋白质是由氨基酸所组成的长链、复杂大分子，氨基酸的种类包括 20 种。在一个基因内，三个 DNA 碱基（密码子）所构成的不同特定序列可以引导细胞的蛋白质合成机制添加相应的特定氨基酸。例如，碱基序列 ATG 编码蛋氨酸（任何生物课本中都有氨基酸及其相应密码子的完整列表）。因此，遗传代码就是一系列密码子，它们指定了需要哪些氨基酸来构成一个由基因编码的特定蛋白质。遗传代码在所有生物体内都是通用的。

并非所有基因都可在任意组织中表达。比如，玉米（玉蜀黍属）植株上的穗和棒分别产生出玉米花粉和胚胎，进而生成种子。最终是由基因表达来控制这两个植物部分的差异。基因在不同组织中的不同表达是受启动子控制的。植物中的个别基因表达也受环境因素（如阳光、温度和日长）所控制。这三个因素在促使植物开花方面起着重要的作用。

2. 生物技术的应用

生物技术包括在生物系统研究与改造过程中所使用的大量技术手段。这些技术包括遗传图谱（鉴定染色体上某个基因的位置并阐明基因序列）、分子疾病诊断（鉴定引起遗传疾病的特定等位基因）、基因治疗（用正常功能的基因替代有缺失或缺陷的基因）、法医技术（破案和鉴定人体遗骸）和转基因（一个或一组基因从一个生物体转化到另一个生物体中的技术，也称作基因工程）。

（1）转基因（基因工程）

转基因曾在生物技术领域产生了巨大的轰动，今后也会继续成为研究热点。携带来自另一生物体遗传物质的生物通常称作转基因生物（GMO）。自古以来，所有粮食、家禽、家畜在遗传学上都已经发生了变化，所以从技术上可以称其为转基因生物。不过，将携带来自另一物种基因的生物体称作转基因生物才更为确切。

生物技术的应用已经有许多年的历史。例如，使用来自猪、牛的胰岛素治疗糖尿病和其它疾病。然而，这类胰岛素现在并没有得到继续应用，因为有些病人的身体会将这些胰岛素视为异物并产生免疫反应，从而产生副作用。人胰岛素是通过克隆技术并在细菌中嵌入人基因而生产出的、不会产生免疫反应的胰岛素。这是通过生物技术生产的第一种药物，保证了持续、稳定的人胰岛素来源。

基因在经过鉴定、分离、克隆后才能转化到另一个生物体中。在实验室中，可以分离要表达的目的基因的 mRNA 分子，再将其用作合成互补 DNA 链（cDNA）的模板。分离的互补 DNA 链可以通过克隆（复制），转化到另一个物种中。可以用互补 DNA 链来定位染色体上的相应基因，或者绘制相应的遗传图谱。

一般通过使用根瘤土壤杆菌或者粒子加速及基因枪来完成转化。根瘤土壤杆菌是自然界中的一种细菌。它包含一个被称为肿瘤诱导质粒（Ti 质粒）的环状小 DNA。当这种细菌感染木本物种时，Ti 质粒就进入宿主植物细胞中。Ti 质粒的特定区域会嵌入到宿主细胞基因组中，这种嵌入发生在 DNA 链的特定序列区域。然后，宿主细胞会表达来自细菌的基因，诱导细胞及相应愈伤组织急剧增长。生物技术利用这一自然转化过程，在特定区域去除细菌要转入宿主的基因，植入目的基因。利用根瘤土壤杆菌进行转化是有局限的，因为它只能感染特定的双子叶植物。

另一种转化过程是用基因枪将涂有目的基因涂层的显微金颗粒射入目的植物的单细胞中，这就是通常所说的粒子加速。转化的基因会融入宿主基因组的一个 DNA 链中，不过具体过程尚不清楚。这一转化过程虽然也不完善，但没有根瘤土壤杆菌宿主物种的局限性。

上述两种转化过程都需要利用植物组织培养。首先对要转化的植物细胞进行培养，然后再进行基因转化。未转化的细胞必须清除出去。这是通过选择标记基因来完成的。以耐草甘膦基因为例，将草甘膦直接用作选择标记基因，因为它会杀死未转化细胞。如果有其它特征基因转化到作物中，还可使用抗生素或抗除草剂药之类的选择标记基因。培养细胞经过除草剂或抗生素处理后，只有转化了这两种基因的细胞才可以存活，这样即可从存活的单细胞中再生整个植株。

在基因转化与植株再生之后，需要对转基因植株进行田间试验来确定转基因是否成功。并非所有的转基因植株都能正确地表达基因特征或产物。一旦鉴别出稳定表达特征基因的转基因植株，就采用传统的植物育种方法，将特征植株培养成适应不同生长环境条件的栽培品系。

（2）基因工程的具体应用

基因工程不仅应用范围广，且数量与日俱增。基因工程目前在药物生产、基因治疗和转基因动、植物开发中均有应用。

① 药物

人类的药物如治疗糖尿病的胰岛素、治疗垂体性侏儒症的生长激素、治疗心脏病的组织纤溶酶原激活剂以及动物类药物（如生长激素，牛、猪促生长素等），一般通过已经植入人类、牛或猪源的某些基因的工程菌发酵来生产。

② 基因治疗

第一种接受临床基因治疗的疾病是矫正酶缺陷症，又称作儿童腺苷脱胺酶缺乏症。治疗中先移除骨髓细胞，骨髓细胞中的缺陷 DNA 用正常 DNA 的拷贝来补充，然后再造细胞移回病人体内。

③ 转基因植物

自 1987 年以来，人们开始在室外实验点种植和实验耐除草剂、耐昆虫或耐有毒害虫的转基因植物，以及经改良的水果或花卉。通过转基因工程技术，可以将其它无亲缘关系的植物、细菌或病毒特征基因转化到植物中。

④ 转基因动物

目前，大多数转基因动物用于协助研究者进行人类疾病的诊断与治疗。一些公司已经计划并正在测试转基因哺乳类动物，以便利用动物的奶来生产重要的药物。目前利用转基因工程菌发酵生产出的产品，如胰岛素、生长激素和组织纤溶酶原激活剂，今后将会利用转基因牛、绵羊或山羊的奶来获得这些产品。

3. 生物技术在诊断中的应用

每个生物体都是独一无二的，因此对每个生物体所用的 DNA 诊断方法也不相同。一个物种、品种或杂交品系中的任何个体都可以通过 DNA 序列的小小差异鉴别区分开来，相当于 100 万个字母中只有 1 个字母不同也能鉴别出来。利用 DNA 指纹分析技术及聚合酶链反应（PCR），科学家们能够诊断出病毒性、细菌性或真菌性感染，区分联系紧密的个体，或在细胞中冗长的 DNA 分子序列中确定特定基因的位置。

（1）鉴别生物体

利用限制性片段长度多态性技术（RFLP），可以进行 DNA 指纹分析。指纹分析可以精确地鉴别任何生物体。因此，指纹分析技术可以用于确定亲子关系诉讼中的家庭关系，匹配移植中的捐赠者与接受者器官，根据遗留在犯罪现场的 DNA 证据（头发或血液）确定嫌疑犯，或者作为植物或畜禽育种的谱系鉴定方法。

（2）鉴别基因

遗传工程的一个重要应用是鉴别控制特定特征的 DNA 基因。比如，一位来访者会用州、城市、街道和房间号码来定位朋友的住址。同样，基因工程师可以利用遗传图谱定位特定的基因。遗传图谱是通过统计分析、PCR、RFLP 和 DNA 测序来建立的。目前人们已开始建立人、鼠、猪、牛、玉米、小麦和其它具有商业及研究价值的动植物图谱。

（3）诊断传染性疾病和遗传性疾病

诊断传染性疾病是 DNA 技术的最新深入应用。利用 PCR 技术，数小时内就可诊断肺结核、艾滋病、乳头状瘤及许多其它传染性疾病，此外还有囊性纤维化遗传性疾病或镰状细胞性贫血病，而传统方法却需要费时数日或数周。与传统方法相比，PCR 技术的检测灵敏度与速度大为提高，可以更早地实施疾病干预与治疗。PCR 检测技术也将很快应用于动植物的疾病诊断。

练习参考答案 *(Reference answers of exercises)*

1. 配对 *(Matching)*

① —(c); ②—(e); ③—(d); ④—(a); ⑤—(f); ⑥—(b)

2. 用词或短语填空，根据需要变换形式 *(Fill in the blanks with the words or expressions given below, and change the form where necessary)*

① brewing	② genome	③ gene
④ Genetic engineering	⑤ DNA fingerprinting	⑥ DNA gene

Chapter Two

Fermentation Engineering

Unit 1　Wine Fermentation

Reading Material

The process of **fermentation in wine** is the catalyst function that turns grape juice into an alcoholic beverage. During fermentation yeast interacts with sugars in the juice to create ethanol, commonly known as ethyl alcohol, and carbon dioxide (as a by-product). In winemaking the temperature and speed of fermentation is an important consideration as well as the level of oxygen present in the must at the start of the fermentation. The risk of stuck fermentation and the development of several wine faults can also occur during the stage which can last anywhere from 5 to 14 days for primary fermentation and potentially another 5 to 10 days for a secondary fermentation. Fermentation may be done in stainless steel tanks, which is common with many white wines like Riesling, in an open wooden vat, inside a wine barrel and inside the wine bottle itself as in the production of many sparkling wines.

The natural occurrence of fermentation was probably first observed long ago by humans. The earliest use of the word "Fermentation" in relation to winemaking was in reference to the apparent "boiling" within the must that came from the anaerobic reaction of the yeast to the sugars in the grape juice and the release of carbon dioxide. The Latin "fervere" means, literally, to boil. In the mid-19th century, Louis Pasteur noted the connection between yeast and the process of the fermentation in which the yeast acts as catalyst and mediator through a series of a reaction that convert sugar into alcohol. The discovery of the Embden–Meyerhof–Parnas pathway by Gustav Embden, Otto Fritz Meyerhof and Jakub Karol Parnas in the early 20th century contributed more to the understanding of the complex chemical processes involved the conversion of sugar to alcohol.

In winemaking there are distinctions made between ambient yeasts which are naturally present in wine cellars, vineyards and on the grapes themselves and cultured yeast which are specifically isolated and inoculated for use in winemaking. The most common genera of wild yeasts found in winemaking include *Candida, Klöckera/Hanseniaspora, Metschnikowiaceae, Pichia* and *Zygosaccharomyces*. Wild yeasts can produce high-quality, unique-flavored wines; however, they are often unpredictable and may introduce less desirable traits to the wine, and can even contribute to spoilage. Traditional wine makers, particularly in Europe, advocate use of ambient yeast as a characteristic of the region's terroir, nevertheless, many winemakers prefer to control fermentation with predictable cultured yeast. The cultured yeasts most commonly used in winemaking belong to the *Saccharomyces cerevisiae* (also known as "sugar yeast") species. Within this species are several hundred different strains of yeast that are used during fermentation to affect the heat of the process and enhance certain flavor characteristics of the varietal. The use of different strains of yeasts is a major contributor to the diversity of wine, even among the same grape variety.

The addition of cultured yeast normally occurs with the yeast first in a dried or "inactive" state and is reactivated in warm water or diluted grape juice. To thrive and be active in fermentation, the yeast needs access to a continuous supply of carbon, nitrogen, sulfur, phosphorus as well as access to various vitamins and minerals. These components are naturally present in the grape, but their proportion may be corrected by adding nutrient packets to the wine, in order to foster a more encouraging environment for the yeast. Oxygen is needed as well but in wine making the risk of oxidation and the lack of alcohol production from oxygenated yeast requires the exposure of oxygen to be kept at a minimum.

Upon the introduction of active yeasts to the grape must, phosphates are attached to the sugar and the six-carbon sugar molecules begin to be split into three-carbon pieces and go through a series of rearrangement reactions. During this process the carboxylic carbon atom is released in the form of carbon dioxide with the remaining components becoming acetaldehyde. The absence of oxygen in this anaerobic process allows the acetaldehyde to be eventually converted, by reduction, to ethanol. During the conversion of acetaldehyde a small amount is converted, by oxidation, to acetic acid which, in excess, can contribute to the wine fault known as volatile acidity (vinegar taint). After the yeast has exhausted its life cycle they fall to the bottom of the fermentation tank as sediment known as lees.

The metabolism of amino acids and breakdown of sugars by yeasts have affect of creating other biochemical compounds that can contribute to the flavor and aroma of wine. These compounds can be considered "volatile" like aldehydes, ethyl acetate, ester, fatty acids, fusel oils, hydrogen sulfide, ketones and mercaptans) or "non-volatile" like glycerol, acetic acid and succinic acid. Yeast also has the effect during fermentation of releasing glycoside hydrolase which can hydrolyse the flavor precursors of aliphatics, benzene derivities, monoterpenes, norisoprenoids, and phenols. Some strains of yeasts can generate volatile thiols which contribute to the fruity aromas in many wines such as the gooseberry scent commonly associated with Sauvignon blanc. Brettanomyces yeasts are responsible for the "barnyard aroma" characteristic in some red wines like Burgundy Pinot noir.

During fermentation there are several factors that winemakers take into consideration. The most notable is that of the internal temperature of the must. The biochemical process of fermentation itself creates a lot of residual heat which can take the must out of the ideal temperature range. Typically white wine is fermented between 64-68°F (18-20℃) though a wine maker may choose to use a higher temperature to bring out some of the complexity of the wine. Red wine is typically fermented at higher temperatures up to 85°F (29℃). Fermentation at higher temperatures may have adverse effect on the wine in stunning the yeast to inactivity and even "boiling off" some of the flavors of the wines. Some winemakers may ferment their red wines at cooler temperatures.

To control the heat generated during fermentation the winemaker has to choose a suitable vessel size or to use various sorts of cooling devices from the ancient Bordeaux traditions of placing the fermentation vat on top of blocks of ice to today's modern use of sophisticated fermentation tanks with built-in cooling rings. A risk factor involved with fermentation is the development of chemical residue and spoilage which can be corrected with the addition of sulfur dioxide (SO_2), although excess SO_2 can lead to a wine fault. A winemaker who wishes to make a wine with high levels of residual sugar (like a dessert wine) may stop fermentation early either by dropping the temperature of the must to stun the yeast or by adding a high level of alcohol (like brandy) to the must to kill off the yeast and create a fortified wine.

Glossary

1. ethyl	*n.* 乙醛，乙烷基
2. must	*n.* 葡萄汁，果汁；霉，发霉
3. rehydration	*n.* 再水化，再水合，补液
4. riesling	*n.* (欧洲、美洲产的)一种葡萄；用此酿造的白葡萄酒
5. vat	*n.* (染色、酿造等用的)大桶，盆，缸；染缸 *vt.* 把……盛入大桶，大桶里染(处理)
6. ambient	*a.* 周遭的，环绕的，外界的
7. cellar	*n.*地下室，地窖，酒窖；*vt.* 把……藏入地窖
8. vineyard	*n.* 葡萄园
9. blush	*n.* 脸红，羞愧，红色；*vi.* 脸红，变成红色
10. volatile	*a.* (液体等)易挥发的，易发作的，爆炸性的，易变的，反复无常的，轻浮的，活泼的，轻快的，飞逝的，短暂的
11. lees	*n.* 渣滓，沉淀物；酒泥，酒糟
12. aldehydes	*n.* 醛类
13. ethyl acetate	*n.* 醋酸乙酯
14. ester	*n.* 酯
15. fusel	*n.* 杂醇
16. aliphatics	*n.* 脂肪族化合物
17. oak	*n.* 橡树，橡木，橡木家具，橡木色，棕色
18. benzene	*n.* 苯
19. monoterpene	*n.* 单萜烯, 半萜
20. phenol	*n.* 酚,石炭酸
21. norisoprenoid	*n.* 萜烯
22. thiol	*n.* 硫醇
23. gooseberry	*n.* 醋栗；醋栗树丛
24. stun	*vt.* 击晕, 打晕；使大吃一惊,使震惊；给（某人）以深刻印象；使深深感动

Exercises

1. Matching

① cellar

(a) a fragrant colorless flammable volatile liquid ester made from ethanol and acetic acid; used in flavorings and perfumes and as a solvent for plastics

② ambient   (b) 1. any of a class of weakly acidic organic compounds; molecule contains one or more hydroxyl groups; 2. a toxic white soluble crystalline acidic derivative of benzene; used in manufacturing and as a disinfectant and antiseptic; poisonous if taken internally

③ stun   (c) 1. a rosy color (especially in the cheeks) taken as a sign of good health; 2. sudden reddening of the face (as from embarrassment or guilt or shame or modesty). *v.* turn red, as if in embarrassment or shame; become rosy or reddish

④ ethyl   (d) formed by reaction between an acid and an alcohol with elimination of water

⑤ rehydration   (e) a colorless liquid hydrocarbon; highly inflammable; carcinogenic; the simplest of the aromatic compounds

⑥ blush   (f) 1. make senseless or dizzy by or as if by a blow; 2. surprise greatly; knock someone's socks off; 3. hit something or somebody as if with a sandbag; 4. overcome as with astonishment or disbelief

⑦ benzene   (g) n.absorb or cause to absorb moisture

⑧ phenol   (h) completely enveloping

⑨ ester   (i) the univalent hydrocarbon radical C_2H_5 derived from ethane by the removal of one hydrogen

⑩ ethyl acetate   (j) 1.the lowermost portion of a structure partly or wholly below ground level; often used for storage; 2. an excavation where root vegetables are stored; 3. storage space where wines are stored

2. Fill in the blanks with the words or expressions given below, and change the form where necessary.

do	occur	catalyst	distinction	contribute
release	consider	type	relate	note

① Fermentation may be_____in stainless steel tanks, which is common with many white wines.

② The natural_____ of fermentation means it was probably first observed long ago by humans.

③ There are_____made between ambient yeasts which are naturally present in wine cellars, vineyards and on the grapes themselves and cultured yeast which are specifically isolated and inoculated.

④ The use of different strains of yeasts are a major_____to the diversity of wine.

⑤ Yeast also _____ glycoside hydrolase to hydrolyse some biochemical substrates.

⑥ During fermentation there are several factors that winemakers take into_____.

⑦ _____white wine is fermented between 64~68 °F (18~20℃).

⑧ The earliest uses of the word "Fermentation" is _____ to winemaking.

⑨ The most_____is that of the internal temperature of the must.

⑩ Louis Pasteur noted the yeast act as_____through a series of a reaction that convert sugar into alcohol.

酒的发酵

酒的发酵过程是将葡萄汁转变成酒精饮料的催化过程。在发酵时，酵母与葡萄汁中的糖类相互作用，并产生醇类，我们熟知的是乙醇，还有作为副产物的二氧化碳。在制酒时，发酵开始时的温度和速度是很重要的因素，葡萄汁中的氧气含量也很重要。深层发酵的风险和酿酒失误的几个过程都有可能在这里发生，初级发酵阶段需要 5～14 天，如发展得好进入到第二阶段则需 5～10 天。发酵过程可在不锈钢容器里完成，这在许多白葡萄酒酿制过程中很常见，例如雷司令白葡萄酒；也可在开口木桶里，里面有酒桶或酒瓶，可以酿造发泡的白葡萄酒。

很久以前人们可能首先观察到自然发生的发酵现象。"发酵"这个术语最早应用于造酒业，是指在葡萄汁里有很明显的"沸腾"现象，这是由于酵母菌发生了厌氧反应，将葡萄汁里的糖类分解掉并释放出二氧化碳的缘故。拉丁词 *"fervere"* 字面上的意思就是指"沸腾"。在 19 世纪中期，路易斯·巴斯德注意到酵母和发酵过程有联系，即在糖类转变成酒精的过程中，酵母起着催化剂和媒介的作用。20 世纪早期由古斯塔夫·埃姆登、奥托·迈尔霍夫、雅库布卡罗尔·帕尔纳斯这三位科学家发现的 EMP 途径使人们更容易理解糖转变成酒精的复杂化学过程。

在制酒业中，环境中的酵母菌和分离纯培养的酵母菌有着明显的区别。环境中的酵母菌天然存在于酒窖中、葡萄园里和葡萄上；分离并培养出来的纯培养酵母菌专门用于酒的制造。在制酒业中发现的最普通的野生酵母属包括假丝酵母属、克勒克酵母/汉生酵母、*Metschnikowiaceae*、毕赤酵母属和接合酵母属。野生酵母能产生高质量并有独特香味的酒，但是有时候也很难预测，例如会使酒带上令人难以接受的味道，甚至会造成腐败。很多传统的酒厂，特别是在欧洲，提倡使用当地的野生酵母菌，而也有很多酒厂更愿意使用纯培养的酵母菌，这样能控制发酵。制酒业中很多时候用的纯培养酵母菌属于酿酒酵母，也就是糖酵母。这个种的酵母有好几百种菌株用于发酵，会影响到发酵过程中产生的热量并提高酒品种的风味。使用不同菌株的酵母发酵是酒类多样性的一个主要影响因素，甚至利用同一葡萄品种也能生产不同品种的酒。

一般加入的培养好的酵母菌种以干燥或休眠状态存在，遇到温水或稀释的葡萄汁后就会重新恢复活力。在发酵中为了繁盛和具有活力，酵母菌需要得到源源不断的碳、氮、硫、磷，也需要得到各种维生素和无机盐。这些成分天然存在于葡萄汁中，但是它们的比例对酵母的生长并不是很合适，需要额外加入一些营养物质才能创造更好的生长环境。在制酒过程中，需要氧气，但是对氧气的量也有一定的要求，酵母菌在过多的氧气环境下会导致乙醇产量的降低，因此要维持最小量的氧气浓度。

一旦葡萄汁接入有活力的酵母菌，磷酸就连接到葡萄糖分子上，随后这个六碳糖分子开始分解成三个碳原子的分子，再发生一系列的分子重排反应。在这个过程中，羧基碳以二氧化碳形式释放出来，剩下的就变成了乙醛。如果缺少氧气，就会发生无氧氧化，乙醛发生还原反应，最终变成乙醇。乙醛转变时，有少量的乙醛通过氧化变成乙酸，如果这种酸过量，会使酒出现挥发性的酸味（醋味）而导致制酒失败。当酵母耗尽生命，就沉入发酵罐底部，这种沉淀就是人们熟知的酒糟。

由酵母引起的氨基酸代谢和糖类的分解能产生其它一些使酒具有芳香和特殊香味的生化物质。这些化合物包括易挥发的物质如醛类、乙酸乙酯、脂类、脂肪酸、杂醇油、硫化氢、酮类化合物、硫醇类化合物，也有一些非挥发性化合物如甘油、乙酸和琥珀酸。发酵过程中酵母通过分泌的糖苷水解酶而产生作用，这种酶能水解脂肪族类化合物的前体、苯类化合物衍生物、单萜烯、降异戊二烯和酚类化合物。酵母菌的一些菌株能产生具有挥发性的硫醇类化合物，这些化合物引起很多酒类具有水果的芳香味道，如醋栗香味，这样的香味经常和白沙威浓葡萄酒联系起来。Brettanomyces 酵母菌生产的红酒如 Burgundy Pinot noir 具有独特的"稗芳香"。

在酒发酵中，酿酒师需要考虑很多因素。影响最显著的因素是葡萄汁发酵液内部的温度。发酵本身是一个生化过程，产生大量的余热会使葡萄汁发酵液的温度超过制定的标准温度。虽然有的酿酒师会选择更高的温度将酒中的一些复杂成分去掉，但是典型的白酒是在 64～68℉（18～20℃）下进行发酵。典型的红酒是在 85℉（29℃）下进行发酵。在更高的温度下发酵可能会对制酒有很大的副作用，表现为酵母菌失去活力，酒中的芳香类物质被蒸发掉。有些酿酒师在较低的温度下发酵制作红酒。

为了控制在发酵过程中产生的热量，酿酒师选择大小合适的容器或者多种装置来降温，这些装置包括：古代的传统发酵设备，在这种设备的上面放置冰块来降低温度；现代采用带有冷却环的先进的发酵罐。发酵制酒的一个危险因素是化学物质残留和酸败，这些可以通过加入二氧化硫加以消除，然而二氧化硫一旦过量就会导致制酒失败。酿酒师都希望制造出含糖量较高的红酒，就像甜酒，那么他会在发酵的早期通过降低葡萄汁的发酵温度，或者加入高浓度的乙醇（如白兰地）停止发酵，这样可以使酵母菌死亡并得到质量稳定的酒。

练习参考答案 *(Reference answers of exercises)*

1. 配对 *(Matching)*

①—(j)；②—(h)；③—(f)；④—(i)；⑤—(g)；⑥—(c)；⑦—(e)；⑧—(b)；⑨—(d)；⑩—(a)

2. 用词或短语填空，根据需要变换形式 *(Fill in the blanks with the words or expressions given below, and change the form where necessary.)*

① done	② occurrence	③ distinctions	④ contributor
⑤ release	⑥ consideration	⑦ Typically	⑧ in relation to
⑨ notable	⑩ catalyst		

Unit 2 Fermentation

Reading Material

Fermentation is the process of deriving energy from the oxidation of organic compounds, such as carbohydrates, using an endogenous electron acceptor, which is usually an organic compound. This is in contrast to cellular respiration, where electrons are donated to an exogenous electron acceptor, such as oxygen, via an electron transport chain. Fermentation does not necessarily have to be carried out in an anaerobic environment. For example, even in the presence of abundant oxygen, yeast cells greatly prefer fermentation to oxidative phosphorylation, as long as sugars are readily available for consumption.

Sugars are the most common substrate of fermentation, and typical examples of fermentation products are ethanol, lactic acid, and hydrogen. However, more exotic compounds can be produced by fermentation, such as butyric acid and acetone. Yeast carries out fermentation in the production of ethanol in beers, wines and other alcoholic drinks, along with the production of large quantities of carbon dioxide. Fermentation occurs in mammalian muscle during periods of intense exercise where oxygen supply becomes insufficient, resulting in the genenration of lactic acid.

Fermentation products contain chemical energy (they are not fully oxidized) but are considered as waste products, since they cannot be metabolized further without the use of oxygen (or other more highly-oxidized electron acceptors). A consequence is that the production of adenosine triphosphate (ATP) by fermentation is less efficient than oxidative phosphorylation, whereby pyruvate is fully oxidized to carbon dioxide.

Ethanol fermentation (performed by yeast and some types of bacteria) breaks the pyruvate down into ethanol and carbon dioxide. It is important in bread-making, brewing, and wine-making. Usually only one of the products is desired; in bread-making, the alcohol is baked out, and, in alcohol production, the carbon dioxide is released into the atmosphere or used for carbonating the beverage. When the ferment has a high concentration of pectin, minute quantities of methanol can be produced.

Lactic acid fermentation breaks down the pyruvate into lactic acid. It occurs in the muscles of animals when they need energy faster than the blood flow can supply oxygen. It also occurs in some kinds of bacteria (such as lactobacilli) and some fungi. It is this type of bacteria that converts lactose into lactic acid in yogurt, giving it its sour taste. These lactic acid bacteria can be classed as homofermentative, where the end product is mostly lactate, or heterofermentative, where some lactate is further metabolized and results in carbon dioxide, acetate or other metabolic products.

Hydrogen gas is produced in many types of fermentation (mixed acid fermentation, butyric acid fermentation, caproate fermentation, butanol fermentation, glyoxylate fermentation), as a way to regenerate NAD^+ from NADH. Electrons are transferred to ferredoxin, which in turn is oxidized by hydrogenase, producing H_2. Hydrogen gas is a substrate for methanogens and sulfate reducers, which keep the concentration of hydrogen sufficiently low to allow the production of such an energy-rich compound.

Dark fermentation is the fermentative conversion of organic substrate to biohydrogen, it is a complex process manifested by diverse group of bacteria by a series of biochemical reactions involving three steps similar to anaerobic conversion. Dark fermentation differs from photofermentation because it proceeds without the presence of light.

Fermentative/hydrolytic microorganisms hydrolyze complex organic polymers to monomers which are further converted to a mixture of lower molecular weight organic acids and alcohols by obligatory H_2 producing acidogenic bacteria.

Utilization of wastewater as a potential substrate for biohydrogen production has been drawing considerable interest in recent years especially in dark fermentation process. Industrial wastewater as fermentative substrate for H_2 production addresses most of the criteria required for substrate selection viz., availability, cost and biodegradability. Chemical wastewater, cattle wastewater, diary process wastewater, starch hydrolysate wastewater and designed synthetic wastewater have been reported to produce biohydrogen apart from wastewater treatment from dark fermentation process using selectively enriched mixed culture under acidophilic conditions. Various wastewaters viz., paper mill wastewater, starch effluent, food processing wastewater, domestic wastewater, rice winery wastewater, distillery and molasses based wastewater, wheat straw wastes and palm oil mill wastewater were also studied as fermentable substrates for H_2 production along with wastewater treatment. Using wastewater as a fermentable substrate facilitates both wastewater treatment apart from H_2 production. The efficiency of dark fermentative H_2 production process was found to depend on the pre-treatment of the mixed consortia used as biocatalyst, operating pH, organic loading rate apart from wastewater characteristics.

Employing mixed culture is extremely important and well-suited to the non-sterile, ever-changing, complex environment of wastewater treatment. Typical anaerobic mixed cultures can not produce H_2 as it is rapidly consumed by the methane-producing bacteria. Successful biological H_2 production requires inhibition of H_2 consuming microorganisms, such as methanogens and pre-treatment of parent culture is one of the strategies used for selecting the requisite microflora. The physiological differences between H_2 producing bacteria (also referred to as acidogenic bacteria) and H_2 consuming bacteria (methanogenic bacteria) form the fundamental basis in the development of various methods used for the preparation of H_2 producing seeds. When parent inoculum was exposed to extreme environments such as high temperature, extreme acidity and alkalinity, spore forming H_2 producing bacteria such as *Clostridium* survived, but methanogens had no such capability. Pre-treatment helps to accelerate the hydrolysis step, thus, reducing the impact of rate limiting step and augment the anaerobic digestion to enhance the H_2 generation. Several pre-treatment procedures viz., heat-shock, chemical, acid, alkaline, oxygen-shock, load-shock, infrared, freezing, etc., were employed on a variety of mixed cultures for selective enrichment of acidogenic H_2 producing inoculum. pH also plays a critical role in governing the metabolic pathways of the organism where the activity of acidogenic group of bacteria is considered to be crucial. Optimum pH range for the methanogenic bacteria is reported to be between 6.0 and 7.5, while acidogenic bacteria functions well below 6 pH. The pH range of 5.5-6.0 is considered to be ideal to avoid both methanogenesis which is the key for effective H_2 generation.

Glossary

1. carbohydrate	*n.* 碳水化合物
2. endogenous	*adj.* 内长的，内生的
3. exogenous	*adj.* 外成的，外生的
4. acceptor	*n.* 接受者，接收器，受体
5. respiration	*n.* 呼吸，一次呼吸；(植物的)呼吸
6. oxygen	*n.* 氧；氧气
7. anaerobic	*adj.* 厌氧菌的；厌氧菌产生的

8. yeast	*n.* 酵母；酵母菌；发酵粉；发面饼
9. hydrogen	*n.* 氢，氢气
10. exotic	*adj.* 1.由外国引进的，非本地的；2.奇异的，醒目的，吸引人的
11. butyric	*adj.* 奶油的，由奶油中提取的，酪酸的，butyric acid 丁酸
12. acetone	*n.* 丙酮
13. carbon dioxide	*n.* 二氧化碳
14. mammalian	*n.* 哺乳动物；*adj.* 哺乳动物的
15. adenosine triphosphate (ATP)	*n.* 三磷酸腺苷
16. pyruvate	*n.* 丙酮酸盐(或酯)
17. carbonate	*n.* 碳酸盐；*vt.* 充二氧化碳于
18. pectin	*n.* 胶质
19. methanol	*n.* 甲醇；差异法
20. sour	*adj.* 1.有酸味的，酸的；2.有发酵味道的，酸腐的，馊的；3.坏脾气的，别扭的；4.关系、态度、人等（使）变坏，恶化；*vt. & vi.* (使某物)变酸，变馊，(使某人)阴郁
21. homofermentative	*adj.* 同型发酵的
22. heterofermentative	*adj.* 异型发酵的
23. acetate	*n.* 醋酸盐；醋酸纤维(制品)
24. caproate	*n.* 己酸盐
25. butanol	*n.* 丁醇
26. glyoxylate	*n.* 乙醛酸
27. ferredoxin	*n.* 铁氧化还原蛋白
28. hydrogenase	*n.* 氢化酶
29. methanogens	*n.* 产甲烷菌
30. biohydrogen	*n.* 生物产氢的
31. anaerobic	*adj.* 厌氧菌的，厌氧菌产生的；(细菌等)能在无空气(或无氧)情况下生活(或成长)的
32. photofermentation	*n.* 光发酵
33. hydrolytic	*adj.* 水解的,产生水解(作用)的
34. polymers	*n.* 高分子材料，聚合物
35. monomers	*n.* 单体
36. acidogenic	*adj.* 引起酸化的
37. dairy	*n.* 牛奶场，乳品店；*adj.* 牛奶的，奶制的，乳品的，乳品业的
38. starch	*n.* 淀粉；淀粉类食物
39. hydrolysate	*n.* 水解产物
40. acidophilic	*adj.* 嗜酸的；耐酸的
41. mill	*n.* 磨坊；面粉厂
42. domestic	*adj.* 家庭的，家事的；国家的；国内的；一心只管家务的；一心追求家庭乐趣的；驯养的
43. winery	*n.* 酿酒厂；酿葡萄酒厂
44. distillery	*n.* 蒸馏室；酿酒厂
45. molasses	*n.* 糖蜜；糖浆

46. straw	*n.* 稻草，麦秆
47. palm	*n.* 手掌，手心；(四足动物的)前足掌；棕榈(树)，棕榈叶
48. consortia	*n.* 公会
49. biocatalyst	*n.* 生物催化剂
50. microflora	*n.* 微小植物，微生物菌群
51. inoculum	*n.* 接种体，种菌，种子培养物
52. methanogenesis	*n.* 产甲烷[作用]

Exercises

1. Matching

① starch — (a) in the formation of a coordinate bond it is the compound to which electrons are donated

② carbohydrate — (b) a nonmetallic univalent element that is normally a colorless and odorless highly flammable diatomic gas; the simplest and lightest and most abundant element in the universe

③ oxygen — (c) the metabolic processes whereby certain organisms obtain energy from organic molecules; processes that take place in the cells and tissues during which energy is released and carbon dioxide is produced and absorbed by the blood to be transported to the lungs; the bodily process of inhalation and exhalation; the process of taking in oxygen from inhaled air and releasing carbon dioxide by exhalation

④ methanol — (d) archaebacteria found in anaerobic environments such as animal intestinal tracts or sediments or sewage and capable of producing methane; a source of natural gas

⑤ acceptor — (e) a light volatile flammable poisonous liquid alcohol; used as an antifreeze and solvent and fuel and as a denaturant for ethyl alcohol

⑥ biocatalyst — (f) a commercial leavening agent containing yeast cells; used to raise the dough in making bread and for fermenting beer or whiskey

⑦ hydrogen — (g) an essential structural component of living cells and source of energy for animals; includes simple sugars with small molecules as well as macromolecular substances; are classified according to the number of monosaccharide groups they contain

⑧ methanogens — (h) a complex carbohydrate found chiefly in seeds, fruits, tubers, roots and stem pith of plants, notably in corn, potatoes, wheat, and rice; an important foodstuff and used otherwise especially in adhesives and as fillers and stiffeners for paper and textiles

⑨ yeast — (i) a biochemical catalyst such as enzyme

⑩ respiration — (j) a nonmetallic bivalent element that is normally a colorless odorless tasteless nonflammable diatomic gas; constitutes 21 percent of the atmosphere by volume; the most abundant element in the earth's crust methanol

2. Fill in the blanks with the words or expressions given below, and change the form where necessary.

| donate | carry out | draw | result | efficiency |
| different | consume | extreme | capable | use |

① This is in contrast to cellular respiration, where electrons_____to an exogenous electron acceptor.

② Fermentation does not necessarily have to_____in an anaerobic environment.

③ Utilization of wastewater as a potential substrate for biohydrogen production has_____considerable interest in recent years especially in dark fermentation process.

④ Fermentation occurs in mammalian muscle during periods of intense exercise where oxygen supply becomes limited,_____in the creation of lactic acid.

⑤ A consequence is that the production of adenosine triphosphate (ATP) by fermentation is less_____than oxidative phosphorylation. less efficient.

⑥ _____wastewater as a fermentable substrate facilitates both wastewater treatment apart from H_2 production.

⑦ The physiological_____between H_2 producing bacteria and H_2 consuming bacteria form the fundamental basis.

⑧ Typical anaerobic mixed cultures can not produce H_2 as it is rapidly_____by the methane-producing bacteria.

⑨ Employing mixed culture is_____important and well-suited to the non-sterile, ever-changing, complex environment of wastewater treatment.

⑩ When parent inoculum was exposed to extreme environments such as high temperature, extreme acidity and alkalinity, spore forming H_2 producing bacteria survived, but methanogens had no such_____.

Translation

发　酵

发酵是指利用有机物（例如碳水化合物）的内在电子受体将其氧化，并释放能量的过程。和发酵相比，细胞呼吸将电子通过电子传递链，最后交给外来的电子受体，例如O_2。发酵并不一定要在无氧条件下进行，例如，在充足氧气存在时，只要有足够的糖供酵母消耗，细胞更容易进行发酵而不是氧化磷酸化过程。

糖类是发酵过程最常见的底物，典型的发酵产物有乙醇、乳酸和氢气。然而通过发酵还可以产生更有用的化合物，如丁酸和丙酮。啤酒、白酒和其它醇类饮料中的乙醇都是通过酵母发酵生产出来的，其中伴随着大量二氧化碳的产生。在哺乳动物肌肉剧烈运动并且氧气供应不足时发生发酵，导致了乳酸的生成。

由于在没有可以利用的氧气或者没有其它更高氧化势能的电子受体存在时，发酵的产物不能被进一步代谢，没有完全被氧化。它们含有一定的化学能，却被认为是无用的产物。这样的结果是，通过发酵产生的三磷酸腺苷（即 ATP）的产量比氧化磷酸化产生的 ATP 的产量低很多，在氧化磷酸化过程中，丙酮酸被完全氧化成了二氧化碳。

由酵母和一些细菌发酵引起乙醇发酵是将丙酮酸分解成乙醇和二氧化碳，这在制作面包、酿造和制酒业中相当重要。通常乙醇和二氧化碳只有一个被保留下来，例如，做面包时，通过烘烤将乙醇除去，而在制酒时，就把二氧化碳释放到空气中，或者用来制作碳酸饮料。如果发酵底物中含有高浓度的胶质，就会产生少量的甲醇。

乳酸发酵是将丙酮酸转变成乳酸。如果哺乳动物肌肉需要能量的速度超过血液提供氧气的速度，那么就会发生这种反应。这种反应也会出现在一些细菌（如乳酸杆菌）和真菌中。正是这种类型的细菌将乳糖转变成乳酸，酸奶才具有酸味。这些乳酸菌要么属于同型发酵，要么属于异型发酵。同型发酵的最终产物大多是乳酸，而异型发酵中，产生的乳酸会进一步代谢，最后产生二氧化碳、乙酸或者其它代谢产物。

许多类型发酵都产生氢气（如混合酸发酵、丁酸发酵、己酸发酵、丁醇发酵、乙醛酸发酵），通过 $NADH + H^+$ 产生 NAD^+ 的方式产生氢气。电子传递给氧化态的铁硫蛋白，脱氢酶再将还原态的铁硫蛋白氧化产生氢气。氢气是产甲烷菌和产硫细菌的底物，这些细菌能维持很低的氢浓度来生产甲烷和硫这类能量高的物质。

暗发酵是将有机物质发酵转化成生物氢，这是一个由多种细菌参与的一系列生物化学反应的复杂过程，涉及三步相似的无氧转化。不同于光发酵，暗发酵不需要光就能进行。

发酵或水解型的微生物将复杂的多聚物水解成单体，进而转变成低分子量的有机酸和醇类。

作为生物制氢的潜在底物——废水，近年来一直引起人们的广泛兴趣，特别是在暗发酵过程中更加如此。能够作为发酵底物来生产氢气的工业废水需要达到一些必需的标准，即底物的选择性、可利用性、成本高低和生物可降解性。已有报道，除了废水处理，利用化工废水、畜牧业废水、奶制品加工废水、制糖业废水和设计合成业废水在酸性条件下用选择性的富集培养基进行暗发酵生产生物氢。在废水处理的时候，对各种废水作为制造 H_2 的发酵底物进行了研究，这些废水包括造纸厂废水、淀粉厂废水、食品加工业废水、家庭生活废水、酒厂废水、制糖业废水等。用废水作为发酵底物可以使废水的处理和制造 H_2 分离开。暗发酵生产 H_2 过程的效率取决于催化剂和废水混合物的处理情况、反应的 pH 以及其它有机物从废水中溢出的速率。

废水处理过程中不用灭菌，条件经常变化且环境相当复杂，用几种微生物混合培养发酵非常重要，也很恰当。典型的厌氧混合培养不能产生 H_2，因为 H_2 很快被产甲烷细菌消耗完了。需要有抑制剂来抑制某些微生物（如产甲烷菌）消耗氢气才能成功地生物制氢，因此对预先培养好的微生物进行前处理是一种用来选择必需微生物菌群的常用策略。产 H_2 细菌（也指产酸细菌）和耗 H_2 细菌（产甲烷细菌）的生理差别是开发各种产 H_2 菌种的制备方法的根本基础。如果把接种的微生物置于极端环境，如高温、强酸或强碱条件下，产 H_2 细菌，如（梭菌 *Clostridium*）的芽孢会存活，而产甲烷菌不能活下来。前处理有助于加快水解步骤，减少限制性步骤和提高无氧代谢，这样能增加 H_2 的产生量。很多预处理过程用于处理各种混合培养基，富集选择出产生 H_2 的产酸细菌，这些过程包括热击、化学处理、酸碱处理、氧击、负荷冲击、红外线处理、冷冻处理等。pH 值在控制这类微生物代谢途径中起着很关键的作用，其中产酸类细菌的作用是最重要的。据报道，产甲烷细菌生长的最适 pH 值在 6.0～7.5 之间，而产酸细菌在 pH6 以下能生长得很好。pH5.5～6.0 是理想的 pH 范围，能避免产甲烷细菌存活，这是在这一 pH 范围内有效产生 H_2 的关键所在。

练习参考答案 *(Reference answers of exercises)*

1. 配对 *(Matching)*

①—(h)；②—(g)；③—(j)；④—(e)；⑤—(a)；⑥—(i)；⑦—(b)；⑧—(d)；⑨—(f)；⑩—(c)

2. 用词或短语填空，根据需要变换形式 *(Fill in the blanks with the words or expressions given below, and change the form where necessary)*

① are donated ② be carried out ③ been drawing ④ resulting ⑤efficient
⑥ using ⑦ differences ⑧ consumed ⑨ extremely ⑩capability

Unit 3 Fungi, Bacteria and Viruses

Reading Material

Fungi

Fungi are an ancient group of organisms at least 400 million, and possibly 800 million years old. This distinct kingdom of organism consists of approximately 100,000 named species, but mycologists, the scientists who study them, believe several times that many may exist.

Many fungi are harmful because they decay, rot and spoil many different materials as they obtain food. They also can cause serious disease in plants and animals, including human beings. Other fungi, however, are extremely useful. The manufacture of both bread and beer depends on the biochemical activities of yeasts, single-celled fungi that produce abundant quantities of ethanol and carbon dioxide. Both cheese and wine achieve their delicate flavors because of the metabolic processes of certain fungi, and other fungi make possible the manufacture of such oriental delicacies as soy sauce and tofu. Vast industries depend on the biochemical manufacture of organic substances such as citric acid by using fungi in culture, and yeasts are now employed on a large scale to produce protein for the enrichment of animal food. Many antibiotics, including the first one widely used, penicillin, are derived from fungi. Other fungi are used to convert complex organic molecules into other molecules, such as in the synthesis of many commercially important steroids. Because so many are harmful and because so many are beneficial, fungi hold great importance for all of us.

Fungi exist mainly as slender filaments, barely visible with the naked eye, which are called hyphae. These hyphae may be divided into cells by cross walls called septa. These septa are rarely from a complete barrier, however, except for those separating the reproductive cells. Cytoplasm characteristically flows freely throughout the hyphae, passing right through the major pores in the septa. Because of this cytoplasmic stream, proteins, which are synthesized throughout the hyphae, may be carried to the actively growing tips of the hyphae. As a result, the growth of fungal hyhae may be rapid with abundant food and water and a high enough temperature.

A mass of hyphae is called a mycelium. Mycelia of fungi constitute a system that may be many kilometers long, although concentrated in a much small area. This system grows through and penetrates the environment of the fungus, resulting in a unique relationship between a fungus and its environment of the fungus. All parts of a fungus are metabolically active, continually interacting with the soil, wood, or other materials in which the mycelia are growing.

In two of the three divisions of fungi, structures composed of interwoven hyphae, such as mushrooms, puffballs and morels are formed at certain stages of the life cycle. These structures may expand rapidly because of cytoplasmic stream and growth in their kilometers of hyphae. For this reason, mushrooms can force their way through tennis court surfaces or appear suddenly in your lawn.

The cell walls of fungi are not formed of cellulose as are those of plants and many groups of protists. Other polysaccharides are typical constituents of fungal cell walls, however, and one of them, chitin, occurs especially frequently. Chitin is the same material that makes up the major portion of hard shells, or exoskeletons, of arthropods, a group of animals that includes insects and crustaceans. Chitin is far more resistant to microbial degradation than is cellulose.

Mitosis in fungi differs from that found in other organisms. The nuclear envelope does not break down and reform, and the spindle apparatus is formed within it. In addition, centrioles are lacking in all fungi. Overall, fungi features suggest that the kingdom oraginated from unknown group of single-celled eukaryotes that lack flagella. Certainly the fungi differ sharply from all other groups of living organisms.

Spores, always nonmotile, constitute a common means of reproduction among the fungi. They may be formed through either asexual or sexual processes. When the spores land in a suitable place, they germinate, giving rise to a new fungal hypha. Since the spores are very small, they may remain suspended in the air for long periods. Because of this property, fungal spores may be blown great distances from their place of origin, a factor explaining the extremely wide distributions of many kinds of fungi. Unfortunately, many fungi that cause diseases of plants and animals are spread rapidly and widely by such means.

Bacteria

We have known that some human diseases, including cholera, bacteria pneumonia, strep throat, are caused by bacteria, so perhaps the first word pop into your mind is 'germ' and that should be gotten rid of all possible when you hear the word 'bacteria'. However, contrary to the popular impression, beneficial bacteria outnumber harmful ones, and most bacteria are helpful to us.

Bacteria are numerous almost everywhere. There are millions of bacteria on our skin, in the air, in garden soil and the human intestine also swarms with bacteria. Bacteria may thrive where few other living things can even survive—in boiling hot spring, in the windswept arctic tundra, in the salty waters and it have even been collected from ocean troughs eleven kilometers deep and from air samples taken at a height of 75 kilometers. Some bacteria can survive for many years in a dried or frozen state and 'come back to life' as soon as conditions are improved. Both plant and animal life depend on the activities of these bacteria, they can prevent the accumulation of dead bodies and metabolic wastes. There are also bacteria in our intestines that synthesize vitamins absorbed by the body and that aid in the digestion of certain materials. Bacteria are of great importance in many industrial processes. Many commercially manufactured substances, such as acetic acid (vinegar), acetone, lactic acid and some vitamins, become easier and cheaper to synthesize by means of bacteria. Bacteria also have the central role in food industry in making butter, cheese, etc. Recently, farmers depend on bacteria to make silage for use as cattle feed, or in controlling of destructive insects. The role of bacteria in production of antibiotics that help control other bacteria is especially interesting. Most recently, bacteria, particularly *E.coil*, have become the workhorse of genetic engineering.

For most of human history, the existence of bacteria has been unaware because they are much too small to be seen with an unaided eye. About 300 years ago, human eyes could see the bacteria for the first time with the appearance of simple single-len microscope. Bacteria belong to the prokaryotic kingdoms. Unlike viruses, bacteria are cellular, they always contain both DNA and RNA, they havc ribosomes, they possess integrated enzyme systems, and they can generate ATP and use it in the synthesis of other organic compounds. Of course, their cells lack a nuclear membrane, mitochondria, lysosomes and other membranous organelles. Most bacteria have a thick and relatively stiff cell wall. If the wall contains a great deal of peptidoglycan, it takes on a blue to purple color when treated with the Gram stain; bacteria with such walls are called Gram-positive. Gram-negative bacteria have an outer membrane of lipopolysaccharides, and contain less peptidoglycan, appear pink to red following Gram stain. This difference is somewhat useful in classifying bacteria.

Most bacteria are classified according to their shapes. Three shapes are particularly common among the bacteria: spherical, the cocci, rod-shaped, the bacilli, or helically coiled, the spirilla. Bacteria often attach together to form chains or grapelike clusters. Most bacteria reproduce by the fission of one cell into two. Chains arise merely by the adhesion of cells after fusion, and bacteria commonly have enormous reproductive potential.

Bacteria often live symbiotically with other species. Some kinds are consistently found living on our skin, others in our interstines. Many bacteria can survive only within the cells of plants, and different ones inhabit animal cells. Many bacteria can move about actively, in most cases, the motion is produced by the rotation of flagella. How does a minute cell without a mouth or stomach feed itself? Bacteria absorb their nutrients directly from the environment around them. They have in them proteins called enzymes that help break down nutrient molecules and so enable the bacteria to extract energy from them. There are two main ways of getting energy out of nutrients. When the nourishing substances are metabolized where there is no oxygen, such bacteria are called obligate anaerobes and the process is called fermentation. Other bacteria, called facultative anaerobes, are more flexible and can live in either presence or absence of O_2, they can obtain energy by fermentation or respiration, and respiration is a much more efficient energy-yielding process than fermentation.

Viruses

The nature of viruses has been really understand only within the last half century, and the first step on this path of discovery was taken by the Russian botanist Dmitri Lvanovsky in 1892 when he studied the tobacco mosaic disease.

Viruses are very small entities, ranging in size from 0.02 to 0.3 microns. Unlike the organisms making up the five taxonomic kingdoms of the living world, viruses are acellular, they don't consist of cells and conduct energy metabolism—they don't produce ATP and are incapable of fermentation, cellular respiration of photosynthesis. As for these, the questions of the viruses origin arise. Do they represent a primitive 'nearly living' stage in the evolution of life? Or are they organisms which have lost all cellular components except the nucleus? Could viruses simply be fragments of genetic material derived from cellular organisms? No one really knows the answers to these questions. But we do know that viruses have been around for a long time, and that almost every form of life is susceptible to viral attack.

The basic units of a virus consist of nucleic acid surrounded by a capsid or coat, composed of one or at most a few kinds of proteins. These proteins are so assembled as to give the virion a characteristic shape. As they bud through host cell membranes, many animal viruses also acquire a membrane consisting of lipids and proteins, and many bacterial viruses have specialized 'tails' made of protein. The viral nucleic acid is usually a single molecule and may be composed of either DNA or RNA, but not both. DNA or RNA can be double-stranded or single-stranded.

Viruses are obligate intracellular parasite, and that is why they must depend upon specific hosts for their reproduction and development. The cells of animals, plants and bacteria can all serve as hosts to viruses. Animal viruses attach to special sites on the plasma membrane of the host cell and are then taken up by endocytosis. A given virus can infect only those cells that have a receptor site for that virus. After the membrane breaks down, the viral protein capsid is broken down by cellular enzymes before the viral nucleic acid is released, then it can take over the host's metabolism, the host cell replicates the viral nucleic acid. In addition, the viral nucleic acid serves to direct the synthesis of new capsid protein by the protein-synthesizing system of the host, and the capsid combine with new viral nucleic acid spontaneously; and in due course, the new virions are released by the host cell.

Plant viruses and bacteriophages must get through a cell wall as well as the host plasma membrane. Infection of a plant usually results from attack by a virion-laden insect vector. The insect uses its proboscis to penetrate the cell wall, and the virions then escape from the insect into the plant. Bacterial viruses are often equipped with tail assemblies that inject the nucleic acid into the host bacterium while the protein coat remains outside. Once inside the host cell, the virus genes take over the metabolic machinery of the cell and generate their own.

Sometimes, viral DNA does not immediately take control of the host metabolism, but inserts itself into the host chromosome and present as 'silent' provirus until the host cell is exposed to some environmental insult, such as ultraviolet light or radiation.

If the viral nucleic acid is RNA, replication needs special enzymes to make the process of RNA-to-RNA synthesis occur. Some RNA viruses called retroviruses do not carry out RNA-to-RNA transcription. Instead, their RNA is transcribed into DNA immediately; this reaction is catalyzed by reverse transcriptase, and then newly formed DNA is inserted into host DNA and then transcribed into RNA and at last new viruses are produced.

After replication and combination, most viruses are released by lysis of the host cell. But in other cases, like that of the retroviruses, viruses are released by extrusion, a process similar to budding thereby the virus becomes enveloped in a small piece of cell membrane as it moves out of the cell. Lysis results in the destruction of the cell, but extrusion allows the cell to remain alive and continue to produce new viruses for a long period of time.

A common way to classify viruses is to separate them first on the nature of the nucleic acid component (DNA or RNA) and then on whether the nucleic acid in the virion is single-or-double-stranded. Further levels of classification depend on such factors as the overall shape of the virus and the symmetry of the capsid. Most capsid may be categorized as helical, icosahedral and so on. Another level of categorization is based on the presence or absence of membranous envelope around the virion; still further subdivision relies on capsid size and other criteria.

Glossary

1. fungi	*n.* 真菌界
2. mycologist	*n.* 真菌学者
3. yeast	*n.* 酵母；酵母菌
4. ethanol	*n.* 乙醇
5. metabolic	*adj.* 代谢作用的,新陈代谢的
6. citric acid	*n.* 柠檬酸
7. steroids	甾体;激素;激素类

8. filament   *n.* 细丝

                                        adj. 细丝状的

9. hyphae   (单 hypha)菌丝

10. septa   *n.* 隔片,隔壁(seprum 的复数)

11. cytoplasm   *n.* 细胞质,细胞浆

12. pore   *n.* 气孔

13. mycelium   *n.* 菌丝体

14. puffballs   *n.* 马勃(菌)

15. morels   *n.* 羊肚菌

16. cellulose   *n.* 细胞膜质;纤维素

17. protists   *n.* 原生生物

18. polysaccharides   *n.* 多糖

19. chitin   *n.* 壳质,角素

20. mitosis   *n.* 有丝分裂,间接核分裂

21. spindle apparatus   纺锤体

22. centriole   *n.* 细胞中心粒,中心体

23. eukaryote   *n.* 真核细胞

24. flagella   *n.* 鞭节,鞭毛

25. nonmotile   *adj.* 不动的,无运动的

26. germinate   *vt. & vi.* (使)发芽

27. human intestine   人体的肠内

28. arctic tundra   北极冻原

29. ocean trough   海槽

30. acetic acid (vinegar)   *n.* 乙酸,醋酸

31. acetone   *n.* 丙酮

32. lactic acid   *n.* 乳酸

33. silage   *n.* 青贮饲料

34. *E.coil*   大肠杆菌

35. ribosome   *n.* 〈生化〉核糖体

36. nuclear membrane   (细胞)核膜

37.mitochondria   *n.* 〈生〉线粒体

38. lysosome   *n.* (细胞中的)溶酶体

39. organelles   *n.* 〈生〉细胞器

40. lipopolysaccharides   脂多糖类

41. cocci   *n.* 球菌

42. bacilli   *n.* 细菌,杆菌

43. spirilla   *n.* 螺旋状菌,螺旋状菌属

44. acellular   *adj.* 非细胞的,非细胞组成的

45. photosynthesis   *n.* 光合作用; 光能合成

46. nucleic acid   *n.* 核酸

47. virion   *n.* 病毒(成熟)粒子,毒粒,病毒体

48. host cell membranes   寄主（宿主）细胞膜

49. lipids   脂类

50. intracellular parasite   胞内寄生物

51. plasma   *n.* 〈解〉血浆

52. endocytosis	*n.* (细胞)内吞作用
53. bacteriophage	*n.* 噬菌体
54. insect vector	昆虫媒介
55. proboscis	*n.* (昆虫等的)喙
56. tail assemblies	尾翼、尾端
57. provirus	*n.* 前病毒
58. retroviruses	逆转录病毒
59. catalyze	*vt.* 催化；促进
60. transcriptase	*n.* 转录酶
61. lysis	*n.* 〈生〉(细胞)溶解
62. extrusion	*n.* 挤出,推出（成形）
63. capsid	*n.* 衣壳
64. helical	*adj.* 螺旋状的
65. icosahedral	*adj.* 二十面的

Exercises

1. *Matching*

① yeast   (a) a structure to most bacteria
② pneumonia   (b) bacterial human disease
③ flagella   (c) obligate intracellular parasite
④ virus   (d) man who study fungi
⑤ bacteriophage   (e) bacterial viruses
⑥ mycologist   (f) single-celled fungus

2. *Fill in the blanks with the words or expressions given below, and change the form where necessary.*

| nonmotile | nucleic acid | germinate |
| catalyzed | metabolic | cellular |

① Both cheese and wine achieve their delicate flavors because of the _____ processes of certain fungi, and other fungi make possible the manufacture of such oriental delicacies as soy sauce and tofu.

② Spores, always _____ , constitute a common means of reproduction among the fungi. They may be formed through either asexual or sexual processes.

③ When the spores land in a suitable place, they _____ , giving rise to a new fungal hypha. Since the spores are very small, they may remain suspended in the air for long periods.

④ Unlike viruses, bacteria are _____ , they always contain both DNA and RNA.

⑤ The basic units of a virus consist of _____ surrounded by a capsid or coat, composed of one or at most a few kinds of proteins.

⑥ Some RNA viruses called retroviruses do not carry out RNA-to-RNA transcription. Instead, their RNA is transcribed into DNA immediately; this reaction is _____ by reverse transcriptase.

真菌，细菌和病毒

真　菌

真菌是一种至少有 4 亿年历史的原始生物群体，甚至可能有 8 亿年之久。这一特别的生物群体包括约 10 万种已命名的物种，但是真菌学家认为现存的物种应是其数倍之多。

许多真菌是有害的，因为它们获取食物的同时会使许多不同的物质腐坏。它们还会引起动、植物包括人类的严重疾病。然而，其它一些真菌却非常有用。面包与啤酒的生产正是依赖酵母的生化活动进行的。酵母是一种能产生大量乙醇和二氧化碳的单细胞真菌。某些真菌的代谢活动能使奶酪和葡萄酒具有鲜美的风味，其它一些真菌则可用来生产像酱油、豆腐之类的东方佳肴。大型工厂利用真菌培养借助生化技术生产柠檬酸等有机物质。目前，还可大规模使用酵母生产蛋白质来强化动物食品。包括第一种广泛使用的抗生素——青霉素在内的许多抗生素都来自真菌。还有一些真菌可将复杂有机分子转化为其它分子，比如合成许多具有重要商业价值的固醇类物质。由于真菌好坏参半，因此对我们至关重要。

真菌主要以肉眼看不到的细丝形式存在，称作菌丝。这些菌丝被隔膜（称为中隔膜）的所分隔。然而，这些隔膜除了分隔生殖细胞，并不会形成一个完整的屏障。细胞质可以经由隔膜中的主要气孔自由地穿过菌丝。借助这一细胞质流，菌丝合成的蛋白质可以运至快速生长的菌丝尖。于是，真菌菌丝就会在充足的食物、水源及足够高的温度下快速生长。

菌丝集合在一起形成的块叫菌丝体。真菌菌丝体的菌丝总长度可能有几十公里长，但集中在一起范围却非常小。菌丝体蔓延生长，渗透在真菌的生长环境周围，从而在真菌及其环境之间产生一种独特的作用关系。真菌的各部分代谢活跃，不断地与土壤、树木或真菌赖以生长的其它环境物质相互作用。

2/3 的真菌，由菌丝交织而成的结构形成，如蘑菇类、马勃菌类和羊肚菌类都是在生命周期的某个特定阶段形成的。这些结构因细胞质流和数十公里长的菌丝的生长而迅速扩张。因此，蘑菇能够冲破网球场地面或突然出现在你的草坪上。

真菌的细胞壁不像植物和许多原生生物那样是由纤维素构成的。真菌细胞壁一般由其它多聚糖构成，其中几丁质尤为常见。几丁质同样是构成软体动物的硬壳、节肢动物（包括昆虫、甲壳动物）的外骨骼主要部分的一种物质。和纤维素相比，几丁质更耐微生物降解。

真菌中的有丝分裂不同于其它生物体的分裂。核膜不分解，不重组，核膜内形成纺锤体。此外，所有真菌都缺少中心粒。总之，真菌的特征表明真菌起源于未知的缺乏鞭毛的单细胞真核细胞类。当然真菌与其它生物类群截然不同。

真菌一般通过非游走的孢子进行繁殖。它们可能通过有性或无性过程形成。当孢子着陆到合适的地方，就开始萌发，产生新的真菌菌丝。由于孢子很小，所以它们可以在空气中停留很长时间。由于这个原因，真菌孢子可能被吹到离原生地很远的地方。这是许多真菌种类分布范围较广的一个原因。不幸的是，许多会使动、植物致病的真菌也是如此传播，速度快，范围广。

细　菌

我们知道，人类许多疾病（包括霍乱、细菌性肺炎、链球菌性喉炎）都是细菌引起的。

"细菌"一词在英文日常口语中一般称为"germ"，但在学术上应严格称为"bacteria"。与人们的平常观念相反，有益的细菌其实多于有害菌，大多数细菌对我们有益。

细菌数量庞大，几乎随处可见。我们的皮肤上、空气中、花园的土壤里有成千上万的细菌，人体肠道内同样存在许多细菌。细菌可以在其它生物体无法生存的环境中生存——在滚烫的沸泉中，在大风肆虐的北极冰原，在盐水中，甚至从数万米深的海沟到海拔 75000 米高的空气中都有细菌存在。一些细菌在干燥或冰冻的状态下可以休眠，只要条件改善它们就立刻可以"复活"。动、植物的生命依赖于这些细菌的活动，它们可以防止尸体和代谢排泄物的累积。我们的肠道内也有细菌，合成身体吸收的维生素，帮助促进一些物质的消化。在许多工业生产过程中，细菌起着至关重要的作用。许多物质如醋酸（醋）、丙酮、乳酸和利用细菌合成的一些维生素变得越来越容易商业化生产，越来越便宜。细菌在黄油、奶酪的制作等食品行业中也非常重要。近年来，农民还利用细菌生产青贮饲料用于喂养小牛或控制害虫。在帮助控制其它细菌的抗生素生产方面，细菌的作用尤为突出。最近，细菌，尤其是大肠杆菌，已成为基因工程的主要载体。

回顾人类历史，细菌由于太微小，肉眼看不到，其存在没有受到重视。大约 300 年前，简单的单透镜显微镜的出现使人类第一次用肉眼看到了细菌。细菌属原核生物。不像病毒，细菌具有细胞结构，它们总是包含 DNA 和 RNA，有核糖体，具有完整的酶系统，能生成三磷酸腺苷（ATP），将之用于其它有机化合物的合成。当然，细菌细胞没有核膜、线粒体、溶酶体和其它膜质细胞器。大多数细菌具有厚而相对较硬的细胞壁。如果细胞壁中包含大量肽聚糖，经革兰染色处理时，会呈蓝到紫色，带有这样细胞壁的细菌叫革兰阳性菌。革兰阴性细菌的细胞壁含有脂多糖外膜，包含的肽聚糖较少，经革兰染色处理后呈粉色到红色。这种差异在某种程度上有益于进行细菌的分类。

大多数细菌按形状来分类，常有三种形状：球状（球菌）、杆状（杆菌）和螺旋状（螺旋菌）。单个细菌常常依附在一起形成链状或葡萄串状。大多数细菌通过细胞一分为二进行繁殖。细菌分裂繁殖之后，通过细胞黏附成链。细菌通常有非常高的繁殖能力。

细菌常与其它物种共生。我们的皮肤上常有一些细菌，肠道内也生活有许多细菌。有些细菌只能生存在植物细胞中，而有些细菌则生活在动物细胞中。许多细菌可以自由游动，大多数情况下，是通过鞭毛的旋转作用而游动的。这种没有嘴、没有胃的微小细胞是如何生存的呢？细菌直接从周围环境中汲取养分。它们自身有被称作酶的蛋白质，帮助降解营养分子，使细菌从中汲取能量。从营养中汲取能量有两种方式。当营养物质在无氧条件下代谢，这些细菌称作专性厌氧菌，该过程称作发酵过程。另外一类细菌更为灵活，称为兼性厌氧菌，在有氧、无氧条件下都可生存，它们可以通过发酵或呼吸作用获取能量。与发酵过程相比，呼吸作用是一种更有效的产能过程。

病　　毒

在 19 世纪后半叶人们才真正了解病毒，1892 年，俄罗斯植物学家伊凡诺夫斯基对烟草花叶病毒的研究迈出了人类了解病毒的第一步。

病毒是非常小的个体，从 0.02～0.3 微米不等。不像组成生命世界的其它五类生物，病毒是非细胞结构的。它们不是由细胞构成的，不能进行能量代谢——它们不产生 ATP，不能发酵，也不能进行光合作用的细胞呼吸作用。由此，病毒的起源问题产生了。它们是生命进化中的原始阶段吗？它们是失去除细胞核外所有细胞成分的生物体吗？病毒有可能只是细胞生物体中遗传物质的片段吗？没人能知道真正的答案，但我们知道病毒的确已经存在了很久，几乎每一种生命形式都易受到病毒的侵袭。

病毒的基本单位是由衣壳或包被所包围的核酸构成，衣壳或包被由一种或最多几种蛋白质组成。这些蛋白质组合在一起，使病毒体形成独特的形状。当萌发穿破宿主细胞膜时，许多动物病毒也会获得由脂肪和蛋白质构成的膜。许多细菌性病毒具有特别的蛋白"尾巴"。病毒核酸通常是一个分子，单独由 DNA 或 RNA 构成，但不会两者都有。DNA 或 RNA 可以是双链或单链。

　　病毒是专性胞内寄生物，这正是它们必须依赖特定宿主繁殖、生长的原因。动物、植物和细菌细胞都可以作为病毒的宿主。动物病毒附着在宿主细胞原生质膜的特定位点，并通过胞吞作用被吸收。一个特定的病毒只会感染对该病毒有受点的那些细胞。原生质膜破裂后，病毒的蛋白质衣壳先被胞内酶分解，然后释放出病毒核酸，接管宿主的代谢过程，宿主细胞开始复制病毒核酸。此外，病毒核酸通过宿主的蛋白质合成系统引导新衣壳蛋白的合成。衣壳与新病毒核酸自发结合，然后宿主细胞适时释放出新的病毒体。

　　除宿主的原生质膜外，植物病毒和噬菌体还必须穿过细胞壁。植物感染通常由带有病毒体的昆虫媒介的侵袭所致。昆虫利用吸管刺破细胞壁，然后病毒体从昆虫导入植物中。细菌病毒通常具有尾部结构，尾部将核酸注入细菌宿主中，而蛋白衣壳则留在外部。一旦进入宿主细胞，病毒基因就会接管细胞的代谢机制，生成自己的遗传物质。

　　有时，病毒 DNA 并不立刻控制宿主的代谢过程，但是将自己嵌入宿主染色体中，以"静默"的前病毒形式呈现，直至宿主细胞受到一些环境损伤，如紫外线照射或辐射。

　　如果病毒的核酸是 RNA，复制时需要特殊的酶来完成从 RNA 到 RNA 的合成。一些被称作逆转录病毒的 RNA 病毒并不进行从 RNA 到 RNA 的转录，相反，它们的 RNA 转录为 DNA，这个反应是由逆转录酶催化而成。然后，新形成的 DNA 嵌入宿主 DNA 中，转录为 RNA，最后生成新的病毒。

　　大多数病毒经过复制与装配之后在宿主细胞溶解时释放。但是，在另外一些时候，例如逆转录病毒，病毒通过芽突过程释放。病毒在排出细胞时，包装在一小片细胞膜中。溶解会破坏细胞，但细胞发生芽突后仍能存活，在相当长的时间内继续生成新的病毒。

　　一种常见的病毒分类方法是先根据核酸成分是 DNA 还是 RNA，再根据病毒体中核酸是单链还是双链进行分类。进一步的分类依据是病毒的整体形状和衣壳是否对称。大多数衣壳可以分为螺旋状、二十面体等形状。另一个分类依据是病毒体周围有无被膜，然后再根据衣壳大小和其它标准进行细分。

练习参考答案 *(Reference answers of exercises)*

1. 配对 *(Matching)*
①—(f)；②—(b)；③—(a)；④—(c)；⑤—(e)；⑥—(d)

2. 用词或短语填空，根据需要变换形式 *(Fill in the blanks with the words or expressions given below, and change the form where necessary)*
① metabolic　② nonmotile　③ germinate
④ cellular　⑤ nucleic acid　⑥ catalyzed

Unit 4 Factors Influencing Optimum Performance of Starter Cultures

Reading Material

As with starter cultures, the proper performance of the lactobacilli requires that the culture receives proper care and handing in uses. The propagation procedures utilized in producing the starter culture are very important. Furthermore, variation among strains of the individual species of lactobacilli must be considered when evaluating optimum performance.

1. Temperature

The optimum performance of the lactobacilli is normally expected to coincide with the optimum growth temperature for each species. In some cases, however, it may be necessary to consider other factors. In the case of yogurt starter cultures, which are mixed species starters usually containing both *L. bulgaricus* and *S. thermophilus*, the two individual species of bacteria exhibit different optimum growth temperatures. Fortunately the temperature (41 to 42 ℃) recommended for maintaining the proper balance between two species of the bacteria is close to that of the optimum growth temperature for *L. bulgaricus*.

2. Treatment of milk prior to inoculation

Other than standardizing the milk with regard to total solids of fat content, the primary treatment that is utilized in preparing the milk for manufacture of cultured milk products is heat processing. This has several functions. Firstly it is the killing of undesirable organisms that might have an adverse effect on the product being manufactured. It is generally accepted that heating of the milk for cultured products improves it as the growth medium for the starter culture bacteria. The effect of heat on the proteins of the milk apparently causes some alteration(s), making them easier to be utilized by the starter bacteria. Since the lactobacilli are microaerophilic in nature, heating of the milk may also play an important role in reducing the amount of oxygen present in the product. This is supported by the fact that the lactobacilli generally grow best in freshly heated milk. The best process of milk may also destroy or at least partially destroy natural inhibitors occurring in raw milk. If sufficiently high temperatures are utilized in heating the milk some formic acid is formed. The presence of this compound in milk can result in stimulation of the growth of certain of the lactobacilli.

3. Nutrient availability

The general requirements for growth of the lactobacilli include water, fermentable sugar, carbon, nitrogen (including preformed amino acids), vitamins, and other cofactors. The organisms are considered to be fastidious in nature. All nutrients essential for growth of the lactobacilli are contained in milk. The key problem is that the nutrients do not necessarily occur in the most easily available forms. For example, the fermentable sugar (lactose) is more difficult to utilize by some cultures than a monosaccharide such as glucose. The necessary amino acids occur in the form of proteins. Thus, the organism must be able to hydrolyze both lactose and at least partially hydrolyze milk protein in order to obtain the nutrients needed for growth. In some cases poor performance of the lactobacilli in producing the desired change(s) in the milk during the culturing process may be due to limitations in their ability to hydrolyze lactose and/or proteins.

L. bulgaricus and *S. thermophilus* used as yogurt cultures produce acid faster in milk in which the lactose had been prehydrolyzed by treatment with β-galactosidase. In some cases however, stimulation is not obtained by prehydrolyzing the lactose. This difference in response is probably due to variations in the cultures being tested. For those starters that can hydrolyze the lactose as rapidly as it can be used for growth and acid production prehydrolysis of lactose may not provide a benefit. In milk treated with β-galactosidase to prehydrolyze the lactose, *L. bulgaricus* uses only the glucose portion of the molecule.

Some lactobacilli, when growing in a medium containing lactose as the sugar source, will excrete the galactose and not utilize it for growth. These observations suggest that the lactobacilli, in addition to exhibiting a preference for glucose, are also utilizing the hexose moiety of lactose that yields the most energy per molecule.

The nonprotein nitrogen fraction of milk would be inadequate to meet the needs of growing lactobacilli. To grow exponentially in milk, the proteinase activity of the lactobacilli must function effectively in order for the organism to obtain sufficient amino acids for growth. Slow growing strains for lactobacilli may have inadequate proteinase activity. The growth of *L. casei* is slower when casein is the nitrogen source than when peptones are supplied to the culture. During growth in milk, *L. bulgaricus* apparently exhibits a preference for utilizing β-casein as a nitrogen source over the other proteins, indicating that the type of protein is also an important factor in influencing the growth of these cultures.

4. Stimulatory

In efforts to improve growth and acid production by lactic acid bacteria in milk, a number of substances have been evaluated for possible stimulatory effects over the years. Yeast extract, various peptones, liver extract, corn steep liquor, and tomato juice are some of the materials that have been found to contain substances that stimulate the growth and action of starter culture bacteria in milk. While such materials may be stimulatory when added to milk for cultured dairy products, their use in most cases has not been practical due to undesirable flavors that accompany them. In general, the stimulants in these products include such compounds as peptones, amino acids, vitamins, and other co-factors. Corn steep liquors, for example, contains amino acids and peptides that are stimulatory for *L. casei*. Tomato juice contains both stimulants and inhibitors for the lactobacilli. The stimulants in this material include both adenine and adenosine. The inhibitor is a nucleotide containing adenine and xylose. Pancreas extract has shown promise as a source of stimulants for starter cultures used in the manufacture of milk products since it dose not impart an undesirable flavour in the milk. However, it is rather expensive and thus is not often utilized as a stimulant. The main stimulatory components from pancreas extract have been identified as peptides, especially when *L. casei* is used as the test organism.

Other compounds stimulatory for the lactobacilli include oleic acid and formate. Formate added to milk can reduce the stimulatory effect that *S. thermophilus* has toward *L. bulgaricus* during yogurt manufacture. Thornhill and Cogan reported that certain fruit preparations added to yogurt resulted in increased acid production by the yogurt culture. They concluded, however, that such additions did not result in a major stimulation for the culture.

5. Metabolites produced by lactobacilli

The major metabolite produced by the lactobacilli that makes them important in cultured milk products is lactic acid. Even though the lactobacilli are considered acid tolerant, sufficient lactic acid will limit their growth. It is possible that in some cases, variations observed among species and/or strains of lactobacilli with the rapidity of growth and acid production in milk may be due to variations in their sensitivity to lactic acid.

The lactobacilli, being catalase negative, do not have the usual mechanism for destroying metabolically produced hydrogen peroxide. For this reason the cultures can accumulate hydrogen peroxide in the growth medium. Some lactic acid bacteria produce autoinhibitory levels of hydrogen peroxide. The addition of catalase to milk cultures often stimulates acid production by *Lactic streptococci*, but not *L. acidophilus* and *L. bulgaricus*. However, the lactobacilli produce more total peroxide than the streptococci. This indicates that the lactobacilli are more tolerant to hydrogen peroxide than the streptococci. In another study on the evaluation of the possibility of adding cells of *L. acidophilus* to yogurt cultures, the *L. acidophilus* cells died during storage due to hydrogen peroxide produced by *L. bulgaricus* in the yogurt culture. It is possible that hydrogen peroxide produced by some strains of lactobacilli may limit their growth and acid production in milk. Most likely these is considerable variation among strains of different species with regard to this characteristic.

The inability of the lactobacilli to destroy metabolically produced hydrogen peroxide may, at least partially, explain there poor growth under highly aerobic conditions. This suggests the importance of avoiding excessive agitation when mixing the starter into the milk to be cultured. The inability to grow under highly aerobic conditions may also be related to oxygen toxicity. In many bacteria superoxide dismutase serves as a defense against oxygen toxicity, however, the lactobacilli do not contain this enzyme. Some lactobacilli contain dialyzable manganese that may replace the function of superoxide dismutase. The intracellular manganese serves as an oxygen scavenger. This emphasizes the importance of providing adequate manganese for the culture during growth.

6. Interactions with other starter bacteria

In yogurt starter culture, *L. bulgaricus* and *S, thermophilus* growing together produce acid more rapidly than either of the individual species alone. This appears to be a two-way beneficial interaction. During growth in milk the *L. bulgaricus* cells produce sufficient free amino acids, particularly histidine, to stimulate growth and acid production by *S. thermophilus*, the *S. thermophilus*, on the other hand, produces formic acid, which is stimulatory for *L. bulgaricus*. Also, *S. thermophilus* produces sufficient amounts of carbon dioxide to stimulate the growth and action of *L. bulgaricus*. In addition to the beneficial interaction between these two species, a competitive interaction has also been reported. Even though acid production by both is greater than either one alone, the total growth of *L. bulgaricus* is less in the associative culture. This is apparently due to the streptococci utilizing some component essential for maximum growth of the lactobacilli.

7. Treatment of starter culture in uses

As with other starter cultures the temperature at which the culture is stored influences its subsequent performance in milk. Storage at – 30 to 0℃ causes reduced activity compared to storage at 14℃. Storage at 8℃ results in a culture having intermediate activity. This suggests that refrigerated storage of the lactobacilli just prior to use may be slightly detrimental to their performance in the manufacture of cultured milk products. Smittle et al. reported variation among strains with regard to survival of *L. bulgaricus* stored at - 196℃. However, all strains of the lactobacilli grown in the presence of Tween 80 or oleic acid survived freezing better than those grown without these materials. The improved survival was related to the level of a C19 cyclopropane fatty acid in the cellular lipids of the lactobacilli. Growth of the organisms in the medium containing oleic acid resulted in increased levels of this fatty acid. Similar findings were reported with regard to storage of the lactobacilli at - 17℃. Cells grown in a medium containing oleic acid survived freezing better than those grown without the fatty acid. The increased survival was attributed to an increased ratio of unsaturated to saturated fatty acids (the C19 cyclopropane fatty acid was included as an unsaturated fatty acid).

8. Bacteriophage

As with the lactic streptococci and other bacterial species there are bacteriophage specific for the lactobacilli. While there have been few reports of bacteriophage for lactobacilli occurring in dairy products it is important that caution be used in handling the cultures to control bacteriophage. Host specificity appears to exist for the phages for lactobacilli as is observed with other bacterial species. Many of the lactobacilli exhibit lysogeny. Within the streptobacterium group there is a very narrow range for host specificity that has been attributed immunity caused by frequent lysogeny within this group. In some species attempts to induce plaque formation from lysogenic lactobacilli through treatment of the cultures with mitomycin have resulted in the release of phage-like structures. However, in several cases no plaques were formed, indicating a relatively low activity with regard to the lytic action of these types of bacteriophage. This lack of plaque formation could be due to insufficient knowledge of all the factors necessary to ensure proliferation of these phages. The bacteriophage for *L. casei* requires calcium ions for penetration into the host cell. These phages also exhibit an optimum pH range of 5.5 to 6 and an optimum temperature of 30℃.

Glossary

1. starter culture	*n.*	发酵剂
2. lactobacilli	*n.*	乳酸杆菌
3. propagation	*n.*	传播；繁殖；增殖
4. optimum	*adj.*	最适宜的
	n.	最佳效果；最适宜条件
5. *L. bulgaricus*	*n.*	保加利亚乳杆菌
6. *S. thermophilus*	*n.*	嗜热乳链球菌
7. inoculation	*n.*	接种；接木

8. microaerophilic	*adj.* 微量需氧的
9. fastidious	*adj.*（微生物等）需要复杂营养地
10. lactose	*n.* 乳糖
11. monosaccharide	*n.*〈化〉单糖，单糖类（最简单的糖类）
12. hydrolyze	*vi.* 水解 *vt.* 使水解
13. galactose	*n.*〈化〉半乳糖
14. hexose	*n.*〈生化〉己糖
15. proteinase	*n.*〈生化〉蛋白酶；〈生化〉朊酶
16. peptone	*n.* 蛋白胨，胨
17. peptide	*n.* 缩氨酸
18. xylose	*n.*〈化〉木糖
19. pancreas	*n.* 胰腺
20. *L. casei*	*n.* 干酪乳杆菌
21. Metabolites	*n.*〈生〉代谢物
22. catalase	*n.*〈化〉接触酵素；过氧化氢酶
23. streptococci	*n.* 链球菌（streptococcus 的复数）
24. histidine	*n.* 组氨酸
25. Tween	*n.* 非离子活性剂, 吐温
26. cyclopropane	*n.*〈化〉环丙烷
27. oleic acid	*n.*十八烯酸，油酸
28. bacteriophage	*n.* 噬菌体
29. lysogeny	*n.* 溶原现象；〈微生物〉溶原性
30. mitomycin	*n.* 丝裂霉素
31. lytic	*adj.* 细胞溶素的；促使细胞溶解的；渐退的
32. calcium ions	*n.* 钙离子

Exercises

1. *Matching*

① optimum

(a) taking a vaccine as a precaution against contracting a disease

② inoculation

(b) enzyme found in most plant and animal cells that functions as an oxidative catalyst; decomposes hydrogen peroxide into hydrogen and water

③ stimulatory materials

(c) the killing of undesirable organisms that might have and adverse effect on the product being manufactured.

④ catalase

(d) a virus that is parasitic in bacteria; it uses the bacterium's machinery and energy to produce more phage until the bacterium is destroyed and phage is released to invade surrounding bacteria

⑤ heat processing

(e) substances that stimulate the growth and action of starter culture bacteria in milk

⑥ bacteriophage

(f) most favorable condition or greatest degree or amount possible under given circumstances

2. *Fill in the blanks with the words or expressions given below.*

| streptococci | oleic acid | lactobacilli |
| bacteriophage | lactic acid | propagation |

① The _____ procedures utilized in producing the starter culture are very important.

② The presence of this compound in milk can result in stimulation of the growth of certain of the_____.

③ Other compounds stimulatory for the lactobacilli include _____and formate.

④ The major metabolite produced by the lactobacilli that makes them important in cultured milk products is _____.

⑤ Even though acid production by both was greater than either one alone, the total growth of *L. bulgaricus* was less in the associative culture. This was apparently due to the _____ utilizing some component essential for maximum growth of the lactobacilli.

⑥ As with the lactic streptococci and other bacterial species there are _____ specific for the lactobacilli.

Translation

影响微生物发酵剂活力的主要因素

发酵剂就是要使乳酸细菌表现其优越性能。不仅关注菌体的培养情况，还要注意处理的方式。细菌培养方法的正确与否对于发酵剂的功能非常重要。而且，对于不同种的菌株必须采用不同的处理方式。

1. 温度

乳酸菌要发挥最佳的性能，不同的菌种就需要用不同的培养温度。但是，在一些情况下，还需要考虑其它因素。例如，酸奶中用的是保加利亚乳杆菌与嗜热乳链球菌的混合菌种，这两种菌的最适生长温度不一致，比较值得庆幸的是，通常推荐的 41~42℃ 的温度能够平衡这两种菌株的生长，且这一温度也与保加利亚乳杆菌的最适生长温度接近。

2. 接种前的处理

不同于奶中的脂质总固形物的标准化，在制备发酵型奶产品的准备步骤中最基本的一步就是热处理。这样的热处理有几个方面的作用，其中一项就是杀死那些不需要的菌株，因为这些菌株有可能会对产品质量产生负面的效应。通常认为，经过热处理的作为加工用的奶，可以被用来作为微生物发酵剂的初始培养基。热处理可以引起牛奶中的部分蛋白质发生变化，使蛋白质变得更容易被发酵菌株所利用。因为乳酸菌在自然界中本来就是微好氧的，热处理可以使奶中的溶氧量降低，乳酸菌总是在刚经过热处理的牛奶中长得很好，这一事实可以证明这一点。最好的牛奶加工工艺能够去除或者部分去除原料奶中的营养抑制因子。如果在牛奶处理中用较好的热处理温度，就能够形成蚁酸，该物质能够促进牛奶中乳酸菌的生长。

3. 可用的营养物

乳酸菌生长所需要的基本营养物质包括：水、可发酵的糖、碳源、氮源（包括一些氨基酸）、维生素等。这类微生物从本质上来说对营养是很苛求的。牛奶能够提供乳酸菌生长所需的所有营养成分，关键问题是这些营养元素在牛奶中是否以直接被微生物可利用的形式存在。例如，可发酵性的糖（乳糖）对于一些微生物来说就不如单糖（如葡萄糖）好利用。必需性氨基酸也往往以蛋白质的形式存在。因此，微生物就既需要降解乳糖，也需要能够部分降解牛奶中的蛋白质，从而能够获得供给其生长的营养物质。有时在奶制品发酵过程中乳酸菌不能表现其应有的性状，就是因为没有能力降解上述两类物质。

保加利亚乳杆菌与嗜热乳链球菌作为酸奶的发酵剂，经过 β-半乳糖苷酶水解乳糖处理后，具有产酸快的特点。在某些情况下，是没有这样的激活方式的，这是因为菌种发生了某些变异而丧失了这一特点。对于有些自身能够快速水解乳糖的菌株，是可以满足菌体生长产酸的，对于这些菌株进行前期的乳糖前处理是无益的。牛奶经过 β-半乳糖苷酶水解乳糖后，保加利亚乳杆菌只优先利用葡萄糖。

对于有些乳酸菌，当生长在只有乳糖作为糖源的培养基上时，就会产生半乳糖，而不加以利用。这一特征说明，乳酸细菌可以表现出另一种功能，即利用乳糖的六碳糖分子产生能量。

牛奶中的非蛋白质氮不能满足乳酸菌的生长需要，为了达到对数生长的速度，乳酸菌中的蛋白酶活力必须发挥其优越的性能，以获得供给菌体生长所必需的氨基酸。对于那些生长缓慢的菌株，一个可能的原因就是蛋白酶的活力不足。当供给的是酪蛋白而不是蛋白胨时，干酪乳杆菌的生长速度就会降低。保加利亚乳杆菌在牛奶中生长时，会优先利用 β-酪蛋白作为氮源，这表明蛋白质的类型也是影响发酵剂生长的一个重要因素。

4. 激活物质

数年来人们试验了很多种物质，希望能够加快牛奶中乳酸菌的生长以及加快其产酸。酵母膏、不同的蛋白胨、肝浸提物、玉米浆以及西红柿汁中含有能够促进微生物生长以及促进微生物发酵剂发挥正常功效的物质。这些物质加到奶中能够促进微生物发酵剂的生长，但是这些物质中的促进因子即为蛋白胨、维生素、氨基酸类物质。例如，玉米浆中含有氨基酸和肽，就能够促进干酪乳杆菌的生长。西红柿汁中同时含有乳酸菌生长的刺激因子与营养抑制因子，刺激因子是腺嘌呤与腺苷，营养抑制因子是一种含有腺嘌呤与木糖的核苷。胰腺提取物中含有对微生物发酵剂生长有很好促进作用的刺激因子，可以用于奶制品的生产，但是因为其价格昂贵，所以一般不添加；这种刺激因子已经被证实是一些短肽，它们对于干酪乳杆菌的生长有很强的促进作用。

对乳酸杆菌具有刺激作用的化合物包括油酸和甲酸盐，向牛奶中添加甲酸盐会减弱酸奶发酵过程中嗜热链球菌对保加利亚乳杆菌的促进作用。Thornhill 和 Cogan 研究证实往酸奶中添加水果汁加酸的产生，然而他们总结说这样的添加并不在培养过程起主要刺激作用。

5. 乳酸菌代谢物

乳酸菌在酸奶产品中起作用的主要因素及其主要代谢产物就是乳酸，尽管乳酸菌是耐酸的菌株，但是酸量过大也能够抑制乳酸菌的生长。某些情况下，不同的乳酸菌或不同的菌株，在牛奶中快速生长与乳酸的产生是不同的，这是由于它们对乳酸的敏感性有所不同。

乳酸菌过氧化氢酶阴性，没有降解其代谢产物中的过氧化物的能力，就是因为这个原因，在乳酸杆菌的培养基中往往会积累一些过氧化物。有些乳酸菌能够产生达到抑制自身生长水平的过氧化物。在牛奶培养基中添加过氧化氢酶能够刺激乳酸链球菌产酸，但是对于保加利亚乳杆菌与嗜热乳链球菌却不起作用，它们却会产生比链球菌多的过氧化物。这表明乳杆菌要比乳球菌更耐受过氧化氢。另一个实验是在普通的酸奶中添加乳球菌活细胞，在酸奶的贮藏过程中，这些乳球菌因为保加利亚乳杆菌产生的过氧化物而致死。乳杆菌产生的过氧化物能够抑制菌的生长和产酸，这因不同的菌种或菌株而异。

乳酸菌不能够消除其代谢过程中产生的过氧化物对自身的抑制，至少也部分地解释了一点，即乳酸菌在高氧的情况下不能很好地生长，这就要求在发酵剂的培养过程中要尽量避免搅拌。另一个不能在高氧的条件下生长的原因也可能与氧的毒理学作用有关。很多细菌中都有超氧化物歧化酶，以解除高氧对菌体的危害，但是乳酸菌中就没有。一些乳酸菌中含有可以被透析的锰，可以作为超氧化物歧化酶的替代物，这就要求在这些菌株的培养基中要添加足够量的锰元素。

6. 发酵剂之间的相互作用

酸奶发酵剂中，用保加利亚乳杆菌与嗜热乳链球菌共同培养，产酸的速度要比单独任何一个菌株的培养都要快得多，这得益于两方面的作用：一方面是保加利亚乳杆菌在生长过程中产生大量的自由氨基酸，特别是组氨酸，能够促进嗜热乳链球菌的生长与产酸；另一方面，嗜热乳链球菌产生蚁酸，又能对保加利亚乳杆菌起到促进作用，嗜热乳链球菌还产生大量的碳水化合物供给保加利亚乳杆菌的生长和代谢所需。得益于这两方面相互之间的关系，获得了这两种菌株的互惠关系。尽管混合培养的产酸量比单独培养的产酸量要高，但是保加利亚乳杆菌的生长量要低一些，这是因为乳球菌在生长中消耗了部分乳杆菌生长所必需的营养物质。

7. 发酵剂使用中的处理

正如其它发酵剂受温度影响一样，乳酸菌发酵剂要在牛奶中发挥应有的功效也受其保藏温度的影响。在-30～0℃保存要比在14℃保存活力下降很多。在8℃保存活力大小居中。这表明乳杆菌在使用之前的储藏温度能够对奶制品加工过程中发酵剂的功能起到一定的削弱作用。Smittle 等建议将保加利亚乳杆菌的菌株保藏在-196℃。但是所有乳杆菌在添加吐温 80 或油酸后冷冻保藏后的存活率要优于没有添加此类物质的菌种，存活率的提高与乳酸菌中脂肪酸所含 C19 环丙烷脂肪酸有关。添加此类物质能够导致乳杆菌细胞油脂中 C19 环丙烷脂肪酸含量的升高；微生物在含有油酸的培养基中生长时其细胞中这种脂肪酸含量会上升。乳杆菌在-17℃也表现出此类情况，细胞在含有油酸的培养基中冷冻后的存活率更高，添加不饱和脂肪酸要比添加饱和脂肪酸的效果更好。

8. 噬菌体

与乳酸链球菌和其它细菌一样，乳杆菌也有其特异的噬菌体。下面列出了一些在酸奶制作过程中对发酵剂起重要作用的部分噬菌体。乳杆菌的噬菌体也同所观察到的其它细菌一样具有宿主特异性，即很多的乳杆菌表现出溶原性现象。在乳酸链杆菌群中因为这一类群中频繁发生的溶原性引起的免疫现象，导致这一类群中噬菌体的宿主范围很小。乳酸链杆菌群的有些种在添加丝裂霉素的培养基中生长会因为噬菌体类似结构物质的形成而产生类似于溶原性白斑。但是在有些情况下也不产生溶原性白斑，这表明这种类型的噬菌体的活性比较低，这是因为缺乏足够的促使噬菌体形成的因子而造成的。如干酪乳杆菌的噬菌体就需要一定的钙离子才能进入宿主细胞。这些噬菌体所需要的最佳 pH 值范围是 5.5～6，最佳温度是 30℃。

练习参考答案 (Reference answers of exercises)

1. 配对 (Matching)

①—(f)；②—(a)；③—(e)；④—(b)；⑤—(c)；⑥—(d)

2. 用词或短语填空，根据需要变换形式 (Fill in the blanks with the words or expressions given below)

① propagation	② lactobacilli	③ oleic acid
④ lactic acid	⑤ streptococci	⑥ bacteriophage

Chapter Three

Enzyme Engineering

Unit 1   Introduction of Enzyme

Reading Material

Enzymes are biomolecules that catalyze (i.e., increase the rates of) chemical reactions. Nearly all known enzymes are proteins. However, certain RNA molecules can be effective biocatalysts too. These RNA molecules have come to be known as ribozymes. In enzymatic reactions, the molecules at the beginning of the process are called substrates, and the enzyme converts them into different molecules, called the products. Almost all processes in a biological cell need enzymes to occur at significant rates. Since enzymes are selective for their substrates and speed up only a few reactions from among many possibilities, the set of enzymes made in a cell determines which metabolic pathways occur in that cell.

Like all catalysts, enzymes work by lowering the activation energy for a reaction, thus dramatically increasing the rate of the reaction. Most enzyme reaction rates are millions of times faster than those of comparable un-catalyzed reactions. As with all catalysts, enzymes are not consumed by the reactions they catalyze, nor do they alter the equilibrium of these reactions. However, enzymes do differ from most other catalysts by being much more specific. Enzymes are known to catalyze about 4,000 biochemical reactions. A few RNA molecules called ribozymes catalyze reactions, with an important example being some parts of the ribosome. Synthetic molecules called artificial enzymes also display enzyme-like catalysis.

Enzyme activity can be affected by other molecules. Inhibitors are molecules that decrease enzyme activity; activators are molecules that increase activity. Many drugs and poisons are enzyme inhibitors. Activity is also affected by temperature, chemical environment (e.g., pH), and the concentration of substrate. Some enzymes are used commercially, for example, in the synthesis of antibiotics. In addition, some household products use enzymes to speed up biochemical reactions (e.g., enzymes in biological washing powders break down protein or fat stains on clothes; enzymes in meat tenderizers break down proteins, making the meat easier to chew).

Etymology and history

As early as the late 1700s and early 1800s, the digestion of meat by stomach secretions and the conversion of starch to sugars by plant extracts and saliva were known. However, the mechanism by which this occurred had not been identified. In the 19th century, when studying the fermentation of sugar to alcohol by yeast, Louis Pasteur came to the conclusion that this fermentation was catalyzed by a vital force contained within the yeast cells called "ferments", which were thought to function only within living organisms. He wrote that "alcoholic fermentation is an act correlated with the life and organization of the yeast cells, not with the death or putrefaction of the cells." In 1878, German physiologist Wilhelm Kühne (1837—1900) first used the term *enzyme*, "in leaven", to describe this process. The word *enzyme* was used later to refer to nonliving substances such as pepsin, and the word *ferment* was used to refer to chemical activity produced by living organisms.

In 1897, Eduard Buchner began to study the ability of yeast extracts that lacked any living yeast cells to ferment sugar. In a series of experiments at the University of Berlin, he found that the sugar was fermented even when there were no living yeast cells in the mixture. He named the enzyme that brought about the fermentation of sucrose "zymase". In 1907, he received the Nobel Prize in Chemistry "for his biochemical research and his discovery of cell-free fermentation". Following Buchner's example, enzymes are usually named according to the reaction they carry out. Typically, to generate the name of an enzyme, the suffix *-ase* is added to the name of its substrate (*e.g.*, lactase is the enzyme that cleaves lactose) or the type of reaction (*e.g.*, DNA polymerase forms DNA polymers).

Having shown that enzymes could function outside a living cell, the next step was to determine their biochemical nature. Many early workers noted that enzymatic activity was associated with proteins, but several scientists (such as Nobel laureate Richard Willstätter) argued that proteins were merely carriers for the true enzymes and that proteins *per se* were incapable of catalysis. However, in 1926, James B. Sumner showed that the enzyme urease was a pure protein and crystallized it; Sumner did likewise for the enzyme catalase in 1937. The conclusion that pure proteins can be enzymes was definitively proved by Northrop and Stanley, who worked on the digestive enzymes pepsin (1930), trypsin and chymotrypsin. These three scientists were awarded the 1946 Nobel Prize in Chemistry.

This discovery that enzymes could be crystallized eventually allowed their structures to be solved by x-ray crystallography. This was first done for lysozyme, an enzyme found in tears, saliva and egg whites that digests the coating of some bacteria; the structure was solved by a group led by David Chilton Phillips and published in 1965. This high-resolution structure of lysozyme marked the beginning of the field of structural biology and the effort to understand how enzymes work at an atomic level.

Structures and mechanisms

Enzymes are generally globular proteins and range from just 62 amino acid residues in size, for the monomer of 4-oxalocrotonate tautomerase, to over 2,500 residues in the animal fatty acid synthase. A small number of RNA-based biological catalysts exist, with the most common being the ribosome; these are referred to as either RNA-enzymes or ribozymes. The activities of enzymes are determined by their three-dimensional structure. However, although structure does determine function, predicting a novel enzyme's activity just from its structure is a very difficult problem that has not yet been solved.

Most enzymes are much larger than the substrates they act on, and only a small portion of the enzyme (around 3–4 amino acids) is directly involved in catalysis. The region that contains these catalytic residues, binds the substrate, and then carries out the reaction is known as the active site. Enzymes can also contain sites that bind cofactors, which are needed for catalysis. Some enzymes also have binding sites for small molecules, which are often direct or indirect products or substrates of the reaction catalyzed. This binding can serve to increase or decrease the enzyme's activity, providing a means for feedback regulation.

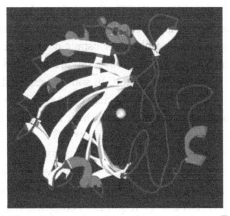

Ribbon diagram showing carbonic anhydrase Ⅱ
The grey sphere is the zinc cofactor in the active site

Like all proteins, enzymes are made of long, linear chains of amino acids that fold to produce a three-dimensional product. Each unique amino acid sequence produces a specific structure, which has unique properties. Individual protein chains may sometimes group together to form a protein complex. Most enzymes can be denatured—that is, unfolded and inactivated—by heating or chemical denaturants, which disrupt the three-dimensional structure of the protein. Depending on the enzyme, denaturation may be reversible or irreversible.

Enzymes are usually very specific as to which reactions they catalyze and the substrates that are involved in these reactions, and there are serval *models to* explain it.

"Lock and key"model

Enzymes are very specific, and it was suggested by Emil Fischer in 1894 that this was because both the enzyme and the substrate possess specific complementary geometric shapes that fit exactly into one another. This is often referred to as "the lock and key" model. However, while this model explains enzyme specificity, it fails to explain the stabilization of the transition state that enzymes achieve. The "lock and key" model has proven inaccurate, and the induced fit model is the most currently accepted enzyme-substrate-coenzyme figure.

Induced fit model

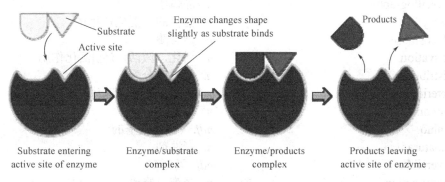

| Substrate entering active site of enzyme | Enzyme/substrate complex | Enzyme/products complex | Products leaving active site of enzyme |

Diagrams to show the induced fit hypothesis of enzyme action

In 1958, Daniel Koshland suggested a modification to the lock and key model: Since enzymes are rather flexible structures, the active site is continually reshaped by interactions with the substrate as the substrate interacts with the enzyme. As a result, the substrate does not simply bind to a rigid active site; the amino acid side chains which make up the active site are moulded into the precise positions that enable the enzyme to perform its catalytic function. In some cases, such as glycosidases, the substrate molecule also changes shape slightly as it enters the active site. The active site continues to change until the substrate is completely bound, at that point the final shape and charge is determined.

Enzymes can act in several ways, all of which lower $\Delta G^{\ddagger}$:

• Lowering the activation energy by creating an environment in which the transition state is stabilized (e.g. straining the shape of a substrate—by binding the transition-state conformation of the substrate/product molecules, the enzyme distorts the bound substrate(s) into their transition state form, thereby reducing the amount of energy required to complete the transition).

• Lowering the energy of the transition state, but without distorting the substrate, by creating an environment with the opposite charge distribution to that of the transition state.

• Providing an alternative pathway. For example, temporarily reacting with the substrate to form an intermediate ES complex, which would be impossible in the absence of the enzyme.

• Reducing the reaction entropy change by bringing substrates together in the correct orientation to react. Considering $\Delta H^{\ddagger}$ alone overlooks this effect.

• Increases in temperatures speed up reactions. Thus, temperature increases help the enzyme function and develop the end product even faster. However, if heated too much, the enzyme's shape deteriorates and only when the temperature comes back to normal does the enzyme regain its shape. Some enzymes like thermolabile enzymes work best at low temperatures.

Glossary

1.	biomolecules	*n.*	生物分子
2.	protein	*n.*	蛋白质
3.	molecule	*n.*	分子
4.	metabolic	*adj.*	代谢作用的，新陈代谢的
5.	synthesis	*n.*	〈化〉合成
6.	pepsin	*n.*	胃蛋白酶
7.	crystallography	*n.*	晶体学
8.	catalytic	*n.*	催化的；催化作用的
9.	glycosidase	*n.*	糖苷酶
10.	activation	*n.*	活化，激活，[化]活化作用
11.	distribution	*n.*	分发，分配
12.	deteriorate	*v.*	恶化，变坏，退化
13.	monomer	*n.*	单体
14.	amino	*adj.*	〈化〉氨基的
15.	denaturant	*n.*	变性剂
16.	reversible	*adj.*	可逆的
17.	modification	*n.*	修饰，修改

Exercise

Fill in the blanks with the words or expressions given below, and change the form where necessary.

identify	lower	conclude
inhibitor	product	

① Louis Pasteur came to the _____ that this fermentation was catalyzed by a vital force contained within the yeast cells called "ferments", which were thought to function only within living organisms.

② In enzymatic reactions, the molecules at the beginning of the process are called substrates, and the enzyme converts them into different molecules, called the _____.

③ Like all catalysts, enzymes work by _____ the activation energy for a reaction, thus dramatically increasing the rate of the reaction.

④ Enzyme activity can be affected by other molecules. _____ are molecules that decrease enzyme activity; activators are molecules that increase activity.

⑤ As early as the late 1700s and early 1800s, the digestion of meat by stomach secretions and the conversion of starch to sugars by plant extracts and saliva were known. However, the mechanism by which this occurred had not been _____.

Translation

酶的简介

酶是能够催化（如加快反应速度）化学反应的生物大分子。目前已知的酶几乎都是蛋白质，但某些 RNA 分子也具有生物催化活性，这些 RNA 被称为核酶。在酶促反应中，初始阶段存在的物质为底物，底物在酶的作用下被转化成为不同的分子，称为产物。几乎所有发生在生物细胞中的过程都需要酶的催化才能发生，因为酶对底物具有选择性，只催化众多可能性中的少数反应，因此在一个细胞中酶的表达决定了哪种代谢途径在细胞中发生。

同其它催化剂一样，酶也是通过降低化学反应的活化能来显著提高化学反应的速度，这个速度要比没有酶催化的化学反应的速度快几百万倍；并且在化学反应前后没有量的变化，不改变化学反应的平衡。然而，酶与其它催化剂不同的是其具有高效性，它能够催化大约 4000 种生物化学反应。另外，核酶（其实质是小分子的 RNA，核糖体的组成成分）和人工酶同样也能展示与酶一样的催化作用，是酶的种类的补充。

酶活性可以受到很多其它分子的影响。比如抑制剂可以降低酶活性，而激活剂可以提高酶活性。很多药物和毒物均可作为抑制剂。同时，酶活性也会受到温度、化学环境（比如 pH）和底物浓度的影响。目前，很多酶都被用于商业化生产过程中，比如抗生素的合成。另外，在一些家庭日常用品中添加酶用于加快相应的生化反应（例如，加酶洗衣粉可以加速分解粘在衣服上的蛋白质或脂肪，嫩化剂中加入酶可以加快蛋白质的降解使肉更易于咀嚼）。

酶的起源与历史

早在 18 世纪末 19 世纪初，人们就知道胃分泌物能够消化肉类，以及植物浸出物和唾液可以将淀粉转化为糖，但是其发生的机制却不得而知。到了 19 世纪，巴斯德在研究酵母把糖转变为酒精的发酵过程中发现，发酵过程是被酵母细胞中一种叫做"酵素"的生命物质所催化，并且他认为这种物质只能在活体细胞中发挥功能。于是他认为"酒精发酵只发生在活的酵母细胞或组织中，对于死的细胞和腐烂物中是无法完成的"。1878 年，德国生理学家威廉·屈内(1837—1900)第一次使用"酶"这个词来描述酒精发酵的过程，"酶"是"在酵母中"的意思。后来，"酶"这个词用来指没有生命的物质，比如胃蛋白酶，而"发酵"一词特指由活体物质产生的化学活性。

1897 年，爱德华·毕希纳开始在柏林大学研究不含有任何活的酵母细胞的酵母提取物发酵糖的能力。他通过一系列的实验发现，即使在没有活酵母细胞的混合物中，糖也能被发酵产生醇。后来，他把这种可以引起蔗糖发酵的酶命名为"酿酶"。正是由于爱德华·毕希纳在生物化学方面的研究和胞外发酵作用（无细胞发酵）的发现，使其获得了 1907 年的诺贝尔化学奖。同爱德华·毕希纳把引起蔗糖发酵的酶命名为"酿酶"一样，酶通常根据它所催化的化学反应来命名。比较典型的是在酶催化的底物或反应类型上加上后缀"酶"来完成一个酶的命名（如乳糖酶就是催化乳糖的酶，DNA 聚合酶就是催化 DNA 聚合反应的酶）。

现有证据表明，酶可以在活体外行使功能，接下来就要探究酶的生物化学本质。一些早期的研究者曾认为酶活性和蛋白质有很大的联系，但一些科学家（比如曾获得诺贝尔奖的里夏德·维尔施泰特）反驳说蛋白质仅仅是真正的载体，并且蛋白质本身不具有催化能力。然而，到了 1926 年，詹姆斯·B·萨姆纳证明了脲酶的本质是蛋白质，并获得了结晶，1937 年，萨姆纳用同样的方法得到了过氧化氢酶。后来，纯的蛋白质可以成为酶的结论被致力于胃蛋白酶、胰蛋白酶和糜蛋白酶等消化酶研究的诺思罗普和斯坦利所证明。这三人由于在此方面的研究在 1946 年被授予诺贝尔化学奖。

酶可以被结晶的发现使通过 X 射线衍射晶体分析法分析酶的结构成为可能。这种方法首先应用在溶菌酶上，溶菌酶通常存在于泪水、唾液和蛋清中，其功能是降解一些细菌的外被；溶菌酶的结构被 David Chilton Phillips 领导的小组成功破解并于 1965 年公布于众。溶菌酶的高分辨率结构的发现标志着结构生物学的兴起，并为在原子水平上理解酶的作用机理提供了帮助。

酶的结构与作用机制

酶大多数是球状蛋白质，其组成从 62 个氨基酸残基（如 4-草酰巴豆酯互变异构酶）到超过 2500 个氨基酸残基（如动物脂肪酸合成酶）不等。另外一小部分酶是以 RNA 为化学本质，称为 RNA 酶或核酶，常伴随核糖体而存在。所有酶的活性都是由其三维结构决定的。然而，虽然结构决定功能，要想仅仅通过其结构来预测一个新酶的活性，到目前为止依然是一件尚未解决并且非常困难的事情。

大多数酶都要比它们作用的底物大得多，但真正行使催化活性的只是酶的一小部分（大约 3～4 个氨基酸）。这个包含催化残基、结合底物以及实现催化反应的区域常称为活性位点。在酶分子结构上，也常存在结合辅助因子的位点，辅助因子对于整个催化过程是必需的。另外，一些酶分子上也存在小分子结合位点，这些小分子常常是酶所催化反应的直接或间接的产物或底物。这些连接位点可以通过反馈调节的方式增长或削弱酶的活性。

碳酸酐酶 II 连续剖面图

灰色区域是存在于活性位点的辅助因子锌

如同所有的蛋白质一样，酶也是由长的、直链的氨基酸组成，并折叠成为三维结构。每一个独特的氨基酸顺序形成特殊的结构，并具有独特的功能。有些情况下，单个的蛋白质链可以聚合形成一个蛋白复合物。大多数蛋白质在加热或化学变性剂作用下，三维结构被破坏，出现解聚和灭活，从而发生变性。变性由于酶的不同可以分为可逆和不可逆两种情况。

酶通常情况下对其催化的反应以及该反应中的底物具有特异性，关于这个特异性的机制有如下学说来解释：

"锁与钥匙"学说

该学说在 1894 年由德国化学家埃米尔·费雪提出，他认为酶的特异性是由于酶和酶催化的底物的几何结构具有特异的互补性，使它们能够完全契合。这就是著名的"锁与钥匙"学说。然而，该学说虽然能够解释酶的特异性，但无法解释酶的过渡态的稳定性。因此，"锁与钥匙"学说被证明是不准确的，而"诱导契合模型"是最广泛接受的酶-底物-辅酶模型。

诱导契合模型

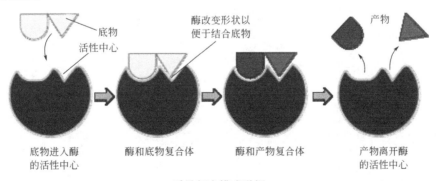

诱导契合模式详解

1958 年，Daniel Koshland 对"锁与钥匙"学说提出了修正。他认为酶具有非常灵活的结构，其活性位点会随着和底物的互相作用不断地进行结构的变化。因此底物不会简单地绑定在一个固定的活性位点；而组成活性位点的氨基酸残基链会趋向形成一个精确的结构使酶发挥其催化功能。比如糖苷酶，其底物分子在进入活性中心时也会发生轻微的变形。同时，活性中心持续发生形变直至与底物完全结合，这样酶-底物-辅酶的最终结构就决定了。

酶在较低的标准自由能变化下，可以通过以下方式行使催化作用：

• 通过营造一个稳定的过渡态环境来降低活化能（如借助结合底物或产物分子的过渡态构象，改变底物的形状，然后通过酶的作用使底物脱离过渡态，这样就减少了完成过渡态所需的能量）；

• 在不需要改变底物的形状的情况下降低过渡态的能量，这种方式是通过在过渡态上形成一个相反的电荷分布微环境而实现的；

• 一种可选途径，比如通过和底物相互作用暂时形成底物-酶中间复合物，这种情况在酶缺失的情况下是不可能形成的；

• 通过指引底物到正确的反应位点来降低反应熵的变化，根据热焓的变化量即可判断此效应。

• 通过提高温度加快反应速度。通过提高温度可以有助酶的功能的行使并加快底物向最终产物的转化。但是，如果温度过高，超过正常值，就会损坏酶的正常结构使其丧失活性。只有温度恢复为正常温度，酶恢复为原来本身的结构才能发挥功能。对于一些不耐热酶来讲，只有在低温下才能发挥催化功能。

练习参考答案 *(Reference answers of exercise)*

用词或短语填空，根据需要变换形式 *(Fill in the blanks with the words or expressions given below, and change the form where necessary)*

① conclusion　② products　③ lowering　④ Inhibitors　⑤ identified

Unit 2 Enzyme classification

Reading Material

Presently more than 2000 different enzyme activities have been isolated and characterized. The sequence information of a growing number of organisms opens the possibility to characterise all the enzymes of an organism on a genomic level. The smallest known organism, *Mycoplasma genitalium*, contains 470 genes of which 145 are related to gene replication and transcription. Baker's yeast has 7000 genes coding for about 3000 enzymes. Thousands of different variants of the natural enzymes are known. The number of reported 3-dimensional enzyme structures is rapidly increasing. In the year 2000 the structure of about 1300 different proteins were known. The enzymes are classified into six major categories based on the nature of the chemical reaction they catalyse:

1. **Oxidoreductases**：catalyse oxidation or reduction of their substrates
2. **Transferases**：catalyse group transfer
3. **Hydrolases**：catalyse bond breakage with the addition of water
4. **Lyases**：remove groups from their substrates
5. **Isomerases**：catalyse intramolecular rearrangements
6. **Ligases**：catalyse the joining of two molecules at the expense of chemical energy

Only a limited number of all the known enzymes are commercially available and even smaller amount is used in large quantities. More than 75% of industrial enzymes are hydrolases. Protein-degrading enzymes constitute about 40% of all enzyme sales. Proteinases have found new applications but their use in detergents is the major market. More than fifty commercial industrial enzymes are available and their number increases steadily.

Glossary

1. sequence	*n.* 有关联的一组事物，序列，顺序
2. organism	*n.* 有机物，有机体；生物
3. category	*n.* 种类，类别
4. hydrolase	*n.* 水解酶
5. proteinase	*n.* 蛋白酶
6. commercial	*adj.* 商业的，商务的，贸易的
7. steady	*adj.* 稳定的，平稳的，坚定的

Exercise

Matching

① Ligases   (a) catalyse group transfer

② Transferases   (b) catalyse bond breakage with the addition of water

③ Isomerases   (c) catalyse oxidation or reduction of their substrates

④ Hydrolases   (d) catalyse the joining of two molecules at the expense of chemical energy

⑤ Oxidoreductases   (e) remove groups from their substrates

⑥ Lyases   (f) catalyse intramolecular rearrangements

Translation

酶的分类

至今已有 2000 多种已成功分离和表征的不同的酶。越来越多的有机体的序列信息使在基因组水平上描述一个有机体的所有酶成为可能。我们已知的最小的有机体——生殖支原体，含有 470 个基因，其中有 145 个与基因的复制和转录相关。面包中的酵母菌有 7000 个基因编码大概 3000 种酶。天然酶的不同种数是以千万计的。报道出三维结构的酶的数量正在迅速增加。到 2000 年，大约有 1300 种不同蛋白质的结构已经研究清楚。酶可以根据它们所催化的化学反应的性质分为六类：

1. 氧化还原酶：催化底物氧化或还原
2. 转移催化酶：催化基团转移
3. 水解酶：加入水后催化化学键断裂
4. 裂解酶：使底物的基团移除
5. 异构酶：催化分子内重排
6. 连接酶：以化学能为代价催化两个分子连接

在所有已知的酶中，只有少数是商业上可以应用的，大量使用的就更少了。工业上用的酶超过 75%是水解酶。在所有的酶的销售中，蛋白质降解酶贡献了大约 40%的销售额。蛋白酶已经被发现有新的应用，但是它们主要还是应用在清洁剂市场上。有超过 50 种已工业化生产的酶，并且用在商业上，而且这个数量还在稳步增长。

练习参考答案 *(Reference answers of exercise)*

配对 *(Matching)*

①—(d); ②—(a); ③—(f); ④—(b); ⑤—(c); ⑥—(e)

Unit 3 Industrial use of enzymes

Reading Material

Large scale enzyme applications

Table 1 summarises major large-scale enzyme applications. Each of them is discussed in the text in some detail.

Table 1. Large-scale enzyme applications

Industry		Effect
Detergent	proteinase	protein degradation
	lipase	fat removal
	cellulase	color brightening
Textile	cellulase	microfibril removal
	laccase	color brightening
Animal feed	xylanase	fiber solubility
	phytase	release of phosphate
Starch	amylases	glucose formation
	glucose isomerase	fructose formation
Pulp and paper	xylanase	biobleaching
Fruit juice	pectinase	juice clarification
	cellulase	juice extraction
	xylanase	
Baking	xylanase	dough conditioning
	alpha-amylase	loaf volume; shelf-life
	glucose oxidase	dough quality
Dairy	rennin	protein coagulation
	lactase	lactose hydrolysis
Brewing	glucanase	filter aid
	papain	haze control

1. Detergents

Detergents were the first large scale application for microbial enzymes. Bacterial proteinases are still the most important detergent enzymes. Some products have been genetically engineered to be more stable in the hostile environment of washing machines with several different chemicals present. These hostile agents include anionic detergents, oxidising agents and high pH.

Late 80s lipid degrading enzymes were introduced in powder and liquid detergents. Lipases decompose fats into more water-soluble compounds by hydrolysing the ester bonds between the glycerol backbone and fatty acid. The most important lipase in the market was originally obtained from *Humicola lanuginose*. It is produced in large scale by *Aspergillus oryzae* host after cloning the *Humicola* gene into this organism.

Amylases are used in detergents to remove starch based stains. Amylases hydrolyse gelatinised starch, which tends to stick on textile fibres and bind other stain components. Cellulases have been part of detergents since early 90s. Cellulase is actually an enzyme complex capable of degrading crystalline cellulose to glucose. In textile washing cellulases remove cellulose microfibrils, which are formed during washing and the use of cotton based cloths. This can be seen as colour brightening and softening of the material. Alkaline cellulases are produced by *Bacillus* strains and neutral and acidic cellulases by *Trichoderma* and *Humicola* fungi.

2. Starch hydrolysis and fructose production

The use of starch degrading enzymes was the first large-scale application of microbial enzymes in food industry. Mainly two enzymes carry out conversion of starch to glucose: alpha-amylase cuts rapidly the large alpha-1,4-linked glucose polymers into shorter oligomers in high temperature. This phase is called liquefaction and is carried out by bacterial enzymes. In the next phase called saccharification, glucoamylase hydrolyses the oligomers into glucose. This is done by fungal enzymes, which operate in lower pH and temperature than alpha-amylase. Sometimes additional debranching enzymes like pullulanase are added to improve the glucose yield. Beta-amylase is commercially produced from barley grains and used for the production of the disaccharide maltose.

In the United States large volumes of glucose syrups are converted by glucose isomerase after Ca^{2+} (alpha-amylase needs Ca^{2+} for activity but it inhibits glucose isomerase) removal to fructose containing syrup. This is done by bacterial enzymes, which need Mg^{2+} ions for activity. Fructose is separated from glucose by large-scale chromatographic separation and crystallized. Alternatively, fructose is concentrated to 55% and used as a high fructose corn syrup in soft drink industry.

3. Drinks

Enzymes have many applications in drink industry. The use of chymosin in cheese making to coagulate milk protein was already discussed. Another enzyme used in milk industry is beta-galactosidase or lactase, which splits milk-sugar lactose into glucose and galactose. This process is used for milk products that are consumed by lactose intolerant consumers.

Enzymes are used also in fruit juice manufacturing. Fruit cell wall needs to be broken down to improve juice liberation. Pectins are polymeric substances in fruit lamella and cell walls. They are closely related to polysaccharides. The cell wall contains also hemicelluloses and cellulose. Addition of pectinase, xylanase and cellulase improve the liberation of the juice from the pulp. Pectinases and amylases are used in juice clarification.

Brewing is an enzymatic process. Malting is a process, which increases the enzyme levels in the grain. In the mashing process the enzymes are liberated and they hydrolyse the starch into soluble fermentable sugars like maltose, which is a glucose disaccharide. Additional enzymes can be used to help the starch hydrolysis (typically alpha-amylases), solve filtration problems caused by beta-glucans present in malt (beta-glucanases), hydrolyse proteins (neutral proteinase), and control haze during maturation, filtration and storage (papain, alpha-amylase and beta-glucanase).

Similarly enzymes are widely used in wine production to obtain a better extraction of the necessary components and thus improving the yield. Enzymes hydrolyse the high molecular weight substances like pectin.

4. Textiles

The use of enzymes in textile industry is one of the most rapidly growing fields in industrial enzymology. Starch has for a long time been used as a protective glue of fibres in weaving of fabrics. This is called sizing. Enzymes are used to remove the starch in a process called desizing. Amylases are used in this process since they do not harm the textile fibres.

Enzymes have replaced the use of volcanic lava stones in the preparation of Denim (special soft cotton based fibre where the dye has been partially faded away) from an indigo-dyed cotton fibre to achieve a high degree of dye fading. The stones caused considerable damage to fibres and machines. The same effect can be obtained with cellulase enzymes. The effect is a result of alternating cycles of desizing and bleaching enzymes and chemicals in washing machines.

Recently, hydrogen peroxides have been tested as bleaching agents to replace chlorine-based chemicals. Catalase enzyme, which destroys hydrogen peroxide, may then be used to degrade excess peroxide. Another recent approach is to use oxidative enzymes directly to bleach textiles. Laccase—a polyphenol oxidase from fungi—is a new candidate in this field.

Laccases are produced by white-rot fungi, which use them to degrade lignin—the aromatic polymer found in all plant materials. Laccase is a copper-containing enzyme, which is oxidised by oxygen, and which in an oxidised state can oxidatively degrade many different types of molecules like dye pigments.

Other enzymes, which interact with textiles, are often added to washing powders. These examples were discussed under detergent enzymes.

5. Animal feed

Intensive study to use enzymes in animal feed started in early 80s. The first commercial success was addition of beta-glucanase into barley based feed diets. Barley contains beta-glucan, which causes high viscosity in the chicken gut. The net effect of enzyme usage in feed has been increased animal weight gain with the same amount of barley resulting in increased feed conversion ratio. Finnfeeds International was the pioneer in animal feed enzymes.

Enzymes were tested later also in wheat-based diets. Xylanase enzymes were found to be the most effective ones in this case. Addition of xylanase to wheat-based broiler feed has increased the available metabolizable energy 7-10% in various studies. Xylanases are nowadays routinely used in feed formulations. Usually a feed-enzyme preparation is a multienzyme cocktail containing glucanases, xylanases, proteinases and amylases. Enzyme addition reduces viscosity, which increases absorbtion of nutrients, liberates nutrients either by hydrolysis of non-degradable fibres or by liberating nutrients blocked by these fibres, and reduces the amount of faeces.

Enzymes have become an important aspect of animal feed industry. In addition to poultry, enzymes are used in pig feeds and turkey feeds. They are added as enzyme premixes (enzyme-flour mixture) during the feed manufacturing process, which involves extrusion of wet feed mass in high temperature (80-90℃). Therefore the feed enzymes need to be thermo tolerant during the feed manufacturing and operative in the animal body temperature.

6. Baking

Similar fibre materials are used in baking than in animal feed. It is therefore conceivable that enzymes also affect the baking process. Alpha-amylases have been most widely studied in connection with improved bread quality and increased shelf life. Both fungal and bacterial amylases are used. Overdosage may lead to sticky dough so the added amount needs to be carefully controlled.

One of the motivations to study the effect of enzymes on dough and bread qualities comes from the pressure to reduce other additives. In addition to starch, flour typically contains minor amounts of cellulose, glucans and hemicelluloses like arabinoxylan and arabinogalactan. There is evidence that the use of xylanases decreases the water absorption and thus reduces the amount of added water needed in baking. This leads to more stable dough. Especially xylanases are used in whole meal rye baking and dry crisps common in Scandinavia.

Proteinases can be added to improve dough-handling properties; glucose oxidase has been used to replace chemical oxidants and lipases to strengthen gluten, which leads to more stable dough and better bread quality.

7. Pulp and Paper

Intensive studies have been carried out during the last twenty years to apply many different enzymes in pulp and paper industry. A real excitement started with the discovery of lignin degrading peroxidases in the early 80s. In spite of extensive research no oxidative enzymes are applied in pulp and paper industry. The major application is the use of xylanases in pulp bleaching. Xylanases liberate lignin fragments by hydrolysing residual xylan. This reduces considerably the need for chlorine based bleaching chemicals. Other minor enzyme applications in pulp production include the use of enzymes to remove fine particles from pulp. This facilitates water removal.

In paper making enzymes are used especially in modification of starch, which is used as an important additive. Starch improves the strength, stiffness and erasability of paper. The starch suspension must have a certain viscosity, which is achieved by adding amylase enzymes in a controlled process.

8. Leather

Leather industry uses proteolytic and lipolytic enzymes in leather processing. The use of these enzymes is associated with the structure of animal skin as a raw material. Enzymes are used to remove unwanted parts. Alkaline proteases are added in the soaking phase. This improves water uptake by the dry skins, removal and degradation of protein, dirt and fats and reduces the processing time. In some cases pancreatic trypsin is also used in this phase.

In dehairing phases enzymes are used to assist the alkaline chemical process. This results in a more environmentally friendly process and improves the quality of the leather (cleaner and stronger surface, softer leather, less spots). The used enzymes are typically alkaline bacterial proteases. Lipases are used in this phase or in bating phase to specifically remove grease. The use of lipases is a fairly new development in leather industry.

The next phase is bating which aims at deliming and deswelling of collagen. In this phase the protein is partly degraded to make the leather soft and easier to dye. Pancreatic trypsins were originally used but they are being partly replaced by bacterial and fungal enzymes.

Future trends in industrial enzymology

Industrial enzyme market grows steadily. The reason for this lies in improved production efficiency resulting in cheaper enzymes, in new application fields and in new enzymes from screening programmes or in engineered properties of traditional enzymes. New applications are to be expected in the field of textiles, new animal diets like ruminant and fish feed. It can be expected that breakthroughs in pulp and paper will materialise. The use of cellulases to convert waste cellulose into sugars and further to ethanol by fermentative organisms has been a major study topic for years. Increasing environmental pressures and energy prices will make this application a real possibility one day.

Glossary

1. chemical	*n.* 化学药品；化学制剂
2. candidate	*n.* 候选人
3. routinely	*adv.* 常规地，惯常地
4. degradable	*adj.* 可降解的
5. poultry	*n.* 家禽
6. operative	*adj.* 有效的，最适合的
7. extensive	*adj.* 广泛的，大规模的
8. cellulase	*n.* 木纤维质酵素，纤维素酶
9. laccase	*n.* 漆酶，虫漆酶
10. xylanase	*n.* 木聚糖酶
11. phytase	*n.* 肌醇六磷酸酶
12. amylase	*n.* 淀粉酶
13. isomerase	*n.* 异构酶
14. glucose	*n.* 〈化〉葡萄糖，右旋糖
15. rennin	*n.* 凝乳酶
16. papain	*n.* 木瓜蛋白酶
17. detergent	*n.* 洗涤剂；去垢剂；洗衣粉
18. textile	*n.* 纺织品，织物
19. starch	*n.* 淀粉，浆粉
20. pulp	*n.* 纸浆
21. brewing	*n.* 酿造
22. dairy	*adj.* 牛奶的；奶制的；乳品的

Exercises

1. *Matching*

Enzyme	Effect
① proteinase	(a) fat removal
② lipase	(b) protein coagulation
③ xylanase	(c) glucose formation
④ amylases	(d) haze control
⑤ lactase	(e) protein degradation

⑥ papain　　　　　　　　　　(f) lactose hydrolysis

⑦ rennin　　　　　　　　　　 (g) fiber solubility

2. *Explain the glossaries below in English*

① Alkaline phosphatase

② Aspartame

③ Dextran

④ DNA-polymerases

⑤ Glucoamylase

⑥ Lyases

⑦ Xylitol

⑧ Pepsin

Translation

酶的工业应用

酶的广泛应用

表1总结了酶的主要应用。本文中会对其作出详细介绍。

表1　酶的主要应用

应用领域		作　　用
清洁剂	蛋白酶	蛋白质降解
	脂肪酶	去除脂肪
	纤维素酶	颜色光亮剂
纺织品	纤维素酶	去除微纤维
	漆酶	颜色光亮剂
动物饲料	木聚糖酶	溶解纤维
	植酸酶	磷释放
淀粉	淀粉酶	形成葡萄糖
	葡萄糖异构酶	形成果糖
造纸业	木聚糖酶	漂白
果汁	果胶酶	澄清果汁 提取果汁
	纤维素酶	
	木聚糖酶	
烘烤	木聚糖酶	面团改良
	α-淀粉酶	增大面包体积；延长储存期
	葡糖糖氧化酶	改善面团品质
奶制品	凝乳酶	凝固蛋白
酿造	乳糖酶	水解乳糖
	葡聚糖酶	助滤
	木瓜蛋白酶	霉控制

1. 洗涤剂

洗涤剂是微生物酶首次大规模的应用。细菌蛋白酶仍然是最重要的洗涤剂酶。部分产品已经可以通过基因工程在加入一些不同的化学试剂后使其在洗衣机的恶性环境里变得更加稳定，这些恶性环境包括阴离子洗涤剂、氧化剂和浓碱性环境等。

20 世纪 80 年代后期脂质降解酶加入到了洗衣粉和洗涤剂中。脂肪酶通过水解甘油骨架和脂肪酸之间的酯键将脂肪分解成水溶性较好的物质。市场上最重要的脂肪酶最开始是从布满绒毛的绿球藻中获得的，在克隆了绿球藻的基因到米曲霉菌的体内后，便开始利用米曲霉菌大量生产我们所需要的酶。

洗涤剂中的淀粉酶用于去除淀粉类污渍。淀粉酶水解那些黏附在纺织纤维或其它染色成分上的胶状淀粉。纤维素酶从 20 世纪 90 年代初成为了洗涤剂的一部分。纤维素酶将纤维素降解为葡萄糖。纤维素酶去除那些在洗涤棉质衣物时产生的纤维素微纤维，这也可以看做是增白或使衣物软化。碱性纤维素酶是由芽孢杆菌产生的，中性和酸性纤维素酶是由木霉菌和绿球藻产生的。

2. 淀粉水解和果糖生产

淀粉水解酶是微生物酶在食品工业的第一次大规模应用。在食品工业中，主要有两种酶将淀粉转化为葡萄糖。在高温下 α-淀粉酶迅速将 α-1,4-糖聚合物分解为低聚物，这一过程称为液化，是由细菌酶完成的。下一阶段叫糖化，糖化酶将低聚物转化成葡萄糖，这一过程在比 α-淀粉酶低一些的 pH 和温度下进行，由真菌酶完成。有时需额外加入普鲁兰酶等脱支酶来增加葡萄糖产量。β 淀粉酶是由大麦中提取并用于麦芽糖的生产。

在美国，大量的葡萄糖浆是由葡萄糖异构酶移除 Ca^{2+}（α-淀粉酶需要 Ca^{2+} 来保持活性，但它抑制葡萄糖异构酶）后将果糖糖浆转化而成，这是通过需要 Mg^{2+} 以保持活性的细菌酶来完成的。果糖是由葡萄糖经大规模色谱分离和结晶得到的。另外，当果糖浓度到 55% 后，可以在软饮料工业中用作高果糖玉米糖浆。

3. 饮料

酶在饮料工业中有很多应用。我们已经讨论过在奶酪制作中使用凝乳酶来凝结牛奶，在牛奶工业中还使用另外一种酶叫 β-半乳糖苷酶或乳糖酶，它将乳糖分解成葡萄糖和半乳糖。这种方法应用于牛奶的生产出，产品适合乳糖不耐症的人。

酶也用于果汁的制造。需要破坏水果的细胞壁来增加果汁的量。果胶是存在于细胞片层和细胞壁中的多糖，细胞壁还含有半纤维素和纤维素。除了果胶酶，木聚糖酶和纤维素酶也帮助提高果汁的释放。果胶酶和淀粉酶用于果汁的澄清。

酿造是一个酶作用的过程。大麦发芽是增加谷物中酶含量的一个过程。在淀粉糖化过程中，酶被释放，它们将淀粉水解成可溶性糖，如二糖麦芽糖。加入其它的酶可以帮助淀粉水解（α-淀粉酶），解决麦芽中 β 葡聚糖的过滤问题（β-葡聚糖酶），解决蛋白质的水解问题（中性蛋白酶），控制后熟、过滤和储存中的浑浊问题（木瓜蛋白酶、α-淀粉酶和 β-葡聚糖酶）。

类似的酶广泛用于酒的生产，使有效成分更好地被提取，以提高产量。酶可以水解像果胶一样的大分子物质。

4. 纺织品

在纺织工业中对酶的应用是工业酶学增长最快的领域之一。淀粉浆作为纤维织物的保护层已经应用很久了，这就是所谓的上浆。可以用酶来去掉这层淀粉浆，这个过程叫退浆。淀粉酶因其不损害纺织纤维而被用于这项工艺。

在制作牛仔布（染料已褪色的特别柔软的纤维棉）的工艺上，酶已经取代了火山石的作用，使靛蓝染的棉纤维高度褪色。火山灰对纤维和机器有损坏，而用纤维素酶，不会有任何破坏却能达到相同的效果。该效应是通过在机器中退浆、漂白酶和化学物质交替循环作用达到的。

最近，过氧化氢被用来测试作为漂白剂，以取代含氯的化学品。过氧化氢酶，通过消耗掉过氧化氢，然后达到降解的作用。最近研究的另一个方法是用氧化酶直接漂白纺织品。漆酶——真菌产生的多酚氧化酶——是这个领域很有潜力的研究对象。

漆酶产自白腐真菌，白腐真菌用漆酶来降解木质素——所有植物中都含有的一种芳香族聚合物。漆酶是一种含铜的酶，它是由氧气氧化而成，它在其氧化态可以氧化降解许多不同类型的分子，比如染料。

其它的酶，它们能和纺织品相互作用，往往被添加到洗衣粉中，这些例子我们在洗涤剂酶部分已进行过讨论。

5. 动物饲料

深入研究动物饲料酶是从 80 年代初开始的。商业上的第一次成功是将 β 葡聚糖酶加入到大麦饲料中。大麦含有 β 葡聚糖，它会使鸡的肠道内容物黏度很高。动物吃同样数量的饲料，添加 β 葡聚糖酶比未添加酶使动物增重更多。芬兰饲料国际有限公司是动物饲料酶行业的先驱。

后来酶添加于小麦饲料中也做了测试。在这种情况下人们发现木聚糖酶是最有效的，在广泛的研究中发现添加木聚糖酶的小麦肉鸡饲料使其有效代谢能增加 7%～10%。现在，木聚糖酶是饲料的常规配方。通常，饲料中的酶制剂是一个混合配方，包括葡聚糖酶、木聚糖酶、蛋白酶和淀粉酶等。加入酶能降低黏度，增加养分吸收，通过水解不可降解的纤维来释放营养素，减少粪便量。

酶已成为饲料工业的重要组成部分。除了家禽，酶还用在猪饲料和火鸡饲料中。在饲料生产过程中，酶作为预混剂（酶粉混合物）加入，它在高温（80～90℃）的湿饲料中受到挤压，因此饲料酶在生产过程中须耐热，而且在动物的体温下它们应当依然有效。

6. 焙烤

与动物饲料相似，纤维材料也加入到了焙烤食品中。因此可以想象，酶也可以影响焙烤过程。人们广泛地研究了 α 淀粉酶对改进面包质量和延长保质期的影响。真菌和细菌淀粉酶都得到了应用。但是过量可能导致面团太黏，所以添加量必须严格控制。

研究酶对于面团和面包质量的影响。目的是为了减少其它添加剂的使用。除了淀粉，面粉通常还含有少量的纤维素、葡聚糖和半纤维素，如阿拉伯木聚糖和阿拉伯半乳聚糖。有证据表明，木聚糖酶的使用减少了水分的吸收，从而降低了焙烤的加水量。这将使面团更加稳定。尤其是木聚糖酶用于全麦黑面包和干薯片的焙烤，在斯堪的纳维亚半岛很常见。

蛋白酶可以添加到面粉中以改善面团的手感；葡萄糖氧化酶已被用来取代化学氧化剂和脂肪酶，用于增加面团的弹性，这将使面团更加稳定而且质量更好。

7. 纸浆和造纸

在过去的 20 年中，深入研究了将不同的酶应用于纸浆和造纸工业。在 20 世纪 80 年代初，发现氧化能降解木质素，这一结果使研究有了一个令人振奋的开始。尽管进行了广泛的研究，但还没有氧化酶应用到纸浆和造纸工业。目前应用较多的是将木聚糖酶用于木浆漂白。木聚糖酶通过水解残余木聚糖，来释放木质素碎片，这将大大减少对氯漂白化学品的使用。在纸浆生产过程中还使用少量其它酶，去除纸浆细小颗粒，利于脱水。

在造纸中，酶特别用在浆粉的改性中，酶主要是作为一种重要的添加剂。浆粉可以改善纸张的强度和耐擦性能。悬浮的浆粉必须有一定的黏度，这是通过加入淀粉来实现的。

8. 皮革

在皮革加工中，主要应用水解酶和酯解酶。这些酶的应用，主要与皮革这种原材料的结构有关，用酶除去不需要的部分。碱性蛋白酶用于浸泡阶段，通过皮子的干燥，蛋白、污物和脂肪的去除和降解，提高吸水性，减少加工时间。在有些情况下，胰蛋白酶也应用于这一过程。

在脱毛阶段，添加酶以促进碱性化学反应，实现更加环境友好的加工过程，提高皮革的质量（表面更干净、更有韧性、皮毛更柔软、瑕疵更少）。此处所用的酶是典型的碱性细菌蛋白酶。脂肪酶应用在这个阶段或软化阶段，专门用于去除油脂。脂肪酶在皮革业的应用是一个新的发展方向。

下一阶段是软化，主要是脱灰和胶原的退胀。在这个阶段，蛋白质部分降解，使皮革变软易于染色。这一阶段原来主要用胰蛋白酶，但现在部分被细菌和真菌酶所替代。

工业用酶的未来趋势

工业酶制剂市场稳步增长，源于生产效率的提高和价格的降低，源于新的应用领域，源于通过筛选而来的新酶的应用，源于具有工程特性传统的酶的应用。酶有望在纺织、动物饲料（如反刍类和鱼类等）领域产生新的应用。可以预见，酶在纸浆和造纸方面的突破将成为现实。近年来利用纤维素酶将废纤维素转化成糖类甚至经微生物发酵转化成乙醇已经成为了一个重大的研究课题。逐渐增长的环境压力和能源价格将促使这些应用在某一天成为现实。

练习参考答案 *(Reference answers of exercises)*

1. 配对 *(Matching)*

①—(e)；②—(a)；③—(g)；④—(c)；⑤—(f)；⑥—(d)；⑦—(b)

2. 对下列单词用英文进行解释 *(Explain the glossaries below in English)*

① **Alkaline phosphatase:** An enzyme that degrades ester bonds in alkaline conditions.

② **Aspartame:** A low calorie high intensive sweetener.

③ **Dextran:** Glucose containing branched polymer used e.g. in blood replacements.

④ **DNA-polymerases:** An enzyme that synthesizes DNA polymers.

⑤ **Glucoamylase:** An enzyme that splits glucose molecules from starch.

⑥ **Lyases:** Enzymes that remove chemical groups from their substrates without addition of water.

⑦ **Xylitol:** A tooth-friendly sugar alcohol used in chewing gums.

⑧ **Pepsin:** An enzyme that degrades proteins and is isolated from animals.

Unit 4 Enzymes：digest、absorb and metabolite

Reading Material

Research has shown that as we grow older, the body's ability to produce enzymes decreases. At the same time, malabsorption of nutrients, tissue breakdown, and chronic health conditions increase. Taking supplemental enzymes can help to ensure that you continue to get the full nutritional value from your foods.

The food we eat cannot nourish us unless it is first prepared for absorption into the body. This is done by enzymes, chemical compounds which digest it and break down large food particles into smaller units. Protein is broken down into amino-acids; complex carbohydrate into simple sugars; fat into fatty acids and glycerol. Every day **10** litres of digestive juices, mainly produced by the pancreas, liver, stomach and intestinal wall, pour into the digestive tract.

For the body to make these enzymes it needs nutrients. If you become nutrient-deficient, enzyme deficiency soon follows (which means your body will be less able to make use of the new nutrients it does take in, which makes you become even more enzyme deficient and so the cycle continues).

What are Enzymes?

The late Dr. Edward Howell, a physician and pioneer in enzyme research, called enzymes the "sparks of life". These energised protein molecules play a necessary role in virtually all of the biochemical activities that go on in the body.

- They are essential for digesting food
- Stimulating the brain
- Providing cellular energy
- Repairing all tissues, organs, and cells

Life as we know it could not exist without the action of enzymes, even in the presence of sufficient amounts of vitamins, minerals, water, and other nutrients.

In their primary role, enzymes are catalysts—substances that accelerate and precipitate the hundreds of thousands of biochemical reactions in the body that control life's processes. If it were not for the catalytic action of enzymes, most of these reactions would take place far too slowly to sustain life. Enzymes are not consumed in the reactions they facilitate.

Each enzyme has a specific function in the body that no other enzyme can fulfil. The chemical shape of each enzyme is specialised so that it can initiate a reaction only in a certain substance, or in a group of closely related chemical substances, and not in others. The substance on which an enzyme acts is called the **substrate**. Because there must be a different enzyme for every substrate, the body must produce a great number of different enzymes.

Facts and Functions of Enzymes

- Enzymes assist in practically all bodily functions.

• Digestive enzymes break down food particles for storage in the liver or muscles. This stored energy is later converted by other enzymes for use by the body when necessary.

• Iron is concentrated in the blood by the action of enzymes; other enzymes in the blood help the blood to coagulate in order to stop bleeding.

• Uricolytic enzymes catalyse the conversion of uric acid into urea.

• Respiratory enzymes facilitate the elimination of carbon dioxide from the lungs.

• They assist the kidneys, liver, lungs, colon, and skin in removing wastes and toxins from the body.

• They also utilise the nutrients ingested by the body to construct new muscle tissue, nerve cells, bone, skin, and glandular tissue.

• One enzyme can take dietary phosphorus and convert it into bone.

• They prompt the oxidisation of glucose, which creates energy for the cells.

• They protect the blood from dangerous waste materials by converting these substances to forms that are easily eliminated by the body.

• The enzyme deficient diet also affects the size of the liver, heart, pituitary, thyroid and other endocrine glands.

The functions of enzymes are so many and so diverse that it would be impossible to name them all. There are three classes of enzymes:

metabolic enzymes, which control the metabolic rate

digestive enzymes, which digest food

food enzymes from raw foods, which start food digestion

Digestive Enzymes

• The digestive enzymes have only three main functions: digesting protein, carbohydrate, and fat.

• The amount of digestive enzymes secreted by the pancreas in response to carbohydrate, protein, and fat was measured in several research studies, and it was found that the strength of each enzyme varied with the amount of each of these food materials it was called upon to digest.

• They are secreted along the gastrointestinal tract and break down foods, enabling the nutrients to be absorbed into the bloodstream for use in various bodily functions.

• There are three main categories of digestive enzymes: **amylase, protease**, and **lipase**.

-**Amylase**, found in saliva and in the pancreatic and intestinal juices, breaks down carbohydrates. Different types of amylase break down specific types of sugars. For example, lactase breaks down milk sugar (lactose), maltase breaks down malt sugar (maltose), and sucrase breaks down cane and beet sugar (sucrose).

-**Protease**, found in the stomach juices and also in the pancreatic and intestinal juices, helps to digest protein.

-**Lipase**, found in the stomach and pancreatic juices, and also present in fats in foods, aids in fat digestion.

Metabolic enzymes

• All the organs and tissues of the body are run by metabolic enzymes.

• They take proteins, fats, and carbohydrates, and structure them to build and carry out the normal functions of the body and to repair damage and decay, and heal diseases.

• These enzymes catalyze the various chemical reactions within the cells, such as energy production and detoxification.

• Found in the blood, organs, and tissues doing their specific work. Each body tissue has its own specific set of metabolic enzymes.

Two particularly important metabolic enzymes are **superoxide dismutase (SOD)** and its partner, **catalase**.

• SOD is an antioxidant that protects the cells by attacking a common free radical superoxide. SOD occurs naturally in a variety of food sources, including barley grass, broccoli, Brussels sprouts, cabbage, wheatgrass, and most green plants.

• Catalase breaks down hydrogen peroxide, a metabolic waste product, and liberates oxygen for the body to use.

Food Enzymes

While the body manufactures a supply of enzymes, it can also obtain enzymes from food. Unfortunately, enzymes are extremely sensitive to heat. Even low to moderate heat (118℉ or above) destroys most enzymes in food. Food irradiation and pasteurisation of milk destroys enzymes. So to obtain enzymes from the diet, one must eat raw foods.

When enzyme deficient food is eaten, the body has to produce its own endogenous (internally produced) enzymes for digestion. Over-taxing the body to produce digestive enzymes can reduce its ability to produce metabolic enzymes. Sometimes it may convert metabolic enzymes to digestive enzymes if necessary. When the body becomes weakened in an enzyme-deficient state, it is a prime target for cancer, obesity, heart disease, endocrine disorder, and other degenerative disorders. The enzyme deficient diet also affects the size of the liver, heart, pituitary, thyroid, and other endocrine glands.

Eating raw foods or, alternatively, taking enzyme supplements (taken at the beginning of every meal—digestive enzyme capsules should contain at least the three basic enzymes: amylase, protease, and lipase) helps prevent depletion of the body's own enzymes and thus reduce the stress on the body.

Enzymes can be found in many different foods, from both plant and animal sources:

bananas	avocados	grapes
mangoes	olives from the tree	fresh raw dates
fresh raw figs	raw honey	raw butter
unpasteurized milk	pineapple	unripe papayas
seeds	tree nuts	raw cereal grains
sprouts (richest source)	germinated inhibitor-free	

The enzymes extracted from papaya and pineapple—papain and bromelain, respectively—are proteolytic enzymes.

Not all raw foods can be eaten directly. Seeds and nuts contain enzyme inhibitors. Eating seeds and nuts with enzyme inhibitors cause the pancreas to secrete digestive enzymes, leading to a decrease in the supply of metabolic enzymes. Raw seeds and nuts contain starch, which is a storage product and a source of future energy when conditions become ideal for them to germinate and grow into a plant.

Enzymes are present in raw seeds and nuts but are prevented from being active by the presence of enzyme inhibitors. Germination (soaking in water) for 24 hours neutralises the inhibitors and releases the enzymes. Germination also greatly increases the enzyme action.

Glossary

1. tissue	*n.* （人、动植物的）组织
2. physician	*n.* 医师
3. metabolic	*adj.* 代谢作用的，新陈代谢的
4. raw	*adj.* 天然的；未加工过的
5. pancreas	*n.* 胰，胰腺
6. lactase	*n.* 乳糖酶
7. maltase	*n.* 麦芽糖酶
8. sucrase	*n.* 蔗糖酶
9. secrete	*vt.* （尤指动物或植物器官）分泌

Exercise

List at least 2 examples of each class of enzymes given below.
① digestive enzymes
② metabolic enzymes
③ food enzymes

Translation

酶——消化、吸收和代谢

研究表明，随着身体逐渐衰老，身体产生酶的能力也在逐渐下降。同时，营养吸收不良、身体组织衰退和慢性健康疾病却在增加。补充酶可以确保你能继续从食物中得到全部的营养。

我们吃的食物不能直接滋养身体，除非它们准备好了让身体吸收，这个过程就是通过酶来完成的。酶是一类化合物，它们能将大的食物颗粒分解成更小的单位供身体吸收。蛋白质被分解成氨基酸；复杂的碳水化合物被分解成单糖；脂肪被分解成脂肪酸和甘油。每天 10 升的消化液，主要是由胰腺、肝、胃和肠壁产生并倾入消化道的。

由于身体产生酶时需要营养，当你营养不良时，酶也会跟着缺乏（这意味着你的身体就不能充分利用新摄入的营养物质，因此又让你身体内的酶更加缺乏——这样恶性循环就开始了）。

什么是酶?

已逝世的爱德华·豪威尔博士是一个医生和酶学研究的先驱者，他称酶为"生命的火花"。这些带电的蛋白质分子在身体内几乎所有的生化活动上发挥了重要的作用。

- 消化食物的必要物质
- 刺激大脑
- 提供细胞能量
- 修复所有的组织、器官和细胞

我们知道，即使有充足的维生素、矿物质、水以及其它的营养物质，如果没有酶的作用，生命也将无法存在。

在它们首要的角色中，酶是催化剂——加速并沉淀身体内成百上千的生化反应，从而控制生命过程。如果没有酶的催化，大部分反应将发生得非常缓慢以至于不能维持生命。在酶参与的反应中，酶本身并不被消耗。

每种酶在身体内都有其它酶不能替代的特定的功能。每种酶特定的化学性状决定了它只能催化一种特定的或是一类密切相关的化学物质，而不能催化其它物质。一种酶作用的特定物质叫底物。由于对每一种底物都有对应的酶，所以身体必须产生大量不同的酶。

酶的应用和作用

- 酶对几乎所有的身体功能有辅助协调作用。
- 消化酶分解食物颗粒并将之储存在肝脏或肌肉中。这些储存的能量在身体需要的时候又被其它酶转化以供利用。
- 在酶的作用下铁被集中在血液中；在需要止血的时候，血液中其它的酶帮助血液凝固。
- 尿酸分解酶催化尿酸向尿素的转化。
- 呼吸酶促进二氧化碳从肺的脱离。
- 它们协助肾、肝、肺、肠和皮肤清除体内的废物和毒素。
- 它们还利用人体所摄入的营养物质来产生新的肌肉组织、神经细胞、骨骼、皮肤和腺体组织。
- 一种酶可以吸收饮食中的磷并将之转化为骨骼。
- 它们推动葡萄糖的氧化作用，为细胞活动生产能量。
- 它们将有害废物转换成容易被身体排除的物质形式，以保护血液。
- 酶缺乏的饮食也将影响到肝脏、心脏、垂体、甲状腺及其它内分泌腺的大小。

酶的种类繁多，功能多样，给所有的酶命名是不可能的。这里我们阐释三种酶：

代谢酶：控制代谢率。

消化酶：消化食物。

食物中的酶：来源于天然食物，启动食物消化。

消化酶

- 消化酶有三大主要功能：消化蛋白质、糖类和脂肪。
- 在一些研究中，研究人员测量了当有糖类、蛋白质和脂肪的刺激下，由胰腺分泌的消化酶的数量，发现了各种酶的浓度与待消化的食物中糖类、蛋白质和脂肪各自的含量多少有关。
- 它们沿着消化道分泌，分解食物，使营养物质吸收到血液中供身体利用，发挥各项机能。

● 消化酶主要有三种：淀粉酶、蛋白酶和脂肪酶。

-淀粉酶：存在于唾液、胰腺和肠道分泌物中，分解糖类。不同类型的淀粉酶分解特定的糖类。例如，乳糖酶分解牛奶（乳糖），麦芽糖酶分解麦芽（麦芽糖），蔗糖酶分解蔗糖和甜菜糖（蔗糖）。

-蛋白酶：存在于胃、胰腺和肠道分泌物中，消化蛋白质。

-脂肪酶：存在于胃和胰液中，在食物的脂肪中也用于消化脂肪。

代谢酶

● 人体所有的组织和器官的运行都有代谢酶的参与。

● 它们协助代谢糖、蛋白质和脂肪，用来维持身体的正常功能，它们还帮助修复损伤或坏掉的细胞，修复病变。

● 它们催化细胞内的各种化学反应，如产生能量或排毒的反应。

● 它们存在于血液、器官和组织中，做着它们特定的工作。每个身体组织有它自己特定的代谢酶。

两种特别重要的代谢酶是**超氧化物歧化酶**（SOD）和**过氧化氢酶**：

● 超氧化物歧化酶（SOD）是一种抗氧化剂，通过攻击超氧阴离子自由基来保护细胞。SOD 广泛存在于自然植物中，包括大麦草、花椰菜、甘蓝、白菜、小麦草和大部分绿色植物。

● 过氧化氢酶分解过氧化氢（一种代谢的废物），并产生氧气供身体利用。

食物中的酶

我们的身体可以自己制造出酶，当然也可以从食物中获取酶。然而，酶对温度非常敏感。即使不在很高的温度（47.8℃）条件下，食物中的大多数酶都会被破坏。食品的杀菌和牛奶的消毒都会破坏酶。因此，想要从食物中获取酶，必须吃生的食物。

当从食物中获取的酶缺乏时，身体就不得不产出内源性（体内产生）的酶来消化食物。过度地依赖身体产生消化酶会减弱身体产生代谢酶的能力，在必要时甚至会将代谢酶转换成消化酶。当身体处在酶缺乏的虚弱状态时，就容易患癌症、肥胖症、心脏病、内分泌紊乱或其它退化性疾病。缺乏酶的饮食习惯也会影响到肝脏、心脏、垂体、甲状腺和其它内分泌腺体。

吃生的食物，或食用酶补充剂（在每一餐开始前服用。消化酶胶囊至少应该包含三种最基本的酶：淀粉酶、蛋白酶和脂肪酶）有助于防止人体自身的酶消耗，从而减少对身体的压力。

在很多不同的食物中都含有酶。如：香蕉、梨、葡萄、橄榄、芒果、鲜枣、无花果、天然蜂蜜、天然黄油、未经高温杀毒的牛奶、菠萝、未成熟的木瓜、种子、坚果、豆芽（含酶量最丰富的）、原生谷物。

从木瓜和菠萝中提取的酶——木瓜蛋白酶和菠萝蛋白酶——是蛋白质水解酶。

并不是所有生的食物都可以直接食用。种子和坚果含有酶抑制剂，吃带有酶抑制剂的种子和坚果引起胰脏分泌消化酶，导致消化酶供应减少。生的种子和坚果含有淀粉，储存着能量，当条件成熟时，它们发芽并长成新的植物。

在酶抑制剂的存在下，生的种子和坚果中的酶被抑制。发芽（浸泡在水中）24 小时中和了酶抑制剂，酶被释放出来。萌芽也大大增强了酶的活性。

练习参考答案 *(Reference answers of exercise)*

以下列出的各种酶类至少各举出 2 例 *(List at least 2 examples of each class of enzymes given below)*

① **digestive enzymes:** amylase, protease, and lipase
② **metabolic enzymes:** superoxide dismutase (SOD), and catalase
③ **food enzymes:** papain, bromelain

Chapter Four

Cell Engineering

Unit 1　Monoclonal antibodies

Reading Material

Monoclonal antibodies are essential tools for many molecular immunology investigations. In particular, when used in combination with techniques such as epitope mapping and molecular modelling, monoclonal antibodies enable the antigenic profiling and visualisation of macromolecular surfaces. In addition, monoclonal antibodies have become key components in a vast array of clinical laboratory diagnostic tests. Their wide application in detecting and identifying serum analytes, cell markers, and pathogenic agents has largely arisen through the exquisite specificity of these unique reagents. Furthermore, the continuous culture of hybridoma cells that produce these antibodies offers the potential of an unlimited supply of reagent.

In 1975, Kohler and Milstein devised a method of growing very large numbers of antibody producing cells from a single B-cell. They did this by the ingenious technique of fusing B-cells from the immunised animal with myeloma cancer cells. The procedure yields a cell line capable of producing one type of antibody protein for a long period. A tumor from this "immortal" cell line is called a hybridoma. The resulting hybridoma retained two main features from its two parent cells. It could grow indefinitely like the cancer cell, yet also produce and secrete antibodies like the B-cell. This was the main discovery leading to hybridoma technology. The antibodies produced by these hybridomas are called monoclonal antibodies (mAbs) because they are derived from a single hybrid cell.

Antibodies

What are antibodies? For a lay person, the response might be that antibodies are special molecules in our blood and tissue fluids that help us fight infection. There are a variety of antibody molecules of different shapes and sizes, although the basic structure is essentially "Y" shaped, with the two tips designed to recognise and bind (Figure 1) foreign agents (for example, bacteria), foreign substances, or harmful cells. The remainder of the molecule is associated with so called "effector functions", which enable the antibody to interact with other immune cells, or serum proteins. In turn, these help do away with most unwanted company. Special molecules termed "monoclonal antibodies" can be obtained from cells grown in the laboratory, and it is these reagents that are useful in research and hospital laboratory diagnostic tests. This is because monoclonal antibodies are very specific for their intended targets. Of course, latterly, monoclonal antibodies have been termed "magic bullets" because they can be used as vehicles for delivering therapeutic agents to cancerous cells in the human body.

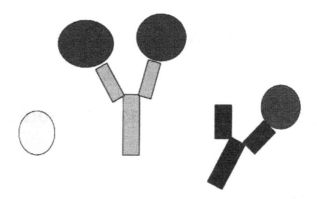

Figure 1 Schematic representation of an antibody molecule highlighting the "Y" shaped structure

Monoclonal antibodies

When a humoral immune response is provoked by an immunogen, such as tetanus toxoid, a plethora of antibodies are produced in an individual against different parts or regions of this foreign substance. These are termed antigenic determinants, or epitopes, which usually comprise six to eight amino acids. It should be appreciated that most antibodies recognise and interact with a three dimensional shape composed of "discontinuous" residues brought into juxtaposition by the folding of a molecule. Alternatively, antibodies can also recognise linear stretches of amino acids or "continuous" epitopes. Of course, an important concept to bear in mind is that each antibody molecule is specific for a single epitope, and that each antibody is the product of a single B cell clone. Thus, an antibody of unique specificity, derived from a single B cell clone, is termed a monoclonal antibody.

In our example cited above, tetanus toxoid would induce antibodies from numerous B cell clones; that is, this immunogen would produce a polyclonal antibody response. In contrast, the propagation of an isolated B cell clone would produce antibody of single specificity. However, a problem arises in that in tissue culture medium, B cells die within a few days of their isolation (for example, from a mouse spleen). Consequently, methods of conferring immortality on to B cells have been investigated. Indeed, immortality has been accomplished by means of viral transformation (for example, using Epstein-Barr virus) and/or fusion to cancerous cells to generate hybrids or "hybridomas". In general, the former technique is used for the immortalisation of peripheral blood B cells (and production of human monoclonal antibodies), whereas myeloma cells have mainly been used in the production of murine monoclonal antibodies.

Why monoclonal as opposed to polyclonal antibodies?

To their advantage, polyclonal antibodies detect a multiplicity of epitopes and therefore recognise antigen from different orientations: this may be important in certain assays where the detection of an analyte would be compromised by the use of a single epitope. In addition, polyclonal reagents are relatively simple and cheap to produce in the short term compared with monoclonal reagents. Furthermore, the use of larger animals (such as horses, goats, and rabbits) enables the recovery of a large volume (for example, 60 ml from a rabbit) of antibody rich serum. However, at some point a fresh batch will be sought as the original stock diminishes, which inevitability leads to the problem of batch to batch variation. This might include differences in antibody reactivity and titre, and thus polyclonal reagents in general suffer from a lack of reproducibility. In contrast, the continuous culture of B cell hybridomas offers a reproducible and potentially inexhaustible supply of antibody with exquisite specificity. Consequently, monoclonal antibodies enable the development of standardised and secure immunoassay systems. Overall, monoclonal antibodies serve as powerful tools for the investigation of macromolecules and cells, and have proved effective reagents in terms of specificity for clinical diagnostic tests. Latterly, of course, murine monoclonal reagents and their humanised counterparts have been used for clinical treatment with varying degrees of success.

So how do you make a monoclonal antibody?

Let us start with a working definition: a monoclonal antibody is regarded as an antibody of single specificity, generated from the immortalisation of a plasma B cell in vitro. Although several recombinant approaches are possible, the process of demystifying monoclonal antibodies is best illustrated by the generation of murine monoclonal reagents. In essence, five main stages (Figure 2) are highlighted: (1) immunisation, (2) fusion and selection, (3) screening, (4) characterisation, and (5) further developments.

stage 1: immunisation

Substances that induce an immune response are usually foreign to the individual and are termed immunogens. In general, protein (50–100 µg), cells (1×10^7), multiple antigenic synthetic peptides, or a short peptide (6–18 amino acids) linked to a carrier protein (for example, keyhole limpet haemocyanin) can be used for the primary immunisation of Balb/c mice. More often than not, an immunogen will be delivered in conjunction with an adjuvant, which is regarded as a non-specific immune enhancer. Typical examples include Freund's complete/incomplete adjuvants and TiterMax™. Invariably, proteins are delivered subcutaneously whereas cells are given intraperitoneally. Regular boosting is needed to augment a polyclonal response, which can be monitored indirectly using tail bleeds. These offer sufficient serum to ascertain the antibody titre to a desired antigen usually in an assay system—for example, enzyme linked immunosorbent assay (ELISA)—that is ultimately required for the monoclonal reagent. The effect of boosting also encourages immunoglobulin class switching and the generation of higher affinity antibodies through somatic hypermutation. In general, IgG monoclonal antibodies are preferred because they are less prone to degradation, and may potentially be more useful as therapeutic reagents.

Of course the end point, particularly for in vivo strategies, is to select an appropriate mouse (generally the best responder from tail bleeds) and remove (aseptically) antigenically responding B cells from its spleen (or lymph node) to obtain viable cells for hybridisation. It is noteworthy that although in vivo immunisation (including intrasplenic administration) is the favourite choice in many laboratories, there is also the opportunity for in vitro immunisation. In this case, cultured splenic cells are stimulated with only a minimal amount of antigen.

Stage 1: Immunisation

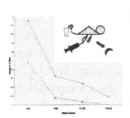

- Animal:mouse,rat
- Antigen:protein,cells, peptide(+carrier)
- Adjuvant such as CFA,IFA
- Immunisation strategy (primary,boosts,dose, site,frequency)
- Antibody response: serial tail bleeds

Stage 2: Fusion and selection

- Myeloma cells such as Sp2,NS1,NSO
- Mouse spleen
- Fusing agent such as PEG
- Plating of cells in HAT selective medium
- Scanning of viable bybridomas
- Propagation in HT medium

Stage 3: Screening

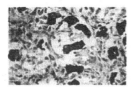

MAb reactivity against human osteoclastoma

- Primary analysis of hybridoma culture supernatants(in:IC/ELISA/HA/WBLOT)
- Tissue culture expansion of selected hybridomas
- Re-evaluation of selected hybridomas
- Cryopreservation of selected hybridomas

Stage 4: Characterisation

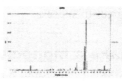

Epitope mapping of MAb A57H(μ isotype)against human IgG

- Isotype determination
- Cloning and cryo preservation
- Purification and verification of specificity
- Reactivity profiling, epitope mapping
- Validation against othger reagents
- Bulk production

Stage 5: Further developments

MAb probing of IgG

- Research applications-for example,as probes,structure-function analyses
- Commercial distribution of single MAb
- Application in diagnostic kits
- Modifications to MAb
- Therapeutic applications and clinical trials

Figure 2　Five stages of generating a murine monoclonal antibody (MAb)

(A) Immunisation, illustrating tail bleeds from mice immunised with Epstein-Barr virus (EBV) latent membrane protein 1 multiple antigenic synthetic peptide. (B) Fusion and selection, showing hybridoma PNG312G. (C) Screening, highlighting reactivity of MAb PNG211D against human osteoclastoma. (D) Characterisation, epitope mapping of MAb A57H against human IgG Fc. (E) Further developments, molecular modelling of monoclonal antibody A57H revealing an epitope (red) in the CH3 domain of IgG. CFA, complete Freund's adjuvant；ELISA, enzyme linked immunosorbent assay；HA, haemagglutination；HAT, hypoxanthine, aminopterin, and thymidine；HT, hypoxanthine and thymidine；IC, immunochemistry；IFA, incomplete Freund's adjuvant；PEG, polyethylene glycol；WBLOT, western blotting.

stage 2: fusion and selection

The hybridisation process centres on the fusion of murine splenic B cells with histocompatible myeloma cells, such as Sp2/0. The latter (and various alternative myeloma cell lines, such as NS1, NSO, and X63Ag8) are preselected for a deficiency in the enzyme hypoxanthine guanine phosphoribosyltransferase (HGPRT)—for example, by culturing in medium containing 8-azaguanine. In essence, this enzyme is fundamental to the post-fusion hybridoma selection process. To understand this process it should be noted that cells possess two pathways of nucleotide biosynthesis: the de novo pathway and the salvage pathway, which uses HGPRT. Consequently, myeloma cells that are HGPRT negative are unable to use the salvage or "alternative" pathway for purine biosynthesis and are thus entirely reliant on the de novo pathway for survival. In the fusion process, splenic B cells are mixed with HGPRT negative myeloma cells and a fusing agent, such as polyethylene glycol. Hopefully, the mixing and centrifugation steps generate myeloma—splenic B cell hybridomas. Once these hybrid cells are formed and plated into tissue culture wells, the priority shifts towards removing unfused myeloma cells. This is necessary because the latter have the potential to outgrow other cells, particularly weakly established hybridomas. This situation is resolved by using a selective medium containing hypoxanthine, aminopterin, and thymidine, otherwise known as "HAT". Of importance is the fact that aminopterin blocks the de novo pathway—the only one available to HGPRT negative cells, and as a consequence all unfused myeloma cells will die. Of course, newly formed hybridomas survive this selection process because the salvage pathway enzyme is provided by its splenic B cell counterpart.

Unfortunately, some hybridomas are unstable and regress. Hence, meticulous attention should be given to the visual examination of hybridomas using an inverted microscope. A record of poorly growing, newly emerging, or established hybridomas provides credibility to immunoassay screening data. Once established, a given hybridoma colony will continually grow in culture medium (such as RPMI-1640 with antibiotics and fetal bovine serum) and produce antibody. Twenty to 30 days post-fusion, hybridomas can be propagated in "HT" medium (hypoxanthine and thymidine only) because aminopterin is no longer required.

stage 3: screening

This stage focuses on identifying and selecting those hybridomas that produce antibody of appropriate specificity. The selection process must be ruthless otherwise numerous unwanted (at least to you!) hybridomas will compete for your time and incur unnecessary expense in terms of culture plates and medium. Invariably, a rapid "primary" screening system is used that tests the hybridoma culture supernatant for antibody reactivity and specificity. As an example, an Epstein-Barr viral associated protein or peptide can be coated on to plastic ELISA plates. After incubation of hybridoma culture supernatant, secondary enzyme labelled conjugate, and chromogenic substrate, a coloured product indicates a positive hybridoma. Alternatively, immunocytochemical screening might be more appropriate.

Ultimately, primary screening is necessary to "weed out" and eliminate non-specific hybridomas at the earliest opportunity. Obviously, it is important to screen supernatants with some degree of equity and, therefore, it might be wise to test hybridomas when at least three quarters confluent. Unfortunately, this approach means that screening becomes an almost daily task because not all hybridomas grow at similar rates. Of particular note is the fact that slow growing (and often very stable) hybridomas can appear after 25–30 days post-fusion, whereas most become established well before this time.

Hybridomas can initially be grown in multiwell plates and then, once selected, expanded to larger tissue culture flasks. This progression is necessary not only to maintain the well being of the hybridomas but also to provide sufficient cells for cryopreservation and supernatant for further investigations. As a rough guide, culture supernatant can yield anywhere between 1 and 60 μg/ml of monoclonal antibody: the latter being maintained at $-20°C$ or lower until required. The numbers of hybridomas that can manageably be "taken through" in a given laboratory require continual validation. Furthermore, if a fusion has been particularly successful, some rationalisation of hybridomas will be needed; that is, selecting only those providing an intense immunocytochemical staining pattern. Of course, less favoured hybridomas can be cryopreserved and examined at a later date. What is important to bear in mind is that the workload in generating hybridomas is generally exponential.

stage 4: characterisation

Further analysis of a potential monoclonal antibody producing hybridoma in terms of reactivity, specificity, and crossreactivity can be achieved using culture supernatant or a purified immunoglobulin preparation. However, before any further work it is often necessary to re-clone hybridomas (for example, by limiting dilution) because an original colony might contain at least two populations of fused B cells. Unless resolved, a consequence of this situation could be ambiguous data resulting from antibodies of differing class, specificity, and affinity. For this reason, isotype determination serves not only to define the murine immunoglobulin class or subclass but also helps identify the presence of a single isotype—for example, IgG1 or a mixture, such as IgM and IgG2b. In addition, knowledge of a monoclonal antibody's isotype will help dictate the most appropriate column purification technique for a culture supernatant—for example, protein G for IgG1.

A crucial aspect of characterisation relates to monoclonal antibody profiling in different assay systems. This is especially pertinent for the antibody's potential as a diagnostic reagent because some monoclonal antibodies perform well in some systems but not others. This phenomenon, termed assay restriction, relates to how an antibody recognises its target epitope in the context of the assay system used. In this case, an important epitope could be masked, denatured, or rendered inaccessible by the immobilisation procedure adopted within a given technique. Characterisation also affords the opportunity to test against a wide panel of related antigens or tissue preparations, particularly if monoclonal antibodies are being targeted for histopathological purposes. Of course, these endeavours and the hand of serendipity might well lead to useful applications elsewhere, and thus help capitalise on the original investment of time, effort, and cost. Once certain of a hybridoma, bulk production of a monoclonal antibody can be achieved using surface expanded tissue culture flasks or hollow fibre systems, such as Technomouse.

It is noteworthy that although a hybridoma may be the fused product of a single B cell and produce a monoclonal antibody of exquisite specificity, this same antibody can in fact crossreact with other antigens or exhibit dual specificity. This corollary arises when an antibody combining site recognises more than one antigenic determinant, either because of some similarity in shape or chemical composition. Furthermore, the nuances of an assay system can also bias the exposure of a particular antigenic determinant or epitope. Consequently, stringent evaluation of a given monoclonal antibody and its target epitope is necessary, which may therefore include epitope mapping. This particular technique allows precise determination of key amino acid residues that are important for antibody recognition and binding. Further characterisation might also include affinity measurements of antigen—monoclonal antibody interactions using surface plasmon resonance (for example, BIACore or IBIS).

stage 5: further developments

Once derived, monoclonal antibodies can serve as investigative research tools, or find applications in diagnostic assays or as therapeutic agents. In addition to potential collaborative opportunities, commercial exploitation of monoclonal antibodies might provide some revenue for future research projects. Furthermore, epitope mapping of monoclonal antibodies in conjunction with molecular modelling can enable the visualisation and localisation of key antigenic regions on a molecule. This information might help to elucidate structure–function relations of proteins, carbohydrates, and other molecules of clinical relevance.

Of course, an ultimate goal of monoclonal specialists is to widen the application of antibodies for the clinical treatment of patients. Certain murine monoclonal antibodies have proved effective (depending on subclass) but might ultimately induce human antimouse responses. This problem has been circumvented either by cleavage of the immunogenic Fc portion of the immunoglobulin molecule or by recombinant methodologies. These have largely focused on producing chimeric antibodies containing a murine antibody recognition unit and human Fc region, or using a human IgG molecule and inserting murine complementary determining residues to retain antibody specificity. Clearly, further advances for so called magic bullets either alone (and reliant on the effector characteristics of the immunoglobulin isotype) or armed with radionucleotides or toxins will undoubtedly obtain further prominence.

Applications

Diagnostic tests

Once monoclonal antibodies for a given substance have been produced, they can be used to detect the presence of this substance. The Western blot test and immuno dot blot tests detect the protein on a membrane. They are also very useful in immunohistochemistry, which detect antigen in fixed tissue sections and immunofluorescence test, which detect the substance in a frozen tissue section or in live cells.

Chimeric and humanized antibodies

One problem in medical applications is that the standard procedure of producing monoclonal antibodies yields mouse antibodies. Although murine antibodies are very similar to human ones there are differences. The human immune system hence recognizes mouse antibodies as foreign, rapidly removing them from circulation and causing systemic inflammatory effects. Such responses are recognised as producing HACA (human anti-chimeric antibodies) or HAMA (human anti-mouse antibodies).

A solution to this problem would be to generate human antibodies directly from humans. However, this is not easy, primarily because it is generally not seen as ethical to challenge humans with antigen in order to produce antibody; the ethics of doing the same to non-humans is a matter of debate. Furthermore, it is not easy to generate human antibodies against human tissues.

Fully human monoclonal antibodies

Since the discovery of in vitro production of monoclonal antibodies, scientists in the plans to produce "all" human antibody in order to avoid the use of humanized antibodies and chimeric antibodies of some of the side effects. Has identified two successful methods: phage antibodies and mice genetically engineered human antibody production class.

Genetically engineered mice, so called transgenic mice, can be modified to produce human antibodies, and this has been exploited by a number of commercial organisations.

Glossary

1. monoclonal	*adj.*〈生〉单克隆的，单细胞繁殖的
	n. 单克隆

2. antibody | *n.* 抗体
3. molecular | *adj.* ①分子的，分子组成的； ②克分子的
4. combination | *n.* 结合；组合；联合；化合
5. epitope | *n.* 表位；〈生化〉抗原决定部位；抗原决定基
6. antigen | *n.* 抗原
7. visual | *adj.* 视觉的，视力的
8. array | *n.* 〈计〉数组，阵列；排列，列阵；
9. clinical | *adj.* 临床的；诊所的
10. diagnostic | *adj.* 诊断的；特征的
n. 诊断法；诊断结论
11. identify | *vt.* 确定；识别
12. serum | *n.* 血清；浆液；免疫血清；乳清；〈植〉树液 [复数 serums 或 sera]
13. cell | *n.* 细胞
14. pathogenic | *adj.* 致病的；病原的；发病的
15. specificity | *n.* 特异性；特征；专一性
16. culture | *vt.* 培养
17. hybridoma | *n.* 〈生〉杂种瘤；杂种细胞（细胞融合后形成的）
18. fuse | *v.* 融化，融合
19. myeloma | *n.* 骨髓瘤
20. hybrid | *n.* 杂种，混血儿；混合物
21. immunogen | *n.* 免疫原
22. residue | *n.* 残渣；剩余；滤渣
23. murine | *n.* 鼠科动物
adj. 鼠科的
24. titre | *n.* 滴定度；最小滴定量
25. inexhaustible | *adj.* 用不完的；不知疲倦的
26. plasma | *n.* 〈物〉等离子体；〈医〉血浆
27. recombinant | *n.* 重组；〈生〉重组体
28. synthetic | *adj.* 综合的；合成的，人造的
n. 合成物
29. peptide | *n.* 缩氨酸
30. adjuvant | *n.* 佐药
adj. 辅助的
31. affinity | *n.* 密切关系；吸引力；姻亲关系；类同
32. somatic | *adj.* 躯体的；肉体的；体壁的
33. propagate | *v.* 传播；传送；繁殖
34. cryopreservation | *n.* 低温贮藏
35. section | *n.* 剖面，截面，切面

v. 被切割成片；被分成部分

36. inflammatory   *adj.* 〈医〉炎症性的；煽动性的；激动的
37. ethical   *adj.* 伦理的；道德的；凭处方出售的
38. encode   *vt.* 编码，译码
39. hybridisation process   *n.* 混合淡化技术（等于 hybridization）

Exercises

1. Matching

① a monoclonal antibody   (a) special molecules in our blood and tissue fluids that help us fight infection.

② hybridoma   (b) any substance (as a toxin or enzyme) that stimulates the production of antibodies.

③ immunogen   (c) mix together different elements.

④ antigen   (d) a hybrid cell resulting from the fusion of a lymphocyte and a tumor cell; used to culture a specific monoclonal antibody.

⑤ fuse   (e) any substance or organism that provokes an immune response (produces immunity) when introduced into the body.

⑥ antibodies   (f) an antibody of single specificity, generated from the immortalisation of a plasma B cell in vitro.

2. Fill in the blanks with the words or expressions given below.

| polyclonal antibodies | hybridisation process | antibodies |
| immunogen | monoclonal antibodies | nucleotide biosynthesis |

① _____ are essential tools for many molecular immunology investigations. In particular, when used in combination with techniques such as epitope mapping and molecular modelling.

② When a humoral immune response is provoked by an_____, such as tetanus toxoid, a plethora of antibodies are produced in an individual against different parts or regions of this foreign substance.

③ _____detect a multiplicity of epitopes and therefore recognise antigen from different orientations: this may be important in certain assays where the detection of an analyte would be compromised by the use of a single epitope.

④ The _____centres on the fusion of murine splenic B cells with histocompatible myeloma cells, such as Sp2/0.

⑤ To understand this process it should be noted that cells possess two pathways of_____: the de novo pathway and the salvage pathway, which uses HGPRT.

⑥ an ultimate goal of monoclonal specialists is to widen the application of _____for the clinical treatment of patients.

Translation

单克隆抗体

单克隆抗体是许多分子免疫学研究必不可少的工具。特别是用于诸如抗原表位标记和分子建模时，单克隆抗体技术的应用可使大分子表面构象可视化。此外，单克隆抗体技术已经成为广大临床实验诊断的一个重要组成部分。由于其特异性和敏感性，单克隆抗体技术广泛应用于检测和鉴定待检血清、细胞标记物和病原微生物等领域。此外，杂交瘤细胞的持续培养能力为单克隆抗体的生产提供了无限供应。

1975 年，Kohler 和 Milstein 设计了一种从单一 B 细胞大量繁殖抗体的方法。他们通过巧妙的技术将骨髓瘤细胞和被免疫动物的 B 细胞融合，应用这一融合技术获得了一种能够长期分泌一种形式抗体蛋白的细胞系，而这个"无限增殖的"瘤细胞系被称为杂交瘤细胞。该杂交瘤细胞保留它的两个亲本细胞的主要特征：既可以像癌细胞一样无限繁殖，也能像 B 细胞一样产生和分泌抗体，这是杂交瘤细胞技术的主要特征。因为抗体是由单一的杂交瘤细胞产生，所以这些由杂交瘤细胞产生的抗体被称为单克隆抗体（mAbs）。

抗体

什么是抗体？对于非专业人士而言，抗体是存在于我们的血液和组织液，帮助我们抵抗感染的一类特殊分子。我们体内存在大量形状和大小均不相同的抗体分子，其基本结构都是"Y"形（图1），两个臂端用来识别和结合侵入物（例如细菌）、外来物质或有害的细胞。抗体分子的柄端则与"效应功能"有关，该部位能使抗体与其它免疫细胞或血清蛋白结合，同时又能使抗体非必要的细胞发生排斥反应。所谓的特殊分子"单克隆抗体"，它们可以通过实验室细胞培养获得，是某些研究机构和医院实验室诊断使用的重要试剂。这是因为单克隆抗体对它们的预定目标具有很高的特异性。后来，单克隆抗体被称为"神奇子弹"，因为它们在人体内被用来传递治疗癌细胞的药物。

图1 抗体的"Y"形结构分子

单克隆抗体

当破伤风类毒素类免疫原激发了机体的体液免疫应答，大量针对这类外源物质不同部位的独特抗体也同时产生。这些部位被称为抗原决定簇或抗原表位，它们通常由 6～8 个氨基酸组成。可以肯定的是，大多数抗体识别和结合的是一个三维立体构型（构象表位），这种立体结构是由免疫原分子引入一些"间断"残基并折叠构成。另外，抗体也可以识别线性氨基酸和线性表位。当然，需要记住这样一个重要的概念：每个抗体分子特异性的对应一个抗原表位，每个抗体是一个单一的 B 细胞克隆的产物。因此，由单个 B 细胞克隆产生的特异性抗体称为单克隆抗体。

在我们上面引用的例子中，似乎破伤风类毒素能够引起众多 B 细胞克隆产生抗体，也就是说，这类免疫原可以引起多克隆抗体应答，单个 B 细胞克隆可以产生单独的特异性抗体。然而，在组织培养中又出现这样一个问题：组织中分离出来的 B 细胞会在几天内死亡（例如老鼠脾脏源 B 细胞）。理所当然的，人们开始研究赋予 B 细胞永生的方法。事实上，B 细胞不断传代可以由病毒转化（例如，使用 EB 病毒）和/或与肿瘤细胞融合来完成，用以产生杂种或"杂交瘤细胞"。一般来说，病毒转化技术用于外周血 B 细胞无限增殖（和人类单克隆抗体的生产），而骨髓瘤细胞主要用于小鼠单克隆抗体的生产。

单克隆抗体与多克隆抗体的比较

两者均有其各自的优势：多克隆抗体可以同时检测多个抗原表位，从各个方向来识别抗原，这点对于检测含有某一单个表位的待测物的定性分析非常重要。此外，在短期内来看，相对于单克隆试剂而言，多克隆试剂的生产相对简单和廉价。再者，使用诸如马、山羊和兔子等大型动物可以回收大量的抗体血清（例如，兔子可以提供 60 毫升抗体血清）。但是，一批又一批新的多克隆抗体的制造，使最原始的多克隆抗体减少，这必然导致了一批批多克隆抗体的差异问题，可能包括抗体滴度和反应性的差异，因此多克隆抗体一般都面临着重复性差的问题。相比之下，连续培养的杂交瘤 B 细胞可以特异性地提供一种可再生的、取之不尽、用之不竭的抗体。因此，单克隆抗体可以发展为一种标准化的、可靠的免疫检测体系。总的来说，单克隆抗体作为一种强有力的工具用于大分子和细胞的检测，并在临床试验的特异性诊断上非常有效。近期，鼠源单克隆试剂和人源化单克隆抗体已被用于临床治疗，并取得了不同程度的成功。

如何生产单克隆抗体

首先，我们认识一个概念：单克隆抗体被认为是一种特异性的抗体，它是由可以持续传代的血浆 B 细胞在体外产生。虽然单克隆抗体的产生有几种可能的重组法，但以小数单克隆抗体来说明单克隆抗体的产生较为恰当。从本质上讲，总共有 5 个重要步骤（图 2）：①免疫接种；②细胞融合和选择培养；③细胞筛选；④抗体性质鉴定；⑤扩大培养。

第一阶段：免疫接种

相对于个体来讲，能够诱导机体产生免疫应答，与机体无关的外来物质称为免疫原。一般来说，蛋白质（50~100 微克）、细胞（1×10^7 个）、多抗原合成肽和短肽（6~18 个氨基酸）结合载体蛋白质（例如，锁孔血蓝蛋白）可以用于 Balb/c 小鼠的首次免疫接种。通常情况下，免疫原结合免疫佐剂同时注射免疫，这被认为是非特异性免疫增强剂。典型的佐剂包括弗氏完全/不完全佐剂和 TiterMax™。通常情况下，蛋白质通过皮下注射，而细胞则是通过腹腔注射。通过小鼠尾部采血定期检测免疫效果，并随时加强免疫。这种检测系统可以提供足够的血清来测定抗体滴度，制备理想的抗原。例如，酶联免疫吸附试验（ELISA）需要单克隆抗体。刺激体细胞突变的结果可以引起免疫球蛋白类转化，并产生高亲和力的抗体。一般来说，首选 IgG 类单克隆抗体，因为它们不容易退化，且有可能作为治疗试剂使用。

(a) 第一阶段：免疫接种

- 动物：小鼠、大鼠
- 抗原：蛋白质、细胞、肽(+携带者)
- CFA和IFA
- 免疫策略(首次免疫，加强免疫，免疫剂量，免疫位点；免疫频率)
- 抗体反应：每次免疫后尾部采血检测

(b) 第二阶段：细胞融合与选择培养

- Sp2,NS1,NSO等多发性骨髓瘤细胞
- 小鼠脾脏
- 融合剂(如PEG)
- 在HAT选择培养基上培养细胞
- 镜检可用的杂交瘤细胞
- 在HT培养基中大量增殖

(c) 第三阶段：细胞筛选

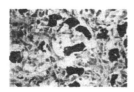

单克隆抗体与人类破骨细胞瘤的反应

- 杂交瘤细胞培养上清的初次分析(IC/ELISA/HA/WBLOT)
- 在组织培养瓶中扩繁选中的杂交瘤细胞
- 进一步检查已选的杂交瘤细胞
- 冷冻保存杂交瘤细胞

(d) 第四阶段：抗体性质鉴定

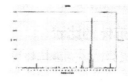

抗人IgG单克隆抗体A57H(μ亚型)的抗原表位图谱

- 同型测定
- 克隆与冷冻保存
- 纯化和验证单克隆细胞的特异性
- 反应性分析抗原图谱
- 用其它试剂验证
- 批量生产

(e) 第五阶段：进一步发展

单克隆抗体探针

- 例如在探针、结构-功能分析等方面的应用研究
- 单克隆抗体的商业贡献
- 在诊断试剂方面的应用
- 单克隆抗体的修饰
- 治疗应用和临床试验

图2　生产鼠源单克隆抗体（MAb）的五个步骤

　　（a）免疫接种，Epstein-Barr 病毒（EBV）潜伏膜蛋白 1 多抗原合成肽免疫小鼠尾部；（b）细胞融合和选择培养，显示杂交瘤细胞 PNG312G；（c）细胞筛选，筛选与人类骨母细胞瘤反应活性高的 PNG211D 单克隆抗体；（d）抗体性质鉴定，检测 A57H 单克隆抗体与人 IgG Fc 反应的抗原表位图谱；（e）扩大培养，单克隆抗体 A57H 的分子建模揭示了 IgG 的 CH3 域表位（红色）

　　CFA—完全弗氏佐剂；ELISA—酶联免疫反应；HA—血凝；HAT—次黄嘌呤，氨基蝶呤，胸腺嘧啶核苷；HT—次黄嘌呤，胸腺嘧啶核苷；IC—免疫组化；IFA—不完全弗氏佐剂；PEG—聚乙二醇；WBLOT—免疫印迹

　　当然，最后体内的试验阶段需要选择一种合适的老鼠（通过小鼠尾部采血来检测免疫效果）和无菌条件下取出脾脏（或淋巴结）中免疫抗原 B 细胞以供杂交。尽管大多数实验室选择体内免疫小鼠，但是也有实验室选择在体外免疫接种。在体外免疫接种情况下，培养的脾细胞只需要少量的抗原刺激。

第二阶段：细胞融合与选择培养

　　杂交瘤细胞制备的关键在于小鼠脾脏 B 细胞与骨髓瘤细胞（如 Sp2/0）的融合过程。缺乏次黄嘌呤鸟嘌呤磷酸核糖转移酶（HGPRT）的骨髓瘤细胞被优先选择（可供选择的骨髓瘤细胞株包括 NS1、NSO 和 X63Ag8），例如在含 8-氮鸟嘌呤的培养基中培养。从本质上讲，这种酶是杂交瘤细胞后期融合过程的基础。而了解细胞核苷酸生物合成的两个途径有助于理解这一过程：从头途径和补救途径均需使用 HGPRT。因此，HGPRT 阴性的骨髓瘤细胞无法利用补救或"替代"途径来合成嘌呤，从而只能完全依赖从头途径生存。在融合过程中，脾脏 B 细胞与 HGPRT 阴性骨髓瘤细胞混合，并且在融合剂作用下融合，如聚乙二醇。两种细胞混匀、离心后产生骨髓瘤-脾脏 B 细胞杂交瘤。一旦这些杂交细胞形成，迅速移走未融合的骨髓瘤细胞，并将融合的细胞放入组织培养板中培养。将未融合的骨髓瘤细胞移走是必要的，因为其长势有可能超过其它细胞，特别是刚刚建立的弱势杂交瘤细胞。当然，这种情况可以通过使用含有次黄嘌呤、氨基蝶呤和胸腺嘧啶（"HAT"）的选择培养基来解决。最重要的是，氨基蝶呤能够阻止从头途径，而这条途径是 HGPRT 阴性细胞所含的唯一一条途径，因此所有未融合的骨髓瘤细胞将会死亡。当然，新形成的杂交瘤细胞将会存活，这是因为其补救途径所需的酶将由相应的脾脏 B 细胞及其类似物提供。

然而不幸的是，一些杂交瘤细胞并不稳定，有些甚至复原。因此，通过倒置显微镜仔细检查杂交瘤细胞。详细记录长势不好、新兴和已确定的杂交瘤细胞，用以为免疫筛选数据提供依据。杂交瘤细胞一旦建立，就继续给予培养基让其生长（如含有抗生素和胎牛血清的 RPMI-1640 培养基）和产生抗体。融合后 20～30 天，在"HT"培养基中杂交瘤细胞可以大量增殖（这种培养基只含有次黄嘌呤和胸腺嘧啶），因为这时杂交瘤细胞已经不再需要氨基蝶呤。

第三阶段：细胞筛选

这一阶段重点是识别和选择产生特异性抗体的杂交瘤细胞。筛选过程必须严格，否则许多非预期的（至少是你不想要的）杂交瘤细胞将消耗你的时间，以及浪费细胞培养板和培养基。用快速的初筛系统来检测杂交瘤细胞培养上清液中的抗体反应性和特异性。例如，可以将 EB 病毒相关的蛋白质或多肽涂到塑料 ELISA 板。孵化后的杂交瘤细胞培养上清、次级酶标结合物和发色底物，有颜色变化的表明是阳性的杂交瘤细胞。另外，免疫细胞化学检查可能更为合适。

最终，初筛要"淘汰"和尽早消除早期非特异性杂交瘤细胞。显然，合适的筛选方法显得非常重要，因此，当杂交瘤细胞长满细胞板 3/4 面积时检测是非常明智的。然而不幸的是，杂交瘤细胞生长速度不一致，采取这种方法也就意味着每天都必须进行筛选。特别值得注意的是，生长缓慢（通常是非常稳定的）的杂交瘤细胞一般在融合后的 25～30 天显现，而多数则在此之前就已经出现。

最初杂交瘤细胞可以培养在多孔细胞板上，然后一旦被选定，便应置于更大的组织培养瓶中培养。转换培养瓶是必要的，因为这时不仅要维持培养中的杂交瘤细胞生长，还要提供充足的细胞以供冷冻保存，并且提供上清进行更进一步的各项指标检查。每毫升培养的上清液大致可以回收 1～60 微克单克隆抗体，然后将其保存在-20℃或更低的温度下直至使用时。大量的杂交瘤细胞可以在一个特定的实验室通过全过程监控管理不断验证。此外，如果杂交瘤细胞选择合理，将会使融合特别成功，即只选择那些免疫细胞化学染色反应强的细胞。当然，如果只有较少特异性的杂交瘤细胞，则可以将其冷冻保存，日后再做筛查。需要记住最重要的一点就是杂交瘤细胞的数量一般是以指数形式增长的。

第四阶段：抗体性质鉴定

通过使用培养上清液和提纯的免疫球蛋白可以进一步分析杂交瘤细胞所产生的单克隆抗

体的反应性、特异性和交叉反应性。然而，在进行下一步的工作之前，常常需要重新繁殖杂交瘤细胞（例如，通过有限稀释），这是因为原代细胞可能含有两种以上的融合 B 细胞。如不解决这个问题，来源、特异性和亲和力均不同的抗体可能会引起数据的不确定性。正是由于这个原因，抗体同型测定不仅可以界定小鼠免疫球蛋白类别或亚类，而且也有助于鉴别某种存在的单一亚型，例如，IgG1 或混合物（如 IgM 和 IgG2b）。此外，掌握单克隆抗体同型相关的知识也有助于选择最合适的培养上清纯化技术，例如从 G 蛋白中纯化 IgG1。

在不同的检测系统中，单克隆抗体特性的一个重要特性与其空间构象有关。作为诊断试剂这点尤为重要，因为单克隆抗体在某些检测中发挥出色，而在有些检测中效果并不好，这种现象称为检测限制，主要取决于在检测系统中抗体是如何识别其目标抗原的抗原表位。在这种情况下，一个重要的抗原表位可以被屏蔽，变性，甚至使用某些技术使这个固定的程序无法正常地递呈。表位结构也为抗原或组织的广泛检测提供了机会，特别是在单克隆抗体以组织病理学切片为检测对象时。当然，这些努力以及一些偶然的机会可能发现单克隆抗体在其它地方的用途，当然这样也有利于缩短研究所花费的时间和精力，以及投资成本的回收。一旦确定了某种杂交瘤细胞的可行性，使用扩大组织培养瓶或中空纤维系统（如Technomouse）可以大量生产的单克隆抗体。

值得注意的是，虽然杂交瘤细胞可能是一个单一的 B 细胞融合产生，并且可以生产出高度特异性的单克隆抗体，如果这种抗体能与其它抗原发生交叉反应，可以说这种抗体具有双特异性。由于抗原在形状或化学成分方面的相似性，一个抗体结合位点可以识别一个或一个以上的抗原决定簇则是一个必然的结果。此外，个别的抗原决定簇和表位的暴露也可以导致检测的细微差别。因此，抗原表位等对于评估一个给定的单克隆抗体及其靶抗原表位严格是非常必要的。利用这种特殊的技术，可以精确地判断识别和结合抗体的关键氨基酸残基。进一步定性筛选还包括使用表面离子共振（例如 BIACore 或 IBIS）来确定抗原与单克隆抗体的亲和力。

第五阶段：扩大培养

一经产生，单克隆抗体就可以作为调查研究工具、诊断分析中的应用基础以及治疗药物。当然还有一些潜在的合作机会，单克隆抗体的商业开发可能为今后的研究提供一些资金上的支持。此外，单克隆抗体的抗原表位标记结合分子模型可以将分子抗原的重点区域可视化，并可进行定位。这点有助于阐明蛋白质、碳水化合物以及与临床有关的其它分子的结构与功能关系。

当然，一个单克隆专家的最终目的是扩大对病人临床治疗中的抗体的应用。某些鼠源单克隆抗体已证明是有效的（取决于鼠亚纲），但最终可能导致人抗鼠的抗体应答反应。这个问题已经通过切割的免疫球蛋白分子的 Fc 片段或基因重组的方法解决。这点主要集中在生产含有小鼠抗体识别单位和人的 Fc 片段的嵌合体，或者使用人 IgG 分子，插入鼠源互补决定簇来保留抗体的特异性。很显然，被称为"神奇子弹"的单克隆抗体（或者凭借免疫球蛋白亚型的效应特点）取得发展，或者借助于放射性核酸或毒素的偶联，无疑将取得进一步发展。

应用

1. 诊断测试

一旦某种物质的单克隆抗体被生产出来，它们可以用来检测该种物质是否存在。在蛋白质印迹试验和免疫斑点杂交试验中，可以用来检测膜上的蛋白质；在免疫组织化学试验中，可以用来检测组织切片上的抗原；在免疫荧光试验中，可以用来检测冰冻组织切片和活细胞中的抗原物质。

2. 嵌合抗体和人源化抗体

单克隆抗体在医疗领域的应用中出现这样一个问题：其标准化生产过程受小鼠抗体限制。虽然鼠源抗体非常类似于人类抗体，但两者还是存在差异。因此，人类免疫系统将鼠源抗体视为外来物，并将它们迅速清除出体内循环，同时引起组织炎症反应。这种反应被认为是导致生产人抗嵌合抗体（HACA）或人抗鼠抗体（HAMA）的原因。

该问题的解决办法是利用人体直接生产人类抗体。然而，想这么做并不容易，主要是因为为了生产抗体而挑战人类伦理并不明智，而且，目前利用动物制造抗体本身就是一个有争议的问题。此外，利用人体组织获得人类抗体也并不容易。

3. "全" 人源单克隆抗体

自从发现单克隆抗体可以在体外生产，科学家就在计划生产"全"人源抗体，以避免使用人源化抗体和嵌合抗体的一些副作用。目前已经确定了两种成功的方法：噬菌体产生的抗体和小鼠基因工程生产的类人源抗体。

基因工程鼠，也就是转基因鼠，经过改造后可以产生人类抗体，这种方法已经被很多商业机构开发利用。

练习参考答案 *(Reference answers of exercises)*

1. 配对 *(Matching)*

①—(f)；②—(d)；③—(e)；④—(b)；⑤—(c)；⑥—(a)

2. 用词或短语填空 *(Fill in the blanks with the words or expressions given below)*

① Monoclonal antibodies　② immunogen　③ Polyclonal antibodies
④ hybridisation process　⑤ nucleotide biosynthesis　⑥ antibodies

Unit 2　Establishment of a Primary Culture

Reading Material

Materials

Chick embryo (approximately 8 days old)
70% (v/v) ethanol for swabbing
Sterile scissors，forceps and probes
Sterile petri plates
Phosphate buffered saline (PBS)
Trypsin,cold sterilized
Minimum Essential Medium（MEM）
Fetal Calf Serum(FCS)
Clinical centrifuge with sterile capped centrifuge tubes
Culture flasks
Inverted phase contrast microscope

Procedure

Candle an 8 days old egg to ensure that it is alive. This is easily accomplished by holding the egg in front of a bright light source；the embryo can be seen as a shadow. Circle the embryo with a pencil.

Place the egg in a beaker with the blunt end up, and wash the top with a mild detergent, followed by swabbing with ethanol.

Carefully puncture the top of the egg with the point of a pair of sterile scissors and cut away a circle of shell, thus exposing the underlying membrane (the chorioallantois).

With a second pair of sterile scissors, carefully cut away and remove the chorioallantoic membrane, exposing the embryo.

Identify and carefully remove the embryo by the neck, using a sterile metal hook or a bent glass rod, and place the embryo in a 100mm petri dish containing PBS. Wash several times with PBS by transferring the embryo to fresh petri plates. After removal of all yolk and blood, move the embryo to a clean dish with PBS.

Using two sterile forceps, remove the head, limbs, and viscera. Be sure to remove the entire limb by pulling at the proximal end. Move the remaining tissues of the embryo to yet another dish and wash with PBS.

Mince the embryo finely with scissors and transfer the minced tissue to a flask containing PBS. Allow the tissue pieces to settle.

Remove the PBS with a sterile pipette and add 25 ml of trypsin, a proteolytic enzyme. Stir the solution gently at 37℃ for 15-20 minutes.

Allow the larger, undigested tissue pieces to settle and decant the supernatant into an equal volume of MEM + 10%FCS. FCS contains protease inhibitors which will inactivate the trypsin.

Centrifuge the cells in MEM at 1000 rpm for 10 minutes in a standard clinical centrifuge. Remove the supernatant and resuspend the pellet in 25 ml of fresh MEM + 10% FCS.

Remove 0.1 ml of the culture and determine cell concentration and viability.

Seed two 25cm^2 plastic culture flasks containing 25 ml of MEM + 10% FCS to a final concentration of 10_5 cells/ml.

Label and place your cultures in the tissue culture incubator at 37° C and examine daily for cell density and morphology.

Note any changes in the color of the media. Tissue culture media has a pH indicator (Phenol Red) added in order to check on the growth of cells. The media initially is a cherry red (with slight blue haze) and turns orange and then yellow as the cells grow, thereby reducing the media. Should this color change occur within 24 hours, the culture is most likely contaminated and should be disposed of it.

Examine the cultures using an inverted phase contrast microscope. This will allow observation of the cells without opening or disturbing the growth.

Make cell density determinations at 10 × magnification using a square ocular grid.

Plot the cell density on a log scale vs. time of culture.

Diagram the shape of the cells at each phase.

Notes:

The cultures will develop differently than the suspension cultures. The viable cells will grow out of the trypsinized pieces of tissue and will remain in contact with the bottom of the culture flask. They will continue to divide and migrate until the entire bottom of the flask is covered with a single layer of cells (contact inhibition and the formation of a monolayer).

Glossary

1. embryo	*n.* 胚，胚胎
2. ethanol	*n.* 乙醇，酒精
3. sterile	*adj.* 无菌的, 消过毒的
4. trypsin	*n.* 胰蛋白酶
5. centrifuge	*n.* 离心机
6. chorioallantois	*n.* 绒毛膜尿囊
7. forcep	*n.* 镊子
8. mince	*vt.* 切碎
9. proteolytic	*adj.* (分)解蛋白的,蛋白水解的
10. stir	*vt.* 搅拌
11. supernatant	*n.* 上清液
12. inhibitor	*n.* 抑制剂
13. label	*n.* 标签
14. incubator	*n.* 孵化器, 恒温箱
15. density	*n.* 密度，密集
16. morphology	*n.* 形态学(尤指动植物形态学或词语形态学)，形态论

17. diagram   *n.* 图表，图解
18. swabbing   *n.*（起模前）刷水；擦（抹）
19. probes   *n.* 探针
20. phosphate buffered saline   磷酸盐缓冲剂
21. Fetal Calf Serum   胎牛血清
22. culture flasks   培养瓶
23. inverted phase contrast microscope   倒置显微镜
24. beaker   *n.* 烧杯
25. detergent   *n.* 清洁剂
26. puncture   *vt.* 刺穿
27. yolks   *n.* 卵黄
28. pipette   *n.* 移液管
29. decant   *vt.* 移入其它仪器，轻轻倒出

Exercises

1. *Matching*

① cell primary culture   (a) an enzyme of pancreatic origin; catalyzes the hydrolysis of proteins to smaller polypeptide units

② contact inhibition   (b) the hydrolysis of proteins into peptides and amino acids by cleavage of their peptide bonds

③ trypsin   (c) a fundamental method to obtain enough amounts of cells for scientific researches

④ PBS   (d) one of the mechanisms related to the migration of cells, and it performs that when the cells contact with others in its migration, they will retract their protrusions and change the direction of motion

⑤ embryo   (e) phosphate buffered saline

⑥ proteolytic   (f) an animal organism in the early stages of growth and differentiation that in higher forms merge into fetal stages but in lower forms terminate in commencement of larval life

2. *Fill in the blanks with the words or expressions given below.*

FCS	embryo	The viable cells
density and morphology	ethanol	an inverted phase contrast microscope

① Place the egg in a beaker with the blunt end up, and wash the top with a mild detergent, followed by swabbing with_____.

② Identify and carefully remove the _____by the neck, using a sterile metal hook or a bent glass rod, and place the embryo in a 100mm petri dish containing PBS.

③ _____contains protease inhibitors which will inactivate the trypsin.

④ Label and place your cultures in the tissue culture incubator at 37° C and examine daily for cell_____.

⑤ Examine the cultures using_____. This will allow observation of the cells without opening or disturbing the growth.

⑥ The cultures will develop differently than the suspension cultures._____will grow out of the trypsinized pieces of tissue and will remain in contact with the bottom of the culture flask.

Translation

原代培养的建立

材料

鸡胚胎（约 8 天）。

70％（体积分数）的乙醇。

无菌剪刀，镊子和探针。

无菌培养皿。

磷酸盐缓冲液（PBS）。

胰蛋白酶，低温灭菌。

MEM 培养基。

胎牛血清（FCS）。

离心机，带无菌离心管。

培养瓶。

倒置相差显微镜。

过程

1. 用光照 8 日龄蛋，以确保它成活。将鸡蛋放在灯前，可以很容易地看到一个阴影，用铅笔圈出，这就是鸡胚。

2. 将鸡蛋放置在烧杯里，大头朝下，先用温和的洗涤剂冲洗顶端，再用乙醇擦抹。

3. 用无菌剪刀小心穿刺，去掉顶部蛋的壳，暴露下面的膜。

4. 用另一把无菌剪刀，小心剪去绒毛尿囊膜，暴露里面的胚胎。

5. 用无菌的金属钩杆或弯曲玻璃棒小心地取出胚胎，并将其放置在盛有 PBS 的 100 毫米培养皿中。用 PBS 清洗胚胎数次，再将其转移到另一个培养皿中。除去蛋黄和血液，将胚胎移至一加入 PBS 的清洁盘中。

6. 使用两个无菌镊子，除去头部、四肢和内脏。一定要近端拉动整个肢体。将剩余的胚胎组织移至另一个盘子，用 PBS 冲洗。

7. 将胚胎组织用剪刀剪碎，放入一个含有 PBS 的培养瓶，静置。

8. 无菌吸管吸去 PBS，加入 25 毫升胰蛋白酶，37℃ 轻轻摇动 15～20 分钟。

9. 沉淀大的、未消化的组织块，将上清移至等量的含有 10％ FCS（胎牛血清）的 MEM（基本培养基）容器中。FCS 含有蛋白酶抑制剂，可灭活胰蛋白酶。

10. 1000 转/分钟离心 10 分钟，弃上清。加入 25 毫升含 10％FCS 的 MEM 中，并重悬沉淀。

11. 取 0.1 毫升的细胞溶液测定细胞的浓度和活力。

12. 取两个 25 厘米塑料培养瓶，加入 25 毫升 MEM+10%FCS，使最终细胞浓度达到 10^5/毫升。

13. 将培养瓶作好标记并放置于恒温箱中，37℃ 培养，每天检测细胞密度和形态。

14. 注意培养液的颜色变化。培养液中加入了酸碱指示剂酚红，以便监测细胞的生长。培养液最初是樱桃红色（显轻微的蓝色烟雾），转橙，然后变为黄色。如果出现这种颜色的变化发生在 24 小时内，培养液有可能已经被污染，应弃去。

15. 倒置相差显微镜下检测。无需打开培养容器，以免干扰其增长。

16. 10 倍的放大倍率下检测细胞密度。

17. 以时间为横坐标、细胞密度为纵坐标绘制工作曲线。

18. 图示各阶段的细胞形态。

注：

这种培养不同于悬浮培养。不受胰蛋白酶的影响，连续分化和迁移，直到整个瓶子的底部形成一个单细胞层（细胞的接触抑制）。

练习参考答案 (Reference answers of exercises)

1. 配对 (Matching)
①—(d)；②—(c)；③—(a)；④—(e)；⑤—(f)；⑥—(b)

2. 用词或短语填空 (Fill in the blanks with the words or expressions given below)
① ethanol   ② embryo   ③ FCS
④ density and morphology ⑤ an inverted phase contrast microscope ⑥ The viable cells

Unit 3 Stem cells

Reading Material

Stem cells are cells that grow and divide without limitation, and given the proper signals, can become any other type of cell.

Some stem cells are embryonic in origin. As a human embryo grows, the early cells start dividing and forming different, specialized cells such as heart cells，bone cells, and muscle cells. Once formed, specialized nonstem cells can only divide to produce replicas of themselves. They can not backtrack and become a different type of cells.

Embryonic stem cells retain the ability to become virtually any cell type. If the cells are harvested from an early embryo (about 5-7 days after conception) and nudged in a particular direction in the laboratory, they can be directed to become a particular tissue or organ。

Tissues and organs grown form stem cells in the laboratory may some day be used to replace organs damaged in accidents or organs that are gradually failing due to degenerative diseases. Degenerative diseases start with the slow breakdown of an organ and progress to organ failure. Additionally, when one organ is not working properly, other organs are also affected. Degenerative disease includes stroke, diabetes, liver and lung diseases, heart disease, and Alzheimer's disease.

Stem cells could provide healthy tissue to replace those damaged by spinal cord injury or burns. New heart muscle could be produced to replace that damaged during a heart attack. A diabetic could have a new pancreas, and people suffering form osteoarthritis could have replacement cartilage to cushion their joints. Thousands of people waiting for organ transplants might be saved if new organs were grown in the lab.

One problem with stem-cell research is that the embryos are destroyed when the stem cells are removed. And many people object to the destruction of early embryos. Currently, the federal government will fund research using leftover embryos from fertility treatments, but will not support research using embryos created solely for research purposes. This ban only applies to federally funded research projects, which means that in the United States, research on embryos can be performed by genetic engineers who obtain grants from nongovernment sources unless they have access to the limited number of embryos created during fertility treatments.

In-vitro (Latin, meaning "in glass") fertilization procedures often result in the production of excess embryos because a large number of egg cells are harvested from a woman who wishes to become pregnant. These egg cells are then mixed with her parent's sperm in a petri dish, resulting in the production of many fertilized eggs that grow into embryos. A few of the embryos are then implanted into the woman's uterus. The remaining embryos are stored so that more attempts can be made if pregnancy does not result or if the couple desires more children. When the couple achieves the desired number of pregnancies, the remaining embryos can, with the couple's consent, be used for stem-cell research.

A solution to the ethical dilemma presented by the use of embryonic stem cells seems to be on the horizon. Scientists have recently discovered that many adult tissues also contain stem cells. Recent studies published in peer-reviewed literature suggest that most adult tissues have stem cells, that these cells can be driven to become other cell types, and that they can be grown indefinitely in the laboratory. Based on success in animal models, there is even evidence that adult stem cells will help cure diseases. In fact, scientists have used stem cells from tissues to treat damage in animals due to heart attack, stroke, diabetes, and spinal cord injury.

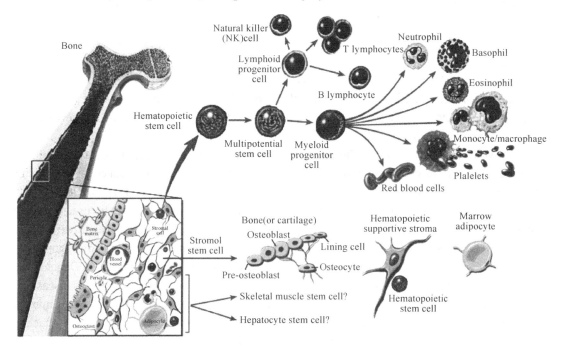

Glossary

1. limitation   *n.* 限制
2. signal   *n.* 信号
3. replica   *n.* 复制品
4. backtrack   *vi.* 返回，退回
5. harvest   *v.* 收获，获得，收集
    n. 收获，收成，结果，成果
6. nudge   *vt.* 轻触，轻推
7. stroke   *n* 中风
8. diabetes   *n.* 糖尿病
9. pancreas   *n.* 胰腺
10. osteoarthritis   *n.* 骨关节炎
11. cushion   *vt.* 放在

12. pregnant	*adj.* 怀孕的，怀胎的
13. implant	*vt.* 植入
14. uterus	*n.* 子宫
15. pregnancy	*n.* 怀孕
16. consent	*vi.* 同意，赞成，答应
	n. 同意，赞成，允诺
17. ethical	*adj.* 伦理的，道德的
18. dilemma	*n.* 进退两难之境；困境
19. stem cell	*n.* 干细胞
20. heart cell	*n.* 心肌细胞
21.degenerative disease	*n.* 退行性疾病
22. Alzheimer's disease	*n.* 阿尔茨海默病
23. organ transplant	*n.* 器官移植
24. have access to	*v.* 有机会得到；能接近；能使用
25. in-vitro fertilization	*n.* 体外受精
26. egg cell	*n.* 卵细胞
27. petri dish	*n.* 培养皿
28. fertilized egg	*n.* 受精卵

Exercises

1. *Matching*

① stem cells

（a）diseases that start with the slow breakdown of an organ and progress to organ failure, including stroke, diabetes, liver and lung diseases, heart disease, and Alzheimer's disease.

② degenerative diseases

（b）the female reproductive cell; the female gamete

③ In-vitro (Latin, meaning "inglass") ferti- lization procedures

（c）copy that is not the original; something that has been copied

④ egg cell

（d）retain the ability to become virtually any cell type. If the cells are harvested from an early embryo (about 5-7 days after conception) and nudged in a particular direction in the laboratory, they can be directed to become a particular tissue or organ。

⑤ replica

（e）often result in the production of excess embryos because a large number of egg cells are harvested from a woman who wishes to become pregnant.

⑥ embryonic stem cells

（f）cells that grow and divide without limitation, and given the proper signals, can become any other type of cell.

2. Fill in the blanks with the words or expressions given below.

early embryos	tissues and organs	embryonic
stem cells	adult tissues	spinal cord injury or burns

① Some stem cells are _____in origin. As a human embryo grows ,the early cells start dividing and forming different, specialized cells such as heart cells，bone cells ,and muscle cells.

② _____grown form stem cells in the laboratory may some day be used to replace organs damaged in accidents or organs that are gradually failing due to degenerative diseases.

③ One problem with stem-cell research is that the embryos are destroyed when the stem cells are removed. And many people object to the destruction of_____.

④ Stem cells could provide healthy tissue to replace those damaged by_____. New heart muscle could be produced to replace that damaged during a heart attack. A diabetic could have a new pancreas, and people suffering form osteoarthritis could have replacement cartilage to cushion their joints.

⑤ A solution to the ethical dilemma presented by the use of embryonic stem cells seems to be on the horizon. Scientists have recently discovered that many adult tissues also contain_____.

⑥ Recent studies published in peer-reviewed literature suggest that most_____ have stem cells, that these cells can be driven to become other cell types, and that they can be grown indefinitely in the laboratory.

3. Translating

① Recent experiments have demonstrated the possibility of cloning differentiated mammalian tissue, opening the door for the first time to practical transgenic cloning of farm animals.

② Transplanted stem cells may allow us to replace damaged or lost tissue, offering cures for many disorders that cannot now be treated. Current work focuses on tissue-specific stem cells, which do not present the ethical problems that embryonic stem cells do.

③ Recent experiments open the way for cloning of genetically altered animals and suggest that human cloning is feasible.

④ Crop foods may be genetically modified to increase their yield, shelf life, and nutritive content.

⑤ There is concern that GM foods may negatively affect the environment or people who consume them.

⑥ Cloning animals with desirable agriculture traits has occurred. It may someday be possible to clone humans, but it is unclear if these humans would be healthy.

⑦ Human cloning occurs commonly in via the spontaneous production of identical twins.

⑧ Cloning offspring from adults with desirable traits has been successfully performed on cattle, goats, mice, cats, pigs, rabbits, and sheep.

⑨ Since the isolation of embryonic stem cells in 1998, labs all over the world have been exploring the possibility of using stem cells to restore damaged or lost tissue.

⑩ The exciting promise of these embryonic stem cells is that, because they can develop into any tissue, they may give us the ability to restore damaged heart or spine tissue.

干细胞

干细胞是一群具有无限生长和分裂能力的细胞，如果有正确的细胞信号，干细胞能发育成任何类型的细胞。

有些干细胞源自胚胎。随着人类胚胎的发育，早期的细胞开始分化并形成不同类型的细胞，如心肌细胞、骨细胞和肌细胞。一旦分化以后，这些非干细胞就只能进行复制，不会再恢复为干细胞而成为其它类型的细胞。

胚胎干细胞具有分化成其它任何类型细胞的能力，如果从一个早期的胚胎中收集这种细胞（大约在受孕后 5 天），然后在实验中对其分化方向进行控制，它们就能直接发育成为某一特定的组织和器官。

将来总有一天，在实验室中利用干细胞培养出来的组织和器官可以替代已损坏的组织和器官——这些组织和器官可能在一场事故中受到损坏，也可能由于退化性疾病造成器官逐渐衰竭。此外，如果一个器官功能不正常，其它的器官也会受到影响。退化性疾病包括中风、糖尿病、肝和肺的疾病、心脏病和阿尔茨海默病。

干细胞能提供健康的组织来替代脊髓受损组织和烧伤的组织。新生成的心肌也可替代心脏受损组织。糖尿病患者可能会有一个新的胰腺，那些正受到骨关节炎病痛折磨的人也可能会有可替代的软骨重新植入他们的关节中。如果能在实验室中生产出来新的器官，将会解救许多正在等待进行器官移植的人。

干细胞研究中出现的一个问题是当干细胞被移出时，胚胎会受到破坏。而许多人反对破坏早期胚胎。目前，联邦政府将资助那些采用受精后剩余胚胎的研究项目，如果在一项研究中，所制备的胚胎单单只是为了研究，那么就不会获得资助。这项规定只适用于联邦基金，这就意味着在美国，进行胚胎研究的科学家只能从非政府机构获得基金资助，除非他们有机会得到数量有限的受精后剩余的胚胎。

体外（拉丁语中意思是"在试管中"）受精步骤通常产生多余的胚胎，因为将有大量想怀孕的妇女捐献卵细胞。将这些妇女卵细胞与她们伴侣的精子在培养皿中混合，结果产生大量的受精卵，这些受精卵最后会发育成胚胎。一些胚胎会被重新植回到子宫里，其余的胚胎将会被保存起来，这样，如果没有怀孕成功或一对夫妻想要更多的孩子，则再进行一次胚胎植入。而当一对夫妻达到目的以后，其余的胚胎在得到当事人的允许之后，将被用于干细胞研究。

似乎已经找到使用胚胎干细胞出现的伦理问题的解决方案。最近，科学家发现成人的许多组织中也含有干细胞。最近发布的同行评审研究成果表明，大多数的成人组织中具有干细胞，这些干细胞同样也能分化成其它类型细胞，而且在实验中这些干细胞能无限制地生长。在成功的动物模型中，甚至有证据表明成人干细胞将有助于治疗疾病。实际上，科学家已经利用从成人组织中分离到的干细胞对患有心脏病、中风、糖尿病和脊髓损伤的动物机体进行修复。

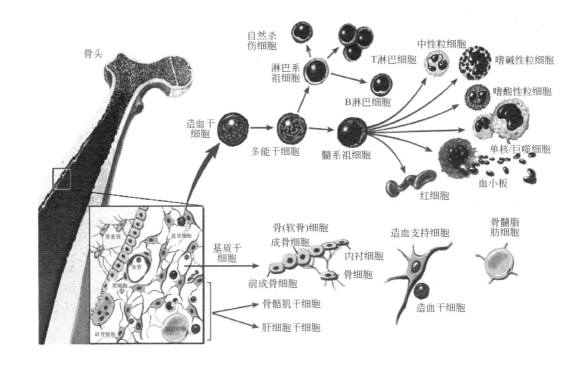

练习参考答案 *(Reference answers of exercises)*

1. 配对（*Matching*）

①—(f)；②—(a)；③—(e)；④—(b)；⑤—(c)；⑥—(d)

2. 用词或短语填空（*Fill in the blanks with the words or expressions given below*）

① embryonic   ② Tissues and organs   ③ early embryos

④ spinal cord injury or burns   ⑤ stem cells   ⑥ adult tissues

3. 翻译（*Translating*）

① 最近的实验显示了克隆不同哺乳动物组织的可能，也首次开启了克隆家畜之门。

② 干细胞移植可能使我们取代损坏或丢失的组织，医治很多现在不能治疗的疾病，目前的工作重点是特定组织干细胞研究，这些研究会出现像胚胎干细胞那样的伦理问题。

③ 近来实验开辟了转基因动物克隆之路，并且预示着人类的克隆是可能的。

④ 农作物经过基因改造可以增加产量、延长食品货架期和增加营养含量。

⑤ 值得关注的是转基因食物可能会对环境或消费它们的人类产生负面的影响。

⑥ 带有预期经济性状的克隆动物已经成功，也许将来某一天克隆人也会成为可能，但是这种人是否健康还不得而知。

⑦ 通常克隆人就像自然生产的双胞胎一样。

⑧ 从具有较好特点的成年动物克隆产生下一代个体技术已经成功应用于牛、山羊、老鼠、猫、猪、兔子和绵羊

⑨ 自从 1998 年分离未发育干细胞以来，全世界的实验室正在探索使用干细胞来修复损坏或丢失组织的可能性。

⑩ 这些未发育干细胞令人激动的前景是它们可以发育成任何组织，这使得人类修复受到损害的心脏和脊髓成为可能。

Unit 4　Animal cell culture

Reading Material

Animal cell culture (ACC) is the process of culture of animal cells outside the tissue (in vitro) from which they were obtained. The process of ACC is carried out under strict laboratory conditions of asepsis, sterility and controlled environment involving temperature, gases and pressure. It should mimic the in vivo environment successfully such that the cells are capable of survival and proliferation in a controlled manner.

Culturable cells

Theoretically, cells of any type can be cultured upon procurement in a viable state from any organ or tissue. However, not all types of cells are capable of strangeness in such an artificial environment because of many reasons on which the artificial environment may fail to mimic the biochemical parameters of the source environment. Some good examples include the absence of growth regulators, cell to cell signal molecules, etc. Under optimal conditions of maintenance, the cell culture established can be sub-cultured (passaging) until a pure-culture of specific cell type is obtained. This can repeatedly sub-cultured to maintain as a cell-line. As a matter of fact, cell lines from cancerous tissues have also been established. The presence of excess growth regulators or other factors may often render the cells to undergo rapid uncontrolled proliferation resulting in a cancerous state. Good examples of established cell lines are HeLa, BHK, Vero, CHO etc.

The artificial environment is generally known as media. A media comprises an appropriate source of energy for the cells which they can easily utilize and compounds which regulate the cell cycle. A typical media may or may not contain serum. The latter is called a serum-free media. Some of the common sources of serum can be fetal bovine serum, equine serum, and calf serum. Both types of media have their own sets of advantages and disadvantages.

Applications

Consider drug testing in the process of discovery of a new drug. The test drug must pass through many phases after which it gets approved and marketed. Among the preliminary phases, one such involves the testing of the test drug on animals for toxicity or efficacy and efficiency. Now this can also be harmful or fatal to the animal on which it is being tested. This can be minimized if the drug is tested on a cell line it is targeted against as a cure, thereby assessing the toxicity on an initial scale thus reducing the probability of death on the test animal.

Production of therapeutically significant biological compounds like hormones and proteins on an industrial scale has been made simpler, faster and more efficient by the use of cell lines in the place of the living animal themselves.

Vaccines effective against many viral infections and diseases require the cultivation and mass production of the virus followed by its attenuation. The drawback in this is that virus requires a living medium to replicate and multiply. Rather than the traditional concept "Sacrifice one life to save many", ACC can be employed to mass produce the virus. Passively, ACC can be employed to reduce the virulence of particular virus strains by cultivating them on cells other than target cells which the virus infects followed by repeated passaging.

Studies on regenerative medicine can be understood on deeper concepts if ACC is fully exploited as cells behave in a spectrum of patterns under various environments which can be simulated in an ACC laboratory and followed in vitro.

Active research on stem cell culture, proliferation leading to organogenesis is at a slow phase due to the non-availability of research materials. This can however be overcome if ACC is fully utilized. The fruits of such a study can be more than overwhelming towards the betterment of human life.

ACC also finds application in the preservation of highly valuable cord blood cells which are nothing but stem cells specific to an individual.

ACC is a potential tool in Assisted Conception which requires the maintenance of sperm and the egg from the donors viable under laboratory conditions after which they are allowed to fertilize (in vitro) followed by re-implantation.

Glossary

1.in vitro		在试管中，在生物体外
2.asepsis	*n.*	无菌操作
3.sterility	*n.*	无菌
4.mimic	*vt.*	模拟，模仿
5.proliferation	*n.*	增殖，繁殖
6.cell-line	*n.*	细胞系，细胞株
7.procurement	*n.*	获得，取得
8.viable	*n.*	能养活的
9.parameters	*n.*	参数，系数，参量
10.cancerous	*adj.*	癌的，恶性肿瘤的
11.media	*n.*	培养基
12.utilize	*vt.*	利用
13.serum	*n.*	血清
14.fetal	*adj.*	胎儿的
15.bovine	*n.*	牛科动物
16.equine	*adj.*	马的
17.toxicity	*n.*	毒性，毒力
18.therapeutically	*adj.*	治疗（学）的，疗法的
19.hormones	*n.*	激素类
20.vaccines	*n.*	疫苗，痘苗
21.infection	*n.*	传染，感染
22.organogenesis	*n.*	器官发生，器官形成
23.sperm	*n.*	精子，精液

24.egg	*n.* 卵子，卵细胞
25.fertilize	*vt.* 受精
26.absence of	缺乏
27.growth regulator	生长调节剂
28. preliminary	*n.* 准备

Exercise

Answer questions:

1. What is ACC?

2. Why some types of cells can not be cultured?

3. How dose a cell-line form?

4. What results in a cancerous state?

5. What dose a media comprise in ACC?

6. What is the applications of ACC?

7. How is ACC applied in drug testing?

8. Comparing to the traditional concept, what are the advantages of ACC in vaccine producing?

Translation

动物细胞培养

动物细胞培养（ACC），是在该组织以外（体外）获得动物细胞的过程。该过程是在严格无菌条件下进行，并控制其温度、气体和压力。它应成功模拟体内环境，使得细胞可以存活并以可控制的方式增殖。

细胞培养

从理论上说，来源于任何器官或组织的任何类型的细胞均可以进行培养，然而，由于种种原因，并非所有类型的细胞都能够适应这样一个人工环境。人工环境可能无法模拟源环境的生化参数。比如，缺乏生长调节剂、缺少细胞间信号分子等。在理想的培养条件下，可以进行传代培养，直到获得纯种的单一细胞。这种细胞可以作为一个细胞系进行反复传代培养。事实上，已建立了从肿瘤组织获得的细胞系。添加生长调节剂或其它因素可使这些细胞如肿瘤组织一样进行快速扩增。建立细胞系的例子有 HeLa、BHK、Vero、CHO 等。

人工环境就是人们通常所说的培养基。培养基包括细胞生长所需的能量及调节细胞周期的因子。一个典型的培养基可能包含血清，也可能不包含，后者被称为无血清培养基。血清可以是胎牛血清、马血清和小牛血清。各种类型的培养基各有优劣。

应用

一种新的药物，必须经过药物测试过程，才能获得批准和进入进一步的销售等各环节。

在最初阶段，应进行一些针对动物的毒性及其效果和效率的药物测试，这对动物来说是有害的，甚至是致命的。使用细胞系可以大大消除这种对动物的危害。

使用细胞系代替活体动物来生产一些药物，如激素、工业化大规模生产的蛋白质等的方法，已经更为简单、快捷和高效。

生产能够对抗病毒感染的疫苗需要培养大量的病毒，并对其进行减毒、弱化。但病毒需要在活的生命体中才能复制和繁殖。传统的方法是，"牺牲一个生命，为了拯救更多的人"，但现在可以采用细胞培养技术，能大规模繁殖这种病毒。继而，通过进一步的细胞培养，还可以降低病毒株的毒性。

如果动物细胞培养能够在细胞培养实验室甚至体外进行，那么对于再生医学的研究就能够更加深入。

基于对干细胞的培养、增殖以至器官形成的研究，进展缓慢，很大程度上由于干细胞很难获得，细胞培养技术能够解决这一难题。这一研究成果可以大大地延长人类的寿命。

细胞培养技术也被应用于保存十分宝贵的脐带血干细胞。每个人脐带血中的干细胞都具有特异性，即每个人都有特定的干细胞。

动物细胞培养可作为一个潜在的辅助工具，帮助完成受孕。这需要在实验室中保存供体的精子和卵子，并且在体外进行受精。

练习参考答案 *(Reference answers of exercise)*

回答下列问题（*Answer questions*）

1. Key：Animal cell culture (ACC) is the process of culture of animal cells outside the tissue (in vitro) from which they were obtained.

2. Key：The artificial environment may fail to mimic the biochemical parameters of the source environment.

3. Key：Under optimal conditions of maintenance, the cell culture established can be sub-cultured (passaging) until a pure-culture of specific cell type is obtained. This can repeatedly sub-cultured to maintain as a cell-line.

4. Key：Undergo rapid uncontrolled proliferation resulting.

5. Key：A media comprises an appropriate source of energy for the cells which they can easily utilize and compounds which regulate the cell cycle. A typical media may or may not contain serum.

6. Key：
① Drug testing.
② Production of therapeutically significant biological compounds.
③ Mass producing the virus.
④ Active research on stem cell culture.
⑤ The preservation of highly valuable cord blood cells.
⑥ A potential tool in Assisted Conception.

7. Key：This can be minimized if the drug is tested on a cell line it is targeted against as a cure,

thereby assessing the toxicity on an initial scale thus reducing the probability of death on the test animal.

8. Key：ACC can be employed to reduce the virulence of particular virus strains by cultivating them on cells other than target cells which the virus infects followed by repeated passaging.

Chapter Five

Gene Engineering

Unit 1　Tomato Engineering

Reading Material

The supermarket tomato, pale red and unyielding to the touch,lacks the vibrant color and luscious flavor of a ripe,fresh-picked fruit. Despite their dissatisfaction with mass-produced tomatoes, U.S. shoppers still buy an impressive 2.8 billion pounds of them every year.

Now, through advances in molecular biology, genetic engineers are gaining more precise control of tomato ripening and its effects on taste, texture, color, and shelf life.

The first of such gene-spliced products is well on its way to market (see Figure 1). Genetic engineers from Calgene Fresh Inc. have created the "FLAVR SAVR", an alternative to the beleaguered supermarket tomato. This engineered tomato, designed to resist softening, will have the fresh flavor consumers desire and an extended shelf life as well.

Figure 1　Transforming tomatoes

Growers of fresh-market　tomatoes harvest their crop firm and green so it can be washed, sorted, packed and shipped without suffering extensive (and expensive) bruising (see Figure 2). Before shipping, commercial packers bathe the tomatoes in ethylene gas for several days to spur ripening. The problem is these artificially ripened tomatoes just don't have the flavor consumers desire (see Figure 3).

Figure 2　Fresh-market Tomatoes

Figure 3　Ripened Tomatoes

From a grower's viewpoint, the ideal mass-production tomato could be left on the vine to build up the sugars and acids critical to fresh taste and aroma, yet remain firm enough to handle without damage.

The Calgene company's FLAVR SAVR is the world's first listing of approved GM foods. FLAVR SAVR for a ripe tomato that produces PG gene was suppressed, so a more unyielding texture can reduce the harvesting, transportation, processing bruises during metamorphism, and therefore preserve flavor. However, the present, the tomato has stopped commercial production.

Tomatoes and many other plants produce ethylene to control the various biochemical processes that cause fruit to ripen, including the breakdown of chlorophyll, the synthesis of the red pigment, the buildup of sugars and acids, and the softening of tomato tissue by PG and other enzymes.

Some genetic engineers have chosen ethylene control as a means of tailoring tomato ripening to growers' needs.An American agricultural research group has outfitted its tomato with a bacterial gene whose enzyme digests and acid called ACC, the raw material that tomato cells convert into ethylene gas. Growers can leave these ethylene-deprived fruits on the vine for three or four more days——just long enough to build up extra flavor.

In addition, genetic engineers want to carve out a place for themselves in the tomato processing industry (see Figure 4). The size of this market is impressive. Every year, U.S. processors transform 12 billion pounds of raw tomatoes into juice, sauce, paste, catsup, and other products.Part of this crop goes into the 315 million cans of Campbell's tomato soup consumed annually in North America.

Figure 4　Tomato processing

The best tomato for making these products is high in solids, chiefly the sugars, fructose and glucose. And tomato solids are no small potatoes. The tomato processing industry estimates that a 1 percent increase in tomato solids could save $ 70 million to $ 80 million a year in processing costs.

Using antisense genetics, Avtar K.Handa of Purdue University created a tomato with 10 percent more solids than current varieties grown for processing. His group used the antisense techniques to block the gene for an enzyme called pectin methylesterase (PME) so he could study its role in fruit softening. The high-solids trait, unexpected though welcomed, showed up during standard testing of the harvested fruit.

In tomatoes, PME works in concert with PG to break down pectin, a major cell-wall building block. During ripening, these enzymes slowly soften tomato tissues, leaving them susceptible to bruising and rot. Currently, Handa does not know exactly why suppressing PME enriches the solids in tomatoes. Handa expects to finish compiling the field testing data on his high-solids tomato by the end of 1995.

Genetic engineers continue to search for patentable tomato genes.Researchers at ICI Seeds in Berkshire, England, have isolated 13 tomato genes that affect fruit quality and have patented five.Other genetically engineered crops will follow. ICI may eventually use its patented genes and techniques to create new kinds of peach and melons.Agritope, a subsidiary of Epitope, Beaverton, Oregon, envisions engineering many different fruits and vegetables, by means of control of ethylene production.For some crops, like broccoli, the goal is to shut down ethylene completely, since broccoli is only consumed when green (ripening turns it yellow). Another project involves raspberries. Oregon grows ninety percent of the U.S. raspberry crop, and consumes most of it, since ripe raspberries don't last more than 48 hours.Scientists see an opportunity for engineering ethylene-controlled raspberries to ship worldwide. DNA Plant Technology Corp. plans to deploy its gene-control techniques further afield.Its managing director of research, Robert Whitaker, envisions bananas, papaya, and cut flowers as logical targets for future efforts to ensure freshness through ethylene control.

Glossary

1. unyielding	*adj.* 坚硬的,不能弯曲的
2. vibrant	*adj.* (尤指颜色)鲜明的, 醒目的
3. luscious	*adj.* 美味的, 香甜的，甘美的
4. texture	*n.* 手感，质感，质地；纹理结构，表面状态
5. gene-spliced	*n.* 基因拼接
6. alternative（to）	*n.* 可供选择的东西
7. beleaguered	*adj.* 受到围困[围攻]的
8. bruise	*v.* (使)碰伤[擦伤], (使)成瘀伤
9. ethylene gas	*n.* 乙烯气体
10. spur	*v.* 刺激，激励
11. vine	*n.* 藤本植物, 藤
12. aroma	*n.* 芳香, 香味

13. antisense	*adj.* 反义的；反向的
14. polygalacturonase (PG)	*n.* 多聚半乳糖醛酸酶
15. enzyme	*n.* 〈生化〉酶
16. messenger RNA	*n.* 信使 RNA
17. ribosome	*n.* 核糖体
18. biochemical	*adj.* 生物化学的
19. chlorophyll	*n.* 叶绿素
20. synthesis	*n.* 〈化〉合成
21. pigment	*n.* 天然色素
22. tailor	*v.* 调整使适应；精心设计巧安排
23. outfit	*v.* 装备；供应；配备；准备
24. bacterial	*adj.* 细菌的
25. digest	*v.* 消化
26. ACC	*abbr.* 1-aminocyclopropane-1-carboxylate 1-氨基环丙烷-1-羧酸
27. raw material	*n.* 原料
28. convert	*v.* (使)转变,(使)转化
29. catsup	*n.* 烹调酱(如番茄酱之类)
30. fructose	*n.* 果糖
31. glucose	*n.* 〈化〉葡萄糖
32. pectin	*n.* 果胶
33. methylesterase	*n.* 甲基酯酶
34. trait	*n.* 特性, 特征, 特点, 特色；品质,
35. susceptible	*adj.* 易受影响的；易受…感染的
36. rot	*v.* 腐烂
37. patentable	*adj.* 可给予（或可取得）专利权的
38. ICI	*abbr.* Imperial Chemical Industries Ltd. 英国化学工业公司
39. isolate	*v.* 分离
40. subsidiary	*n.* 子公司
41. raspberry	*n.* 悬钩子(树), 木莓(树), 山莓(树), 树莓（树）
42. afield	*adv.* 偏离；在野外，在田中
43. envision	*v.* 想象,预想
44. papaya	*n.* 香木瓜

Exercises

1. *Matching*

① enzyme   （a）any of various plants, having long flexible stems that creep along the ground or climb by clinging to a support by means of tendrils, leafstalks, etc

② catsup   （b）any of numerous minute particles in the cytoplasm of cells, either free or attached to the endoplasmic reticulum, that contain RNA and protein and are the site of protein synthesis

③ ribosome   （c）a variant (esp US) of **ketchup**

④ fructose   （d）a white crystalline monosaccharide sugar

⑤ glucose   （e）a white crystalline water-soluble sugar occurring in honey and many fruits.

⑥ vine   （f）any of a group of complex proteins or conjugated proteins that are produced by living cells and act as catalysts in specific biochemical reactions

2. *Fill in the blanks with the words or expressions given below, and change the form where necessary.*

tailor	vibrant	convert
envision	spur	digest

① He always uses_____ colours in his paintings.

② They expected that their effort should _____the market further.

③ Some genetic engineers have chosen ethylene control as a means of_____ tomato ripening to growers' needs.

④ Digestive enzymes can _____food into absorbable substances.

⑤ _____ your success. Write about it. Then read that daily or weekly.

⑥ Cheese does not _____ easily.

Translation

西红柿工程

超市里的西红柿，呈浅红色，摸起来较硬，缺乏新摘果实的鲜艳颜色和香甜味道。在美国，尽管人们对批量生产的西红柿感到不满意，但每年顾客们还是会消费 28 亿磅的西红柿。

如今，随着分子生物学的发展，遗传学的工程师们对西红柿的成熟期可以做到更精确的控制，而且对其味道、质地、颜色和货架期的掌握也可以很好地控制。

第一批基因改造的产品即将上市（图1）。Calgene Fresh 公司的遗传学工程师们已经开发出"佳味"（"FLAVR SAVR"，FLAVR SAVR 西红柿是世界上第一种获准上市的基因改造食品）品种，可替代超市受人欢迎的西红柿。这种借助基因工程开发出来的西红柿能耐软化，且具有消费者喜欢的新鲜风味，货架期也会延长。

新品西红柿的制造者们在西红柿硬实、色绿时进行收获，进而可以轻松地清洗、挑选、包装、运输，而不会遭受大量（且造价昂贵）的损伤（图2）。在装运前，包装货物的批发商们将西红柿在乙烯气体中放几天促使其成熟。问题是这些人为催熟的西红柿其味道满足不了消费者的需求（图3）。

图 1　转基因西红柿

图 2　新鲜上市的西红柿　　　　图 3　催熟的西红柿

有位西红柿栽培者认为，理想中批量生产的西红柿应在成熟后摘取以提高对新鲜味道来说至关重要的糖度和酸度，还要使西红柿足够硬实不至于碰伤。

美国 Calgene 公司的"佳味"（FLAVR SAVR）西红柿是世界上第一种获准上市的基因改造食品。佳味西红柿中促进熟软 PG 基因被抑制，所以质地较坚实，可减少采收、运输、加工处理过程中碰伤变质，因而保存风味。不过，目前该品种西红柿已停止商业生产。

西红柿和其它许多植物会产生乙烯来控制各种生化过程，使果实成熟，包括叶绿素的分解、红色色素的合成、糖和酸的制造，以及通过 PG 和其它酶使西红柿的肉质组织软化。

有些遗传学工程师选择控制乙烯作为控制西红柿成熟的手段，以满足西红柿栽培者的需要。一个美国农业研究小组向西红柿中植入一个带有 1-氨基环丙烷-1-羧酸降解酶的细菌基因，这种酸是西红柿细胞产生乙烯气体的原料。西红柿的种植者可将这些不产生乙烯的西红柿在架上多放 3～4 天——只是为了足以丰富果实的味道。

另外，遗传学工程师们想在西红柿的加工业中谋得一席之地（图 4）。市场潜力非常可观。每年，在美国有 120 亿磅的西红柿被加工成果汁、果酱、番茄酱和其它产品。在北美每年一部分西红柿被制成 3.15 亿个坎贝尔西红柿汤罐头供人们消费。

用于加工这些产品的西红柿最好是固形物含量很高的，主要是糖、果糖和葡萄糖的含量高。西红柿的固形物含量绝非微不足道。西红柿加工业估计，固形物含量每增加 1%，则加工成本一年可节省 7000 万～8000 万美元。

利用反义基因技术，美国普渡大学的 Avtar K.Handa 培育出一种固形物含量比目前种植的品种高 10%的西红柿用于加工。他的研究小组利用反义技术阻碍了编码胶质甲基酯酶（PME）的基因，以便于他对这种酶在果实软化方面的作用进行研究。虽然固形物含量高的特性出人意料地受欢迎，但却只有在成熟果实标准测验时才会表现出来。

在西红柿中，胶质甲基酯酶（PME）与多聚半乳糖醛酸酶（PG）一起分解果胶，果胶是构成细胞壁的主要成分。在成熟期，这些酶慢慢软

图4　西红柿的生产过程

化西红柿组织，使西红柿容易碰伤或腐坏。目前，Handa 尚未明确为何抑制胶质甲基酯酶会使西红柿中的固形物含量丰富，他期望到 1995 年底能完成收集高固形物含量西红柿的实验数据。

遗传学工程师们继续在寻找可取得专利权的西红柿基因。在英格兰的 Berkshire（波克夏，英格兰南部的伯克郡泰晤士河畔的一个城市），从事英国化学工业公司种子研究的研究人员分离出影响西红柿质量的 13 种西红柿基因，有 5 项获得专利。其它基因工程作物也将被培育出来。英国化学工业公司最终会利用其获得专利的基因和技术培育出新品种的桃子和瓜类。Agritope（在美国俄勒冈州比弗顿）为 Epitope 的子公司，其期望通过控制乙烯的产生，对多种不同水果和蔬菜实施基因工程。对于某些作物如花椰菜，目标是完全去除乙烯，因为花椰菜只有绿色时才能享用（成熟后变黄）。另一个项目是对树霉的研究。俄勒冈州出产的树霉占全美国总量的 90%，由于成熟的树霉保质期不超过 48 小时，所以其大部分在该州内消费。科学家们看到了机会：借助基因工程控制乙烯的产生来培育树霉，可将其运往世界各地。DNA 植物技术公司打算将基因控制技术进行更为广泛的应用。总经理 Robert Whitaker 预想：将来通过乙烯控制技术，确保香蕉、木瓜与剪下的花朵的新鲜度，从逻辑上说是可行的。

练习参考答案 (Reference answers of exercises)

1. 配对（Matching）

①—(f)；②—(c)；③—(b)；④—(e)；⑤—(d)；⑥—(a)

2. 用词或短语填空，根据需要变换形式（Fill in the blanks with the words or expressions given below，and change the form where necessary）

① vibrant；② spur；③ tailoring；④ convert；⑤ envision；⑥ digest

Unit 2 Polymerase Chain Reaction

Reading Material

The polymerase chain reaction (PCR) is arguably the most important biotechnological innovation to date, and is rapidly becoming a standard technique in molecular biology research. Since its conception in the mid-1980's by Nobel Prize winner Kary Mullis and other scientists at Cetus Corporation, new and innovative applications for PCR have been and are being developed at an exponentially increasing rate.

The polymerase chain reaction relies on the ability of DNA—copying enzymes to remain stable at high temperatures. DNA polymerase is the Taq polymerase, named for Thermus aquaticus, from which it was isolated. It helps scientists produce millions of copies of a single DNA segment in a matter of hours. In nature, most organisms copy their DNA in the same way. The PCR mimics this process, but only does it in a test tube. When any cell divides, polymerases make a copy of all the DNA in each chromosome. The first step in this process is to "unzip" the two DNA chains of the double helix. As the two strands separate, DNA polymerase makes a copy using each strand as a template.

The four nucleotide bases, the building block of every piece of DNA, are represented by the letters A, T, C, and G, which stand for their chemical names: adenine, thymine, cytosine, and guanine. The A on one strand always pairs with the T on the other, whereas C always pairs with G. The two strands are said to be complementary to each other.

To copy DNA, polymerase requires two other components: a supply of the four nucleotide bases and something called a primer. DNA polymerases, whether from humans, bacteria, or viruses, cannot copy a chain of DNA without a short sequence of nucleotides to "prime" the process, or get it started. So the cell has another enzyme called a primase that actually makes the first few nucleotides of the copy. This stretch of DNA is called a primer. Once the primer is made, the polymerase can take over making the rest of the new chain.

A PCR vial contains all the necessary components for DNA duplication: a piece of DNA, large quantities of the four nucleotides, large quantities of the primer sequence, and DNA polymerase(see Figure 1).

The three parts of the polymerase chain reaction are carried out in the same vial, but at different temperatures(see Figure 2). The first part of the process separates the two DNA chains in

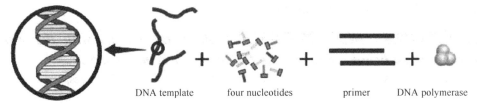

DNA template   four nucleotides   primer   DNA polymerase

Figure 1   All the Necessary Components for DNA Duplication

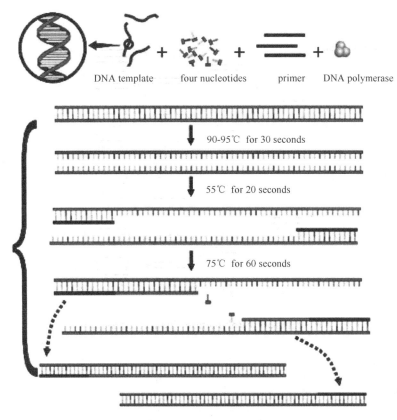

DNA template   four nucleotides   primer   DNA polymerase

90-95℃ for 30 seconds

55℃ for 20 seconds

75℃ for 60 seconds

Figure 2   One PCR Cycle

the double helix. This is done simply by heating the vial to 90-95 degrees Centigrade for 30 seconds. But the primers cannot bind to the DNA strands at such a high temperature, so the vial is cooled to 55 degrees C. At this temperature, the primers bind or "anneal" to the ends of the DNA strands. This takes about 20 seconds. The final step of the reaction is to make a complete copy of the templates. Since the DNA polymerase works best at around 75 degrees C, the temperature of the vial is raised.

The DNA polymerase begins adding nucleotides to the primer and eventually makes a complementary copy of the template. If the template contains an A nucleotide, the enzyme adds on a T nucleotide to the primer. If the template contains a G, it adds a C to the new chain, and so on to the end of the DNA strand. This completes one PCR cycle.

The three steps in the polymerase chain reaction—the separation of the strands, binding the primer to the template, and the synthesis of new strands—take less than two minutes. Each is carried out in the same vial. At the end of a cycle, each piece of DNA in the vial has been duplicated. But the cycle can be repeated 30 or more times (see Figure 3). Each newly synthesized DNA piece can act as a new template, so after 30 cycles, 1 million copies of a single piece of DNA can be produced!Taking into account the time it takes to change the temperature of the reaction vial, 1 million copies can be ready in about three hours.

PCR is valuable to researchers because it allows them to multiply unique regions of DNA so that they can be detected in large genomes. The new uses for PCR are literally transforming the way we do biological research, diagnostics and drug discovery.

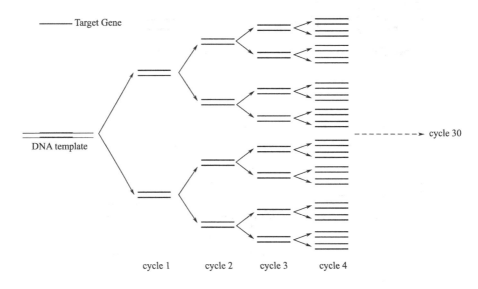

Figure 3   Polymerase Chain Reaction

Glossary

1. polymerase	*n.* 聚合酶	
2. arguably	*adv.* 可论证地	
3. exponentially	*adv.* 以指数方式	
4. segment	*n.* 片段	
5. organism	*n.* 生物，有机物	
6. mimic	*v.* 模仿	
7. chromosome	*n.* 染色体	
8. unzip	*v.* 拉开拉链	
9. helix	*n.* 螺旋结构	
10. strand	*n.* (线、绳、发的)股；链	
11. template	*n.* 模板	
12. nucleotide	*n.* 核苷酸	
13. represent	*v.* 代表，象征，表示	
14. adenine	*n.* 腺嘌呤	
15. thymine	*n.* 胸腺嘧啶	
16. cytosine	*n.* 胞嘧啶	
17. guanine	*n.* 鸟嘌呤	
18. complementary	*adj.* 互补的	
19. primer	*n.* 引物	
20. prime	*v.* 启动	

21. primase	*n.* 引发酶
22. stretch	*n.* 一段
23. vial	*n.* 小(玻璃)瓶
24. duplication	*n.* 复制
25. bind	*v.* (使)结合，黏结
26. anneal	*v.* 退火
27. duplicate	*v.* 复制
28. synthesize	*v.* 使合成，人工合成
29. multiply	*v.* 增加
30. unique	*adj.* 特有的, 少见的
31. genome	*n.* 基因组
32. literally	*adv.* 确实地, 真正地
33. transform	*v.* 改变，使改观
34. diagnostics	*n.* 诊断学

Exercises

1. *Matching*

① prime	（a）to act as or be the authorized delegate or agent for
② segment	（b）a model or standard for making comparisons
③ template	（c）to alter or be altered radically in form, function, etc
④ duplicate	（d）a part of a line or curve between two points
⑤ transform	（e）to prepare (something); make ready
⑥ represent	（f）to make in a pair; make double

2. *Fill in the blanks with the words or expressions given below, and change the form where necessary.*

stretch	unique	organism
bind	complementary	synthesize

① These two aims are not always _____ : at times they conflict.

② It was an infectious _____ that he studied.

③ I see nothing but a small _____ of road immediately ahead.

④ Stones and cement _____ strongly.

⑤ There are many amino acids that the body cannot _____ itself.

⑥ The tranquil beauty of the village scenery is _____.

Translation

聚合酶链反应

聚合酶链反应（PCR）可谓是如今最为重要的生物技术革新，很快就成为分子生物学研究中的核心技术。自从 20 世纪 80 年代中期由获得诺贝尔奖的穆利斯及西斯特公司的其他科学家们提出以来，PCR 技术已经被不断地创新，其发展速度正在以指数形式增长。

聚合酶链反应依赖于 DNA 复制酶类在高温条件下仍然稳定的能力。DNA 聚合酶即 Taq 酶，分离自一种水生嗜热 Taq 菌，正是它帮助科学家在短短几小时内将一个独立的 DNA 片段复制出数百万的拷贝。实际上，大多数生物都是以这种方式复制它们自身的 DNA。PCR 仅仅在一支试管中就可以模仿完成这一过程。任何细胞分裂的时候，聚合酶都会对每条染色体上所有的 DNA 进行一次复制。这一过程的起始步骤是"拉开" DNA 双螺旋结构的两条链（解链）。当两条链分开后，DNA 聚合酶就以每一条链为模板进行一次复制。

用于构成 DNA 链的四种核苷酸碱基分别用字母 A、T、C、G 表示，它们依次代表的化学名称为腺嘌呤、胸腺嘧啶、胞嘧啶和鸟嘌呤。一条链上的 A 总是和另一条链上的 T 配对，而 C 总是和 G 配对，两条链彼此互补。

要想复制 DNA，聚合酶需要另外两种成分，即足量的四种核苷酸碱基和引物。如果没有一小段核苷酸序列"启动"复制程序的话，那么无论是人体、细菌还是病毒的 DNA 聚合酶都无法对 DNA 链进行复制。因此细胞中还有另外一种酶叫做引发酶，它可以指导合成复制最初所需的那一小段核苷酸序列。这一小段核苷酸序列构成的 DNA 就叫做引物。一旦有了引物，聚合酶就可以继续完成新链余下核苷酸序列的复制工作。

一支 PCR 管中包含着所有 DNA 复制所需的成分：一段目的 DNA，大量的四种核苷酸碱基和引物，以及 DNA 聚合酶（见图 1）。

| DNA 模板 | 四种核苷酸 | 引物 | DNA 聚合酶 |

图 1　DNA 复制的所有必需组分

聚合酶链反应的三个步骤均在同一支 PCR 管中完成，但是反应温度各不相同（见图 2）。整个反应过程的第一步是将 DNA 双螺旋结构的两条链分开。该步操作只需将 PCR 管加热到 90～95℃，反应 30 秒即可。但是引物在这么高的温度下无法与 DNA 链结合，所以进行第二步时要将 PCR 管缓慢冷却至 55℃。在这一温度下，引物结合或者说"退火"到 DNA 两链的末端。这一反应过程大概需要 20 秒。整个反应的最后一步是对模板进行复制。由于 DNA 聚合酶的最适作用温度是 75℃，所以需要对 PCR 管进行升温。

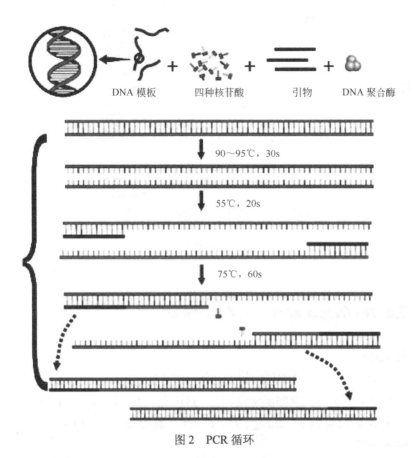

DNA 模板　　　四种核苷酸　　　引物　　　DNA 聚合酶

90~95℃，30s

55℃，20s

75℃，60s

图 2　PCR 循环

DNA 聚合酶将核苷酸加到引物上，最终完成对模板的整体复制。如果模板上有一个腺苷酸，DNA 聚合酶就会往引物上加一个胸腺苷酸，如果模板上有一个鸟苷酸，它就会往新复制链上加一个胞苷酸，如此反应直至 DNA 链的末端。这样就完成了一个 PCR 循环。

聚合酶链反应中的三个步骤，即解链、引物结合模板和合成新链，不到 2 分钟就可以全部完成，每个步骤都在同一个 PCR 管中进行。一个循环下来，每条 DNA 链都完成了复制。这样的循环可以重复 30 次，甚至更多（见图 3）。每一段新近合成的 DNA 链都可以作为一个新的模板，所以 30 个循环下来，原本的一段 DNA 可以得到数百万的拷贝。加上反应管温度改变的时间，完成 100 万个拷贝大概仅需要 3 小时。

PCR 技术对于研究人员而言意义重大，正是利用它，他们才可以对特定区域的 DNA 片段进行扩增，从而使这些特有的区域能够从巨大的基因组群中被查明和发现。PCR 的新用途正在真真切切地改变着我们进行生物研究、诊断和药物研发的方法。

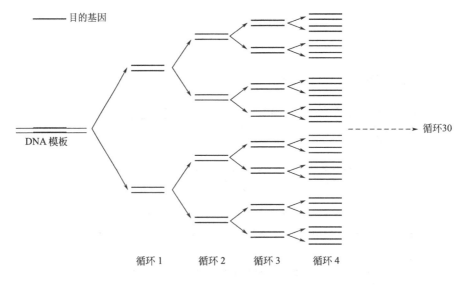

图 3 聚合酶链反应

练习参考答案 *(Reference answers of exercises)*

1. 配对（*Matching*）

①—(e)；②—(d)；③—(b)；④—(f)；⑤—(c)；⑥—(a)

2. 用词或短语填定，根据需要变换形式 *(Fill in the blanks with the words or expressions given below, and change the form where necessary).*

① complementary   ② organism   ③ stretch

④ binds   ⑤ synthesize   ⑥ unique

Unit 3 Transforming Plants

Reading Material

Cloning of Plant Cells and Manipulation of Plant Genes

Plant cells exhibit a variety of characteristics that distinguish them from animals cells. These characteristics include the presence of a large central vacuole and a cell wall, and the absence of centrioles, which play a role in mitosis, meiosis, and cell division. Along with these physical differences, another factor distinguishes plant cells from animal cells, which is of great significance to the scientist interested in biotechnology: Many varieties of full-grown adult plants can regenerate from single, modified plant cells called protoplasts—plant cells whose cell walls have been removed by enzymatic digestion. More specifically, when some species of plant cells are subjected to the removal of the cell wall by enzymatic treatment, they respond by synthesizing a new cell wall and eventually undergoing a series of cell divisions and developmental processes that result in the formation of a new adult plant. That adult plant can be said to have been cloned from a single cell of a parent plant.

Plants that can be cloned with relative ease include carrots, tomatoes, potatoes, petunias, and cabbage, to name only a few (see Figure 1). The capability to grow a whole plant from a single cell means that researchers can engage in the genetic manipulation of the cell, let the cell develop into a completely mature plant, and examine the whole spectrum of physical and growth effects of the genetic manipulation within a relatively short period of time. Such a process is far more straightforward than the parallel process in animal cells, which cannot be cloned into full-grown adults. Therefore, the results of any genetic manipulation are usually easier to examine in plants than in animals.

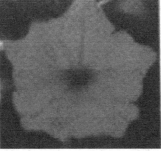

Figure 1 Transforming petunias

A Cloning Vector that Works with Plant Cells

Not all aspects of the genetic manipulation of plant cells are readily accomplished. Not only do plants usually have a great deal of chromosomal material and grow relatively slowly as compared with single cells grown in the laboratory, but few cloning vectors can successfully function in plant cells. While researchers working with animal cells can choose among a wide variety of cloning vectors to find just the right one, plant cell researchers are currently limited to just a few basic types of vectors.

Perhaps the most commonly used plant cloning vector is the "Ti" plasmid, or tumor-inducing plasmid.This plasmid is found in cells of the bacterium known as Agrobacterium tumefaciens, which normally lives in soil (see Figure 2). The bacterium has the ability to infect plants and cause a crown gall, or tumorous lump, to form at the site of infection. The tumor-inducing capacity of this bacterium results from the presence of the Ti plasmid. The Ti plasmid itself, a large, circular, double-stranded DNA molecule, can replicate independently of the A. tumefaciens genome.When these bacteria infect a plant cell, a 30000 base-pair segment of the Ti plasmid—called T DNA— separates from the plasmid and incorporates into the host cell genome. This aspect of Ti plasmid function has made it useful as a plant cloning vector.

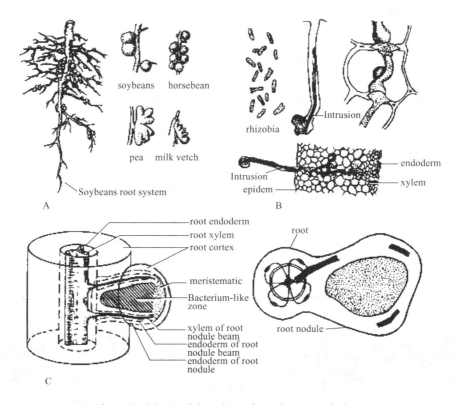

Figure 2   Root Nodule and Agrobacterium Tumefaciens

The Ti plasmid can be used to shuttle exogenous genes into host plant cells. This type of gene transfer requires two steps: 1)the endogenous, tumor-causing genes of the T DNA must be inactivated and; 2)foreign genes must be inserted into the same region of the Ti plasmid. The resulting recombinant plasmid, carrying up to approximately 40,000 base pairs of inserted DNA and including the appropriate plant regulatory sequences, can then be placed back into the A.tumefaciens cell. That cell can be introduced into plant cell protoplasts either by the process of infection or by direct insertion.

Once in the protoplast, the foreign DNA, consisting of both T DNA and inserted gene, incorporates into the host plant genome. The engineered protoplast—containing the recombinant T DNA—regenerates into a whole plant, each cell of which contains the inserted gene. Once a plant incorporates the T DNA with its inserted gene, it passes it on to future generations of the plant with a normal pattern of Mendelian inheritance.

One of the earliest experiments that involved the transport of a foreign gene by the Ti plasmid involved the insertion of a gene isolated from a bean plant into a host tobacco plant. Although this experiment served no commercially useful purpose, it successfully established the ability of the Ti plasmid to carry genes into plant host cells, where they could be incorporated and expressed.

A. tumefaciens Infects a Limited Variety of Plant Types

The fact that only certain types of plants were naturally susceptible to infection with the host bacterial organism initially limited the usefulness of the Ti plasmid as a cloning vector. In nature, *A. tumefaciens* infects only dicotyledons or "dicots" — plants with two embryonic leaves. Dicotyledenous plants, divided into approximately 170,000 different species, include such plants as roses, apples, soybeans, potatoes, pears, and tobacco. Unfortunately, many important crop plants, including corn, rice, and wheat, are monocotyledons—plants with only one embryonic leaf—and thus could not be easily transfected using this bacterium.

Overcoming the Limited Range of *A. tumefaciens* Infection.

Research efforts in the past few years have reduced the limitations of *A.tumefaciens*. Scientists discovered that by using the processes of microinjection, electroporation, and particle bombardment (see Figure 3), naked DNA molecules can be introduced into plant cell types that are not susceptible

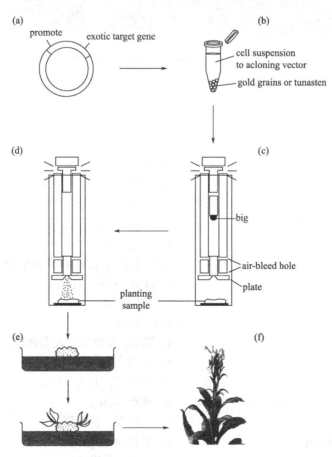

Figure 3   Particle Bombardment

to *A.tumefaciens* transfection.Microinjection involves the direct injection of material into a host cell using a finely drawn micropipette needle. Electroporation uses brief pulses of high voltage electricity to induce the formation of transient pores in the membrane of the host cell. Such pores appear to act as passageways through which the naked DNA can enter the host cell. Particle bombardment actually shoots DNA-coated microscopic pellets through a plant cell wall. These developments, important in the commercial application of plant genetic engineering, render the valuable food crops of corn, rice, and wheat susceptible to a variety of manipulations by the techniques of recombinant DNA and biotechnology (see Figure 4).

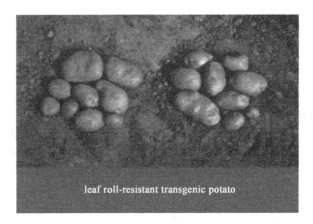 

Figure 4   The pictures about several transgenic plants

Glossary

1. vacuole	*n.* 液泡
2. centriole	*n.* 细胞中心粒,中心体
3. mitosis	*n.* 有丝分裂
4. meiosis	*n.* 减数分裂,成熟分裂
5. cell division	*n.* 细胞分裂
6. full-grown	*adj.* 生长完全的,发育完全的
7. regenerate	*vt. & vi.* 新生; 再生
8. protoplast	*n.* 原生质体
9. enzymatic	*adj.* 酶的
10. synthesize	*v.* 综合, 使合成; 人工合成
11. carrot	*n.* 胡萝卜
12. potato	*n.* 马铃薯, 土豆
13. petunia	*n.* 矮牵牛(花)
14. cabbage	*n.* 洋白菜, 卷心菜
15. genetic manipulation	*n.* 遗传[基因]操纵
16. spectrum	*n.* 范围, 系列

17. straightforward	*adj.* 简单的; 易懂的
18. parallel	*adj.* 类似的; 相对应的
19. cloning vector	*n.* 克隆载体
20. accomplished	*adj.* 已完成的, 熟练的, 有成就的
21. chromosomal	*adj.* 染色体的
22. plasmid	*n.* 质粒,质体
23. tumor-inducing plasmid ="Ti" plasmid	根瘤诱导质粒
24. *Agrobacterium tumefaciens*	根瘤土壤杆菌，根瘤农杆菌
25. crown gall	冠瘿
26. tumorous lump	肿块
27. double-stranded DNA molecule	双链 DNA 分子
28. replicate	*vi.* 复制
29. *A. tumefaciens* genome	根瘤农杆菌基因组
30. base-pair	碱基对
31. exogenous	*adj.* 外源的
32. endogenous	*adj.* 内生的
33. T DNA	转化 DNA（指 T 质粒上能够转移至植物基因组的 DNA）
34. inactivated	*v.* 使不活泼，阻止活动
35. recombinant	*n.* 重组[复合]器官;重组细胞;重组体[子]
36. Mendelian inheritance	孟德尔遗传
37. dicotyledon	*n.* 双子叶植物
38. dicotyledenous	*adj.* 双子叶植物的
39. soybeans	*n.* 大豆, 黄豆
40. monocotyledon	*n.* 单子叶植物
41. transfect	*v.* 使转染，使(细胞)感染病毒核酸
42. microinjection	*n.* (在显微镜下进行的)显微注射
43. electroporation	*n.* 电穿孔(法)
44. particle bombardment	基因枪轰击
45. micropipette	*n.* ①微量吸管；②(在显微镜下进行注射时用的)小型微量吸管

Exercises

1. *Matching*

① vacuole   （a）a small circle of bacterial DNA that is independent of the main bacterial chromosome

② centriole   （b）a unit consisting of the living parts of a cell, including the protoplasm and cell membrane but not the vacuoles or (in plants) the cell wall

③ protoplast （c）either of two rodlike bodies in most animal cells that form the poles of the spindle during mitosis

④ monocotyledon （d）any flowering plant of the class *Dicotyledonae*, normally having two embryonic seed leaves and leaves with netlike veins. The group includes many herbaceous plants and most families of trees and shrubs

⑤ dicotyledon （e）any flowering plant of the class *Monocotyledonae,* having a single embryonic seed leaf, leaves with parallel veins, and flowers with parts in threes: includes grasses, lilies, palms, and orchids

⑥ plasmid （f）a fluid-filled cavity in the cytoplasm of a cell

2. *Fill in the blanks with the words or expressions given below, and change the form where necessary.*

regenerate	exogenous	transfect
vector	replicate	recombinant

① Many varieties of full-grown adult plants can _____ from single, modified plant cells called protoplasts—plant cells whose cell walls have been removed by enzymatic digestion.

② The Ti plasmid can be used to shuttle _____ genes into host plant cells.

③ The resulting _____ plasmid, carrying up to approximately 40,000 base pairs of inserted DNA and including the appropriate plant regulatory sequences, can then be placed back into the *A.tumefaciens* cell.

④ Unfortunately,many important crop plants, including corn, rice, and wheat, are monocotyledons—plants with only one embryonic leaf—and thus could not be easily _____ using this bacterium.

⑤ Perhaps the most commonly used plant cloning _____ is the "Ti" plasmid,or tumor-inducing plasmid.

⑥ If the virus cannot _____, it cannot cause illness.

Translation

转基因植物

植物细胞克隆与基因操作

植物细胞具有不同于动物细胞的种种特性。其中包括植物细胞有中央液泡和细胞壁，没有在有丝分裂、减数分裂以及细胞分裂中发挥作用的中心体（中心粒）。除了这些物理属性的不同，还有另一个区分植物细胞与动物细胞的因素，这对于对生物技术有兴趣的科学家来说有着重要意义：各种发育成熟的植物可以由被称为原生质体的单细胞再生出——原生质体是细胞壁在酶的消化作用下去除后的植物细胞。确切地说，一些植物的细胞经过酶的处理除去细胞壁后，会合成新的细胞壁，最后经过一系列的细胞分裂及发育过程生成一株新植株。发育成熟的植物可以说是从母体植株的单细胞克隆出来的。

比较容易被克隆的植物包括胡萝卜、西红柿、马铃薯、牵牛花，这里只列举了几个例子

（见图1）。把单一细胞培育成完整植物体指的是研究人员可以在相对较短的时间内将经过基因操作的细胞发育成完整成熟的植株，同时研究基因操作对植物外观及生长幅度的影响。这样的过程与动物细胞的类似过程相比要简单得多。动物细胞无法克隆发育成成熟个体。因此，检验植物基因操作的结果比检验动物基因控制的结果容易些。

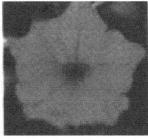

图1　转基因牵牛花

对植物细胞起作用的克隆载体

植物细胞的遗传操作，并非在所有方面都能得以轻易实现。不仅因为植物通常有大量的染色体物质，与在实验室生长的单细胞相比生长得相对缓慢，而且能在植物细胞中成功起作用的克隆载体很少。从事动物细胞研究的人员可以从多种克隆载体中进行选择，找出它们需要的克隆载体，但是植物细胞的研究人员目前仅限于几个基本类型的载体。

也许最常用的植物克隆载体是"Ti"质体，或者说是致瘤质粒。这种质粒是在人们熟知的根瘤土壤农杆菌中发现的，该菌通常存活在土壤中（见图2）。这种菌能侵染植物，产生冠

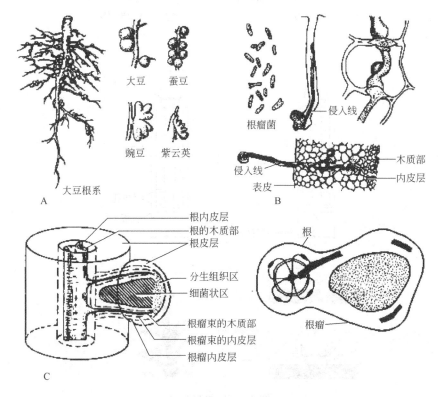

图2　根瘤和根瘤土壤杆菌

状瘤，或叫肿块，形成感染处。这种菌的致瘤性能产生 Ti 质粒。Ti 质粒本身是一种环形的、双链 DNA 分子，能够自主复制根瘤土壤农杆菌基因组。当这些细菌侵染植物细胞时，一个 30000 碱基对的 Ti 质粒片段——叫做 T DNA——从质粒中分离出来，并整合到寄主（宿主）细胞基因组中。Ti 质粒这方面的特性使其能够成为植物的克隆载体。

Ti 质粒可用来将外源基因引入寄主（宿主）细胞中。这种类型的基因转移需要两步：①T DNA 的内源致瘤基因必须失去活性；②外源基因必须插入到 Ti 质粒的相同区域。形成的重组质粒，带有高达近 40000 碱基对插入的 DNA 及相应的植物调控序列，然后重新转入根瘤土壤农杆菌细胞中。通过侵染或直接注入，菌体细胞被转入植物细胞原生质体中。

由 T DNA 和插入基因组成的外源 DNA 一进入原生质体中，便整合到寄主（宿主）植物基因组中。含有重组 T DNA 的基因改造原生质体可重新发育成完整的植株，新生植株的每一个细胞都含有插入基因。一旦植株将 T DNA 与插入的基因整合到一起，它就会以孟德尔遗传方式遗传给下一代。

利用 Ti 质粒载入外源基因的一项早期实验，是将从豆科植物中分离出的基因插入到寄主（宿主）烟草植株中。虽然这项实验没有满足商业用途的需要，但是它成功地证实了 Ti 质粒能将基因携带进植物寄主（宿主）细胞中，在寄主细胞中，基因进行整合并表达出相关性状。

根瘤土壤杆菌对有限的几种植物类型的侵染

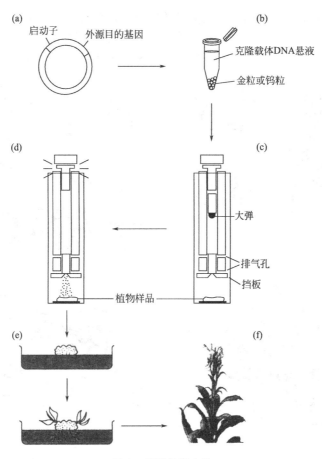

图 3　基因枪轰击法

只有某些类型的植物天生受寄主细菌生物的侵染，这一事实最初限制了 Ti 质粒作为克隆载体的应用。实际上，根瘤土壤农杆菌只侵染双子叶植物，即带有两个胚叶的植物。双子叶植物，可分为近 17 万个不同种属，包括玫瑰、苹果、大豆、马铃薯、梨和烟草等。不巧的是，许多重要的农作物，包括玉米、水稻和小麦都是单子叶植物，即只有一个胚叶，因而不能被该菌轻易地侵染。

克服根瘤土壤农杆菌的局限性

近几年的研究成果已减少了根瘤土壤农杆菌的局限性。科学家发现，通过显微注射，电穿孔及基因枪轰击（见图 3），裸露的 DNA 分子可以被转入不受根瘤土壤农杆菌转染的植物细胞中，显微注射时用极细的小型微量吸管针头将 DNA 分子直接注射进寄主细胞中。电穿孔是用高压电流的短暂脉冲，在寄主细胞膜上瞬间形成微孔，这些微孔充当通道，通过微孔通道，裸露的 DNA 进入到寄主细胞中。基因枪轰击是将带有外源 DNA 的微小颗粒直接射入植物的细胞壁。这些成果对植物基因工程的生产应用十分重要，可使玉米、水稻和小麦等重要的粮食作物，通过重组 DNA 和生物技术，进行各种基因操作（见图 4）。

抗卷叶病毒转基因马铃薯

图 4 几种转基因植物图

练习参考答案 *(Reference answers of exercises)*

1. 配对 *(Matching)*

①—(f)；②—(c)；③—(b)；④—(e)；⑤—(d)；⑥—(a)

2. 用词或短语填空，根据需要变换形式 *(Fill in the blanks with the words or expressions given below, and change the form where necessary）*

① regenerate　　② exogenous　　③ recombinant
④ transfected　　⑤ vector　　　　⑥ replicate

Unit 4 Transgenic Animals

Reading Material

Figure 1　Cloned Sheep Dolly

Manipulating mammalian genes(Figure 1) has broad potential in livestock breeding. The ability to implant new genes in animals will provide a faster way of accomplishing what traditional breeding programs can—namely, creating animals with better-quality meat and improved resistance to diseases.

On a ranch near Houston, Texas, four calves are frolicking(Figure 2). They are unusual because each contains genes from other species, intended to make the animals grow faster and leaner. The genes were inserted into embryos by a team headed by Bert W.O'Maney, a cell biologist at the Baylor College of Medicine.

Look at this giant pig in Germany! It is so tall that the woman farmer standing behind it is nearly blocked. It strains its four legs to support its heavy body when it hobbles hard around in a courtyard—it suffers unbearable pain at every pace. The pig is a product of genetic engineering. Growth hormone taken from a human being has been inserted into its genes. As a result, it has grown twice as big as an ordinary pig, and it will provide twice amount of meat. But unfortunately, the pig suffers from a spectrum of diseases: stomach tumor, pneumonia, heart failure and joint deformity. But the people who created it care little about its sufferings, because more rib, leaner meat for making ham and sausage satisfy consumers—the prime purpose of their efforts.

Figure 2　Transgenic Cattle

To breed more, finer and cheaper animals to meet the needs of insatiable consumers, scientists in more than 3,000 laboratories throughout the world are busy manipulating nuclei of cells taken from animals and crops, inducng mutations in their natural hereditary codes, splicing genes to make artificial hereditary codes representing new species.

At present,many biotechnology companies are adding human genes to laboratory animals to produce "models" of human diseases. Transgenic goats(Figure 3), rabbits and mice are all serving as living drug factories, producing pharmaceutical proteins in their milk, which can be used to produce drugs such as hormone and interferon. Most efforts so far have focused on directing genes to mammary tissue so that the desired substances are secreted in the animals' milk.

The most immediate impact of transgenic animals has been on models for medical research. Instead of finding naturally occurring animal counterparts of human disease or inducing such conditions with surgery or drugs, transgenics researchers can breed animal models with the very genes that cause an illness. Mice have been turned into subjects for studying many cancers as well as viruses such as hepatitis. Mouse models have also been developed for gene-defect disorders such as Duchenne's muscular dystrophy and multiple sclerosis.

The U.S. government is also involved in an effort to use transgenic mice in carcinogenicity testing. The National Institute of Environmental Health Sciences in Research Triangle Park, New Jersey, is testing mice

Figure 3   Transgenic Goats

carrying genes known to be associated with cancers to see if they are more sensitive to carcinogens than their unaltered brethren.

Most of the near-term applications will be slightly better models of diseases in which a single gene is responsible.

Glossary

1. transgenic	*adj.* 转基因的，基因被改变的
2. implant	*v.* 移植，培植，种植
3. frolick	*v.* 嬉戏，玩耍
4. strain	*v.* 强迫，强制，滥用
5. hobble	*v.* 跛行
6. deformity	*n.* 畸形
7. rib	*n.* 排骨
8. sausage	*n.* 香肠
9. insatiable	*adj.* 贪得无厌的，不知足的
10. mutation	*n.* 突变，变异
11. hereditary	*adj.* 遗传(性)的
12. splice	*v.* 拼接
13. artificial	*adj.* 人造的，人工的
14. pharmaceutical	*adj.* 药物的，药用的
15. hormone	*n.* 荷尔蒙，激素
16. interferon	*n.* 干扰素
17. mammary	*adj.* 乳房的，乳腺的
18. secrete	*v.* 分泌
19. counterpart	*n.* 相对物，极相似的物（人）
20. induce	*v.* 引发，诱发
21. subject	*n.* 受实验者，实验材料
22. virus	*n.* 病毒
23. hepatitis	*n.* 肝炎

24. dystrophy	*n.* 营养障碍，营养不良
25. sclerosis	*n.* 硬化症
26. carcinogenicity	*n.* 致癌性
27. carcinogen	*n.* 致癌物质
28. brethren	*n.* 同胞，弟兄们

Exercises

1. *Matching*

① implant	（a）	not able to be satisfied or satiated; greedy or unappeasable
② artificial	（b）	plant, insert or fix (in)
③ deformity	（c）	any substance that produces cancer
④ insatiable	（d）	produced by man; not occurring naturally
⑤ counterpart	（e）	disfigurement
⑥ carcinogen	（f）	a person or thing identical to or closely resembling another

2. *Fill in the blanks with the words or expressions given below, and change the form where necessary.*

mutation	hobble	brethren
subject	virus	transgenic

① The topic of this text is _____ animals.

② The old man _____ along with the help of his son.

③ Many factors of physics and chemistry will induce _____ in animals.

④ The H1N1 swine flu is a disease caused by a _____ .

⑤ Mice have been turned into _____ for studying many cancers.

⑥ My _____, please help me in the critical time!

Translation

转基因动物

　　哺乳动物的转基因技术（见图1）在家畜饲养领域具有广阔的应用潜力。这项技术将会为获得传统育种工艺所期望的更具优质肉类和高抗病力的动物产品提供一条更为快捷的途径。

　　位于得克萨斯州休斯敦附近的一个大牧场中，四头小牛正在顽皮地嬉戏着（见图2）。它们之所以不寻常是因为它们的体内包含了可以使它们长得更快更精瘦的其它物种的基因。这些基因是由医药大学细胞生物学家 Bert W. O'Maney 所领导的工作组插入到小牛初期胚胎中的。

　　再来看看德国培育出的这只巨型猪吧！它是那么高大，以至于站在它后面的女农场主差点儿被挡住了。当它在庭院周围艰难地行走时，其四肢被迫支撑着它那沉重的身躯——每走

图 1　克隆羊多利　　　　　图 2　转基因牛　　　　　图 3　转基因羊

一步它都要承受难以想象的痛楚。这只巨型猪是一个基因工程的产物，一段来自人类的生长激素基因被插入了它的基因组中，结果，它长得有普通猪两倍那么大，并且可提供两倍于普通猪的肉量。然而，非常不幸的是，这只猪患上了一连串的疾病：胃癌，肺炎，心衰以及关节畸形。尽管这样，创造它的人们却并不为此担忧，因为从它的身上得到的排骨和瘦肉比一只普通猪更多，可以制作更多的火腿和香肠来满足消费者的需求——这才是他们的首要目的。

为了饲养出更多、更精瘦、更便宜的动物来满足消费者日益增长的需求，全世界有 3000 多个实验室的科学家们正忙于处理来自动植物体的细胞核，诱发核内自然遗传密码发生变异，进而拼接(重组)基因以再造出具有人工遗传密码的新物种。

目前，许多生物技术公司都在试图将人类基因构建到实验动物基因上以建立起人类疾病模型。转基因山羊（见图 3）、兔和小鼠也都担当起了活性药物工厂的角色，在其乳汁中可以提取出诸如激素和干扰素之类的药用蛋白。迄今为止，绝大多数研究成果都集中于对动物乳腺组织进行基因操作，这样可以使想得到的物质直接分泌到其乳汁中。

转基因动物最为直接的应用就是用于构建医学研究模型。转基因学的研究人员不再寻找动物中自然形成的与人类疾病类似的病，或用手术和药物来诱发这类疾病，而是利用某种疾病的基因来培养动物模型。小鼠已经成为研究许多肿瘤和肝炎一类病毒的实验材料。小鼠模型已经应用于诸如杜氏肌营养不良和多发性硬化症等基因缺陷疾病的研究中。

美国政府也已经介入到使用转基因小鼠来进行致癌性实验的研究中。地处新泽西州研究三角园区的全国环境健康科学研究院正在对携带有已知肿瘤基因的小鼠进行试验，观察其与未携带已知肿瘤基因的同类相比是否能够对致癌物质更为敏感。

近期的研究申请中大多数都较倾向于构建更好的单致病基因动物模型。

练习参考答案 *(Reference answers of exercises)*

1. *配对 (Matching)*
①—(b)；②—(d)；③—(e)；④—(a)；⑤—(f)；⑥—(c)

2. *用词或短语填空，根据需要变换形式(Fill in the blanks with the words or expressions given below, and change the form where necessary).*

① transgenic	② hobbled	③ mutations
④ virus	⑤ subjects	⑥ brethren

Unit 5　DNA Fingerprinting

Reading Material

Recently recombinant DNA techniques have been used in new ways—to identify criminals and to determine paternity. For decades, fingerprints, blood samples, hair, seminal fluids, etc. have been analyzed and used to place criminals at the scene of the crime. Unfortunately, the best these tests could do was to exonerate a falsely accused person or suggest a suspects' guilt. Because every person's DNA is unique, evidence from DNA analysis is different—this information can positively identify a suspect, or completely exonerate them. Although the amount of DNA in a person's cells is enormous, and about 99.9% of everyone's DNA is identical, there are certain regions that vary a great deal from person to person, and it is these 'hypervariable' areas that can be used to distinguish the DNA of one person from that of another. The most variable region are certain sequences of two to 300 base pairs that are repeated over and over a variable number of times. For instance, the sequence CAT may appear in one allele once, but another allele might have three repeats (CATCATCAT), another might have six repeats, etc. Population studies are done to determine the frequency of these variable regions in a specific Population. Using these information geneticists can calculate the probability of DNA samples from two different individual matching by chance; estimates often vary from 1:500,000 to 1:738 trillion. The procedure was first developed by British geneticist Alec Jefferys of the University of Leicester.

Evidence from DNA analysis was first used in the United Stated in a court in Orlando, Florida, in 1987. The defendant was suspected of 23 incidents of prowling, assault, and rape. Because the rapist was very careful not to let his victims see his face, and wore gloves, these were little physical evidence for conviction. The prosecutors had heard of the process of 'DNA fingerprinting', which was used to solve a rape-murder case in Britain, and decided to try the procedure in the Orlando cases.

Since every person's DNA is unique, analysis of DNA from biological sources found at the crime scene can definitively identify or exonerate an individual. The procedures have been well worked. DNA is extracted from a sample of the suspect's blood and from a tissue sample obtained at the scene of the crime. If the sample is sufficiently large, the analysis can proceed directly, but if the sample is small, the DNA must be amplified using the new PCR technique. The amplified genetic information can then be analyzed. The DNA of a single sperm cell, for instance, can be amplified to provide enough material for analysis. Traces of seminal fluid, blood, or even a hair with cells attached left at crime scene are enough to identify an individual.

Once the sample is sufficiently large, the DNA in each sample is cut with the same restriction enzyme, producing DNA fragments of varying lengths. In the areas where the DNA is constant from individual to individual, the resulting fragments are identical, but in the 'hypervariable' regions the fragment lengths vary greatly, depending on the number of repeats. It is these varying fragment lengths that must be compared.

The process of gel electrophoresis is used to separate the DNA fragments on the basis of their charge and size: the DNA samples are placed at the ends of a sheet of a special gel, electrodes are placed at each end, and an electric current is applied across the gel. DNA, because of its many phosphate groups, is strongly negative and will migrate toward the positive electrode. The gel, which is a semisolid material with minute pores, acts as a molecular sieve. The distance the fragments move depends on the charge of the fragments and their sizes: smaller fragments are slowed down less by the gel, and therefore move farther. At the end of the procedure the DNA fragments are nicely separated by size. Because the investigators are only interested in fragments of the variable regions, they must use specific techniques to locate these regions: the DNA bands are treated in such a way that the two strands of DNA separate, leaving exposed nucleotide bases. The DNA pattern is then transferred to a nylon sheet and radioactive DNA probes are added, these probes are radioactive sequences of single-stranded DNA known to be complementary to sequences found in the variable regions of DNA.

The radioactive probes will bind tightly to the bands of DNA containing the complementary sequences. Because the DNA fragments for each individual will be of different sizes, and thus will migrate different distances, the probes will attach at different positions on the sheet. X-ray film is placed against the sheet, and the film is developed. Black bands show the location of probes. This pattern of bands constitutes a 'DNA print' and is unique for each individual. Because there are many different hypervariable regions in the human genome, a number of different probes are generally used and the information is used to produce a 'DNA profile' or 'DNA fingerprint' of the individual.

The band pattern obtained from a suspect's blood can then be compared with seminal fluid obtained from the victim, and if it matches, the suspect can be positively identified. In the Orlando case the jury accepted the DNA evidence, and the suspect was convicted. The 'print' can be made from almost any biological source-hair and skin cells, seminal fluid, blood—and because each individual has a unique pattern, the potential uses of these techniques in criminal investigations are enormous , promising to revolutionize the way such procedures are conducted. To date more than 2,000 U.S. court cases in 49 states have used DNA testing for forensic purpose. Already the Federal Bureau of Investigation is designing its first computer database of DNA fingerprints of convicted criminals. And California already has a law mandating that blood samples be obtained for DNA profiling from all men convicted of sex felonies. The information is computerized, and whenever a sex crime occurs, a DNA profile will be run on the evidence and checked to see if there is a match with a previous offender.

Despite the wide acceptance of DNA evidence, its use is still controversial. Questions of how well the samples match and the reliability of the procedures in different laboratories continue to be an issue. Technical standards have yet to be developed and implemented. Most investigators insist that 'blind-test methodology' must be implemented within the laboratory, so that neither the laboratory nor the examiner knows whether any given sample is actually a test. Congress is, at this writing, considering a DNA Proficiency Testing Act, which will address the issues of quality control.

Glossary

1. recombinant DNA   *n.* 重组基因

（recombinant deoxyribonucleic acid）

2. paternity	*n.* 父权；父系；父系后裔
3. seminal	*adj.* 种子的；精液的；生殖的
4. exonerate	*vt.* 使免罪,使免除
5. hypervariable	*n.* 超变量；高变的，变异度高的
6. CAT（catalase）	*n.* 氧化氢酶
7. allele	*n.* 等位基因
8. prowl	*vi.* 徘徊，潜行
	n. 徘徊，潜行；悄悄踱步
9. PCR（polymerase chain reaction）	*n.*聚合酶链反应
10. gel	*vi.* 胶化
	n. 凝胶，胶体
11. electrophoresis	*n.*〈物〉电泳
12. pores	*n.* 气孔；毛穴
13. sieve	*n.* 筛子；滤网
14. probe	*n.* 探针，探测器
15. genome	*n.*〈生〉基因组；〈生〉染色体组
16. forensic	*adj.* 辩论的；法院的；适于法庭的
17. mandate	*n.* 命令，指令
	vt. 托管；授权
18. felony（复数 felonies）	*n.*〈法〉重罪

Exercises

1. *Matching*

① fingerprinting （a）one of two alternate forms of a gene that can have the same locus on homologous chromosomes and are responsible for alternative traits; "some alleles are dominant over others"

② paternity （b） a long linear polymer found in the nucleus of a cell and formed from nucleotides and shaped like a double helix; associated with the transmission of genetic information

③ allele （c）the ordering of genes in a haploid set of chromosomes of a particular organism; the full DNA sequence of an organism; "the human genome contains approximately three billion chemical base pairs"

④ genome （d）a serious crime (such as murder or arson)

⑤ DNA （e）the procedure of taking inked impressions of a person's fingerprints for the purpose of identification

⑥ felony （f）the state of being a father; "tests were conducted to determine paternity"

2. *Fill in the blanks with the words or expressions given below.*

DNA analysis	DNA fragments	gel electrophoresis
PCR technique	recombinant	genome

① Recently _____ DNA techniques have been used in new ways — to identify criminals and to determine paternity

② Evidence from _____ was first used in the United Stated in a court in Orlando, Florida, in 1987.

③ Once the sample is sufficiently large, the DNA in each sample is cut with the same restriction enzyme, producing _____ of varying lengths.

④ The process of _____ is used to separate the DNA fragments on the basis of their charge and size.

⑤ If the sample is sufficiently large, the analysis can proceed directly, but if the sample is small, the DNA must be amplified using the new_____.

⑥ Because there are many different hypervariable regions in the human_____, a number of different probes are generally used the information is used to produce a 'DNA profile' or 'DNA fingerprint' of the individual.

Translation

DNA 指纹图谱

　　最近 DNA 重组技术有了新的用途，即用于识别罪犯、确定亲子关系。数十年来，指纹、血液样本、头发、精液等已经被用来分析确定犯罪现场的罪犯身份。这些检测的最佳用途在于免除被诬告人的罪行，暗示嫌疑犯的罪行。由于每个人的 DNA 排列都是不同的，来自 DNA 分析的证据也是不同的——此信息能指认一个嫌疑犯，或证明他们无罪。尽管一个人的细胞中 DNA 数量巨大，每个人的 DNA 序列有 99.9%是完全相同的，但某些特定区域人与人之间却大不相同，正是利用高变区来区别人与人之间的 DNA 差异。最可变区是重复多次的 2～300 碱基对的特定序列。如 CAT 序列可能在一个等位基因中出现一次，但是另外一个等位基因也许重复出现 3 次（CATCATCAT），再有一个等位基因重复出现 6 次，等等。人口研究就是在特定人群中确定这些可变区的出现频率。利用这些信息遗传学家能够计算出来自两个个体的 DNA 样本之间偶然匹配的可能性，概率估计在 1:($5 \times 10^5 \sim 738 \times 10^{12}$) 之间。这种方法是由英国莱斯特大学遗传专家 Alec Jefferys 最早提出的。

　　来自 DNA 分析的证据于 1987 年最先在美国佛罗里达州奥兰多市的法庭上使用。被告涉嫌跟踪、攻击、强奸等 23 起案件。由于强奸犯非常小心不让受害者看到他的脸，且戴着手套，几乎没有任何证据来定罪。检察官听说英国用 DNA 指纹分析来侦破强奸谋杀案，因此尝试在奥兰多案中使用该方法。

　　由于每个人的 DNA 序列都不同，对犯罪现场的生物来源的 DNA 分析能指认一个人的罪行或免罪。这个方法很奏效。DNA 取自犯罪嫌疑人的血液样本和犯罪现场的组织样本。如果样本足够大，分析可以直接进行，但如果样本很小，需借助聚合酶链反应（PCR）技术来放大样本。然后对放大的遗传信息进行分析。例如单个精子细胞的 DNA 就可以复制到足够的数量以便进行分析。遗留在犯罪现场的精液、血液的任何痕迹或带有黏附细胞的一根头发都足以辨认某人。

一旦样本足够大，每个样本的 DNA 序列就可以被相同的限制内切酶切割开，形成不同长度的 DNA 片段。在个体间 DNA 排列相同的区域，得到的酶切片段是一样的，但在高变区，酶切片段长度差异就很大，其取决于重复的次数。这些不同长度的酶切片段就需要进行比较。

凝胶电泳是根据电荷数及其大小对 DNA 片段进行分离。将 DNA 样本放在特定凝胶的边缘，电极置于两端，电流穿过凝胶。DNA 由于有许多磷酸基而带有大量负电荷，将移向正极。带有微小孔隙的半液体状凝胶则充当分子筛。片段移动的距离取决于片段的电荷量及片段的大小：较小片段受凝胶阻碍较小，因此移动较远。最终依据 DNA 片段大小可以使其得到很好的分离。因为研究者仅对可变区的片段感兴趣，他们必须利用具体技术定位这些片段：DNA 链被处理后，两条 DNA 链分离，暴露出核苷酸碱基。然后将 DNA 转移到一块尼龙膜上并添加放射性的探针，这些探针是有放射性的单链 DNA 序列，与定位的 DNA 可变区域中的序列互补。

放射性探针与包含互补序列的 DNA 链紧密结合。由于对每个个体来说 DNA 片段大小各异，因此移动距离各异，探针结合到尼龙膜上的不同位置，X 射线胶片紧贴尼龙膜，然后冲洗出胶片。黑带是探针位置，这种带图就构成了 DNA 指纹，而且每个个体都不同。因为人类基因组中有许多高变区，一般使用许多不同的探针，利用信息形成个体 DNA 基因图或 DNA 指纹。

取自嫌疑犯血液样本的带图要与取自受害者体中的精液进行对比，如果匹配，就可以指认嫌疑犯有罪。奥兰多案件的陪审团接受了 DNA 证据，因此嫌疑犯被定罪。任何生物来源（如头发、皮肤细胞、精液、血液）都可制成 DNA 指纹——因为每个人都有不同的图谱，这些技术在犯罪调查方面潜力巨大，将会革新传统的定罪方式。至今在美国已有 49 个州的 2000 个诉讼案中利用 DNA 检测技术达到刑侦目的。联邦调查局已经在设计第一个罪犯 DNA 指纹计算机数据库。加利福尼亚也制定了法律授权从所有性犯罪者体内收集血液样本绘制 DNA 指纹图谱，使信息计算机化，只要有性犯罪，指纹图谱就可作为证据看是否与以往罪犯 DNA 指纹图谱相匹配。

尽管 DNA 证据已得到广泛认可，但其使用仍有争议。在不同实验室样本的匹配程度及该方法的可靠性仍是热点问题。技术标准有待开发与完善。许多研究者坚持认为应在实验室中推广盲测技术，这样无论实验室还是检测者都不知道所给样本是否是真正的检测样本。目前议会正考虑 DNA 技术检测议案，将探讨质量监控问题。

练习参考答案 *(Reference answers of exercises)*

1. 配对 *(Matching)*
①—(e)；②—(f)；③—(a)；④—(c)；⑤—(b)；⑥—(d)

2. 用词或短语填空 *(Fill in the blanks with the words or expressions given below)*

① recombinant	② DNA analysis	③ DNA fragments
④ gel electrophoresis	⑤ PCR technique	⑥ genome

Chapter Six

Protein Engineering

Unit 1　Introduction of Protein engineering

Reading Material

Protein engineering is the process of developing useful or valuable proteins. It is a young discipline, with much research currently taking place into the understanding of protein folding and protein recognition for protein design principles.

There are two general strategies for protein engineering. The first is known as *rational design*, in which the scientist uses detailed knowledge of the structure and function of the protein to make desired changes. This has the advantage of being generally inexpensive and easy, since site-directed mutagenesis techniques are well-developed. However, there is a major drawback in that detailed structural knowledge of a protein is often unavailable, and even when it is available, it can be extremely difficult to predict the effects of various mutations.

Computational protein design algorithms seek to identify amino acid sequences that have low energies for target structures. While the sequence-conformation space that needs to be searched is large, the most challenging requirement for computational protein design is a fast, yet accurate, energy function that can distinguish optimal sequences from similar suboptimal ones. Using computational methods, a protein with a novel fold has been designed, as well as sensors for un-natural molecules.

The second strategy is known as directed evolution. This is where random mutagenesis is applied to a protein, and a selection regime is used to pick out variants that have the desired qualities. Further rounds of mutation and selection are then applied. This method mimics natural evolution and generally produces superior results to rational design. An additional technique known as DNA shuffling mixes and matches pieces of successful variants in order to produce better results. This process mimics recombination that occurs naturally during sexual reproduction. The great advantage of directed evolution techniques is that they require no prior structural knowledge of a protein, nor is it necessary to be able to predict what effect a given mutation will have. Indeed, the results of directed evolution experiments are often surprising in that desired changes are often caused by mutations that no one would have expected. The drawback is that they require high-throughput, which is not feasible for all proteins. Large amounts of recombinant DNA must be mutated and the products screened for desired qualities. The sheer number of variants often requires expensive robotic equipment to automate the process. Furthermore, not all desired activities can be easily screened for.

Rational design and directed evolution techniques are not mutually exclusive; good researchers will often apply both. In the future, more detailed knowledge of protein structure and function, as well as advancements in high-throughput technology, will greatly expand the capabilities of protein engineering. Eventually even unnatural amino acids may be incorporated thanks to a new method that allows the incorporation of novel amino acids in the genetic code.

Glossary

1. discipline	*n.* 1. 学科; 2. 纪律; 3. 处罚, 处分
2. rational	*adj.* 1. 神智清楚的; 2. 理性的, 理智的, 合理的, 出于理性的
3. site-directed	定点诱变
4. mutagenesis	*n.* 突变形成,变异发生
5. drawback	*n.* 缺点, 不利条件; 障碍
6. algorithms	算法式
7. distinguish	*vt. & vi.* 辨别, 区别, 区分, 分清
8. regime	*n.* 1. 政治制度, 政权, 政体; 2. 组织方法, 管理体制
9. DNA shuffling	DNA 重组技术
10. sexual reproduction	*n.* 有性生殖
11. prior	*adj.* 优先的; 在前的; 较早的
12. high-throughput	高流量
13. screened	遮蔽的,筛过的
14. genetic code	遗传密码

Exercises

1. *Matching*

① genetic code

② sexual reproduction

③ *rational design*

④ protein engineering

⑤ mutagenesis

（a）the process of developing useful or valuable proteins.

（b）a specific sequence of three adjacent bases on a strand of DNA or RNA that provides genetic information for a particular amino acid.

（c）an event capable of causing a mutation

（d）the scientist uses detailed knowledge of the structure and function of the protein to make desired changes.

（e）reproduction involving the union or fusion of a male and a female gamete

2. *Fill in the blanks with the words or expressions given below, and change the form where necessary.*

site directed	drawback	screened
distinguish	site-directed	

① Protein engineering and_____mutagenesis have been used to change the active site and alter the substrate specificity of various hydroxynitrile lyases.

② Complacency is a_____to progress.

③ Unsuitable candidates were _____out.

④ The ease with which a line of type or an individual character can be discriminated and recognized. _____from readability which refers to the ease with which a passage can be read and understood.

⑤ *In vitro* _____mutagenesis is an invaluable technique for studying protein structure-function relationships, gene expression and vector modification.

Translation

蛋白质工程简介

蛋白质工程是开发有用或有价值蛋白质的过程。这是一个新兴的学科，目前在蛋白质的折叠和蛋白质的识别方向开展了大量的研究，以便进行蛋白质的设计。

蛋白质工程有两种策略。第一种是理性的设计，是科学家运用蛋白质结构和功能的详细知识进行所需的改造。由于定点突变技术已得到很好的发展，这种设计方式具有价格便宜、操作简便的优势，然而，该方式有一个主要的缺点，那就是蛋白质的详细结构信息往往不清楚，即使搞清楚了，各种突变的影响也很难预料。

计算机蛋白质设计的算法正在寻求如何确定氨基酸序列，以使目标蛋白结构具有较低的能量。然而，对于序列和空间构象之间的关系需要进行大量的研究，计算机蛋白质设计更大的挑战在于如何准确、迅速地通过能量函数区分最佳序列。运用计算机辅助的方法，可以设计一种具有新的折叠方式的蛋白质，以及非天然分子的传感器。

第二种策略是定向进化。这种方式是对蛋白质进行随机突变，然后筛选出具有所需性能的蛋白质。不断地循环运用突变和筛选。该方法模拟自然进化过程，可以取得比理性设计更好的效果。DNA 重组技术将成功改造的各种突变体进行混合和匹配，便产生更好的效果。这个过程模仿天然有性繁殖中发生的重组过程。定向进化技术的巨大优势是，人们不需要事先知道蛋白质的结构知识，也不必预测给定的突变会产生什么影响。事实上，定向进化实验的结果往往出人意料，突变经常产生意想不到的所期望的变化。该方法的缺点是需要较高的通量，这并不是对所有蛋白质都可行。对大量的重组 DNA 进行突变，然后根据所需的性状进行筛选。为了筛选大量的突变体，往往需要昂贵的机器设备，以实现筛选过程的自动化。而且，并非所有需要的活性都可以很容易地筛选获得。

理性设计和定向进化技术并不是相互排斥的，优秀的研究人员往往会两种方法并用。未来随着对蛋白质结构和功能了解的深入，以及高通量技术的进步，将极大地扩展蛋白质工程的能力。甚至可以将非天然氨基酸与天然氨基酸一起运用到遗传密码中。

练习参考答案 (Reference answers of exercises)

1. 配对（Matching）

①—(b)；②—(e)；③—(d)；④—(a)；⑤—(c)

2. 用词或短语填空，根据需要变换形式（Fill in the blanks with the words or expressions given below, and change the form where necessary）

① site directed   ② drawback   ③ screened

④ distinguish   ⑤ site-directed

Unit 2 Proteins

Reading Material

Proteins are molecules of great size, complexity, and diversity. They are the source of dietary amino acids, both essential and nonessential, that are used for growth, maintenance, and the general well-being of man. These macromolecules, characterized by their nitrogen contents, are involved in many vital processes intricately associated with all living matter. Mammals and many internal organs are largely composed of proteins. Mineral matter of bone is held together by collagenous protein. Skin, the protective covering of the body, often accounts for about 10% of the total body protein.

Some protein function as biocatalysts (enzymes and hormones) to regulate chemical reactions within the body. Fundamental life process, such as growth, digestion and metabolism, excretion, conversion of chemical energy into mechanical work, etc, are controlled by enzymes and hormones. Blood plasma proteins and hemoglobin regulate the osmotic pressure and pH of certain body fluids. Proteins are necessary for immunology reactions. Antibodies, modified plasma globulin proteins, defend against the invasion of foreign substances of microorganisms that can cause various diseases; food allergies result when certain ingested proteins cause an apparent modification in the defense mechanism. This leads to a variety of painful, and occasionally drastic, conditions in certain individuals.

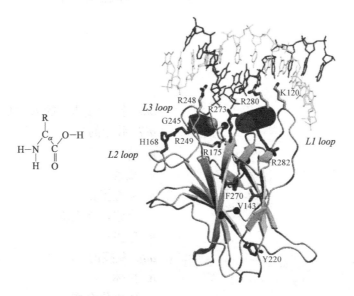

Food shortages exist in many areas of the world, and they are likely to become more acute and widespread as the world's population increases. Providing adequate supplies of protein poses a much greater problem than providing adequate supplies of either carbohydrate or fat. Proteins not only are more costly to produce than fats or carbohydrates but the daily protein requirement per kilogram of bodyweight remains constant throughout adult life, whereas the requirements for fats and carbohydrates generally decrease with age.

As briefly described above, proteins have diverse biological functions, structures, and properties. Many proteins are susceptible to alteration by a number of rather subtle changes in the immediate environment. Maximum knowledge of the composition, structure, and chemical properties of the raw materials, especially proteins, is required if contemporary and future processing of foods is to best meet the needs of mankind. A considerable amount of information is already available, although much of it has been collected by biochemists using a specific food component as a model system。

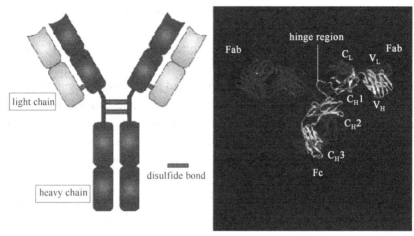

basic structure of immunoglobulin molecular

Glossary

1. intricate	*adj.* 复杂的,错综的,缠结的,难懂的
2. collagenous	*adj.* 胶原的
3. enzyme	*n.* 酶
4. hormone	*n.* 激素
5. hemoglobin	*n.* 血红蛋白
6. plasma	*n.* 血浆，原生质
7. globulin	*n.* 球蛋白
8. immunological	*adj.* 免疫的
9. antibody	*n.* 抗体
10. carbohydrate	*n.* 碳水化合物
11. kilogram	*n.* 千克

Exercises

1. *Matching*

① hormone   （a）a family of proteins found in blood and milk and muscle and in plant seed

② plasma   （b）the secretion of an endocrine gland that is transmitted by the blood to the tissue on which it has a specific effect

③ globulin   （c）any of a large variety of proteins normally present in the body or produced in response to an antigen which it neutralizes, thus producing an immune response

④ antibody   （d）colorless watery fluid of blood and lymph containing no cells and in which erythrocytes and leukocytes and platelets are suspended

⑤ carbohydrate   （e）a hemoprotein composed of globin and heme that gives red blood cells their characteristic color;

⑥ hemoglobin   （f）an essential structural component of living cells and source of energy for animals; includes simple sugars with small molecules as well as macromolecular substances; are classified according to the number of monosaccharide groups they contain

2. *Fill in the blanks with the words or expressions given below, and change the form where necessary.*

intricate	collagenous	immunological
kilogram	antibody	carbohydrate

① One thousand _____ go to the ton.

② I have a novel with an _____ plot.

③ Athletes usually eat a high _____ diet.

④ _____ in breast milk protect babies against infection.

⑤ An _____ agent that increases the antigenic response

⑥ A strong liquid adhesive obtained by boiling _____ animal parts such as bones, hides, and hooves into hard gelatin and then adding water.

Translation

蛋白质

蛋白质是错综复杂、多种多样的大分子物质，是食物必需氨基酸和非必需氨基酸的来源。人体利用这些氨基酸以满足生长发育、修复组织和维持正常健康生活的要求。这些大分子以含氮为其特征，参与了许多与各种有生命物质有复杂联系的生命过程。哺乳动物及其许多内脏器官都是由大量蛋白组成的。骨骼中的矿物质是靠胶原蛋白的作用得以保持在一起。机体的保护层——皮肤中的蛋白质通常占机体蛋白质总量的10%左右。

有些蛋白质有生物催化剂（酶和激素）的作用，以调节体内的化学反应。基本的生命过程如生长、消化、代谢、排泄、化学能转变成机械功等都受酶和激素的控制。某些体液的渗透压和 pH 值受制于血浆蛋白和血红蛋白。蛋白质对免疫反应是必不可少的。抗体、改性的血浆球蛋白能抵御引起疾病的外来杂质和微生物的入侵。当某些摄入的蛋白质使防御机制产生明显的变化时，便发生人体的生物过敏。这就导致某些个体身上出现各种各样的疾病，且有时是急剧的病情。

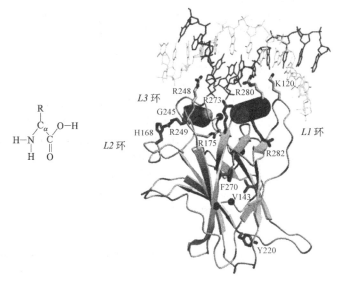

食物短缺现象在世界许多地区存在。随着人口的增加，这个问题很可能愈来愈尖锐、愈来愈普遍。而蛋白质供应不足问题远比碳水化合物或脂肪供应不足更为严重。蛋白质不仅生产成本要比碳水化合物或脂肪高，而且每天每千克体重所需的蛋白质量在成年期是恒定的，每天所需脂肪和碳水化合物的量一般都随着年龄的增长而逐渐减少。

正如上面简述的一样，蛋白质有多种不同的结构、性质和生理功能。许多蛋白质容易受周围环境的一系列相当微妙的影响而发生变化。要想使现在和将来的食品加工能理想地满足人类的需要，就必须彻底了解原料特别是蛋白质的组成结构和化学性质。目前，已经有这方面的大量资料可供利用，不过其中大部分是生物化学家利用某一特定食物成分作为模拟物加以收集的。

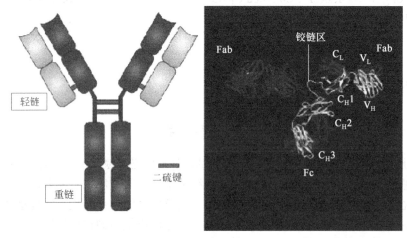

免疫球蛋白分子的基本结构

练习参考答案 *(Reference answers of exercises)*

1. *配对（Matching）*

①—(c)；②—(a)；③—(d)；④—(b)；⑤—(f)；⑥—(e)

2. *用词或短语填空，根据需要变换形式（Fill in the blanks with the words or expressions given below, and change the form where necessary）*

① kilogram   ② intricate   ③ carbohydrate

④ Antibody   ⑤ immunological   ⑥ collagenous

Unit 3 Amino Acids

Reading Material

Amino acids are the "building blocks" of proteins. Therefore, to understand the properties of proteins, a discussion of the structures and properties of amino acids is required. Amino acids are chemical compounds, which contain both basic amino groups and acidic carboxyl groups. Amino acids found in proteins have both the amino and carboxyl groups on the a-carbon atom; a-amino acids have the following general structure:

At neutral pH values in aqueous solutions both the amino and the carboxyl groups are ionized. The carboxyl group loses a proton and obtains a negative charge, while the amino group gains a proton and hence acquires a positive charge. As a consequence, amino acids possess dipolar characteristics.

Several properties of amino acids provide evidence for this structure: they are more soluble in water than in less polar solvents; when present in crystalline form they melt or decompose at relatively high temperatures (generally above 200), and they exhibit large dipole moments and large dielectric constants in neural aqueous solutions.

The R groups or side chains, which can affect the chemical property of amino acids and proteins significantly, may be classified into four groups.

Amino acids with hydrophilic groups can from hydrogen bond with water and are generally soluble in aqueous solutions. The hydroxyls of serine, heroine, and tyrosine; the sulfhydryl of thinly of cysteine, and the amides of asparagines and glutamine are the functional moieties present in r groups of the class of amino acids. Two of these, the toil of cysteine and the hydroxyl of tyrosine, are slightly ionized at pH 7 and can lose a proton much more readily than others in this class. The amides of asparagines and glutamine are readily hydrolyzed by acid or base to aspartic and glutamic acids, respectively.

Amino acids with nonpolar (hydrophobic) groups are less soluble in aqueous solvents than amino acids with polar uncharged groups. Five amino acids with hydrocarbon side chains decrease in polarity as the length of the side chain is increased. The unique structure of praline (and its hydoxylated derivative, hydroxyproline) causes this amino acid to play a unique role in protein structure.

The amino acids with positively charged (basic) groups at pH6-7 are lysine; arginine has a positively charged guanidine group. At pH7.0 10% of the imidazole groups of histidine molecules are protonated, but more than 50% carry positive changes at pH6.0.

The dicarboxylic amino acids, aspartic and glutamic, possess net negative charges at the neutral pH range. An important artificial meal-flavoring food additive is the monosodium salt of glutamic acid.

Glossary

1. amino acid	*n.* 氨基酸
2. acidic carboxyl	*n.* 酸性的羧基
3. basic amino	*n.* 碱性的氨基
4. aqueous	*adj.* 1. 水的; 2. 含水的; 3. 水成的
5. ionize	*v.* 电离
6. proton	*n.* 质子
7. dipolar	*adj.* 偶极的, 两极的
8. zwitterion	*n.* 两性离子
9. solvent	*n.* 溶剂
10. crystalline	*adj.* 1. 结晶的,晶状; 2. 清澈的
11. dipole	*n.* 双极子,偶极
12. dielectric	*adj.* 非传导性的
13. hydrophilic	*adj.* 亲水的,吸水的
14. hydrogen bond	*n.* 氢键
15. hydroxyl	*n.* 羟(基)氢氧基
16. heroine	*n.* 女英雄, 女主角
17. tyrosine	*n.* <化>酪氨酸
18. sulfhydryl	*adj.* 〈美〉巯基,氢硫基
19. cysteine	*n.* 半胱氨酸,巯基丙氨酸
20. asparagine	*n.* 天门冬素,天冬酰胺酸
21. glutamine	*n.* 谷氨酸盐
22. nonpolar	*adj.* 无极的
23. polarity	*n.* <物>极性, 两极并存的状态
24. praline	*n.* 果仁糖
25. derivative	*n.* 派生物, 引出物
26. hydroxyproline	*n.* 羟(基)脯氨酸
27. lysine	*n.* 赖氨酸
28. arginine	*n.* 精氨酸
29. guanidine	*n.* 胍
30. imidazole	*n.* 咪唑
31. histidine	*n.* 组氨酸, 组织氨基酸
32. dicarboxylic	*adj.* 二羧基的
33. glutamic	*adj.* 谷氨酸的
34. monosodium	*n.* 一钠

Exercises

1. *Matching*

① proton   （a）having a strong affinity for water; tending to dissolve in, mix with, or be wetted by water

② solvent   （b）a stable particle with positive charge equal to the negative charge of an electron

③ hydrophilic   （c）a liquid substance capable of dissolving other substances;

④ nonpolar   （d）not ionic; "a nonionic substance"

⑤ polarity   （e）the result of mathematical differentiation; the instantaneous change of one quantity relative to another; df(x)/dx

⑥ derivative   （f）a relation between two opposite attributes or tendencies;

2. *Fill in the blanks with the words or expressions given below, and change the form where necessary.*

dipolar	crystalline	glutamic
polarity	amino acid	carbohydrate

① Lacking distinct _____structure.

② There are also smaller, non-_____ structures in the Earth's field, which change locally and very slightly on a century timescale.

③ The _____ does not change its state in forming a solution

④ _____ inheres in a magnet

⑤ Theanine, the ethyl amide of_____ acid, is the main amino acid in the fresh leaf and contributes 1 to 2 percent of the dried weight, but other amino acids arise during the early part of the processing.

⑥ He has isolated an _____.

Translation

氨基酸

氨基酸是蛋白质的"结构单元"。因此，要了解蛋白质的性质，就需要讨论氨基酸的结构和性质，包括其碱性氨基组和酸性羧基组。蛋白质中的氨基酸在 α-碳原子上同时有氨基和羧基。α-氨基酸具有如下的一般结构：

在中性 pH 水溶液中，氨基和羧基都呈离子状态。羧基失去一个质子而带负电荷，同时氨基得到一个质子而带正电荷。结果氨基酸便具有偶极的特性。

氨基酸有好几种性质都反映了这种结构，这些性质是：它们易溶于水而不易溶于极性很小的溶剂；当以晶体形式存在时，它们要在较高温度（一般在 200℃以上）下熔化或分解；它们在中性溶液中显示出很大的偶极矩和介电常数。

氨基酸的侧链 R 基团对氨基酸和蛋白质的化学性质产生重大的影响。这些侧链可以分为四类。

带有极性非荷电的（亲水的）R 基团的氨基酸能与水形成氢键，通常能溶于水溶液。丝氨酸、苏氨酸和酪氨酸的羟基，半胱氨酸的硫氢基（即硫醇）以及天冬酰胺和谷氨酰胺的酰胺基是出现在这类氨基酸 R 基团中的功能部分，其中半胱氨酸的硫氢基和酪氨酸的羟基在 pH7 时能轻度离子化，因而比此类中其它氨基酸更容易失去质子。天冬酰胺和谷氨酰胺的酰胺基容易被酸和碱水解，分别形成天冬氨酸和谷氨酸。

在水溶液中，带有非极性（疏水的）R 基团的氨基酸溶解性比带极性非荷电的氨基酸要小得多。带有烃侧链的五种氨基酸，其侧链长度增加而在水溶液中的溶解性降低。脯氨酸（以及它的羟基衍生物羟脯氨酸）的独特结构使这种氨基酸在蛋白质结构中有独特的地位。

pH6～7 时带正电荷（碱性的）R 基团的氨基酸有赖氨酸、精氨酸和组氨酸。赖氨酸带正电的原因主要在于氨基，而精氨酸则具有带正电荷的胍基。pH7 时组氨酸分子中的咪唑基有 10%质子化，但在 pH6 时则有 50%以上带正电荷。

二羟基氨基酸（天冬氨酸和谷氨酸）在中性 pH 范围内带净负电荷，谷氨酸钠盐是一种重要的膳食调味用的人造食品添加剂。

练习参考答案 *(Reference answers of exercises)*

1. 配对（*Matching*）

①—(b)；②—(c)；③—(a)；④—(d)；⑤—(f)；⑥—(e)

2. 用词或短语填空，根据需要变换形式（*Fill in the blanks with the words or expressions given below, and change the form where necessary*）

① crystalline   ② dipolar   ③ carbohydrate

④ polarity   ⑤ glutamic   ⑥ amino acid

Unit 4　Peptides

Reading Material

When the amino group of one amino acid reacts with the carboxyl group of another amino acid, a peptide bond is formed and a molecule of water is released. This C—N bond joins amino acids together to form proteins

The peptide bond is slightly shorter than otter single C—N bonds. This indicates that the peptide bond has some characteristics of a double bond, because of resonance stabilization with the carbonyl oxygen. Thus group adjacent to the peptide bond cannot rotate freely, this rigidity of the peptide bond holds the six atoms in a single plane. The amino (—NH—) group does not ionize between pH 0 and 14 due to the double-bond properties of the peptide bond. In addition, r groups on amino acid residues, because of starch hindrance, force oxygen and hydrogen of the peptide bond to exist on a trans configuration. Therefore, the backbone of peptides and proteins has free rotation in two of the three bonds between amino acids.

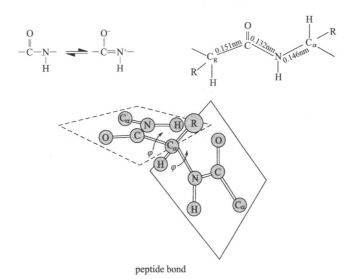

peptide bond

If a few amino acids are joined together by peptide bonds, the compound is called "peptide". Most natural peptides are formed by the partial hydrolytic of proteins; however, a few peptides are important metabolites. Anserine and carnosine are two derivatives of histamine that are found in muscles pf animals. The biochemical function of these peptides is not understood.

Glutathione occurs in mammalian blood, yeast, and especially in tissues of rapidly dividing cells. It is thought to function in oxidative metabolism and detoxification. During oxidation, two molecules of glutathione join via a disulfide bridge (—S—S) between two cysteine is not found in proteins.It is not found the peptide bond between γ-carboxyl group of glutamate and cysteine.

Other peptides function as antibodies and hormones. Oxytocin and hormones. Oxytocin and vasopressin are examples of peptide hormones.

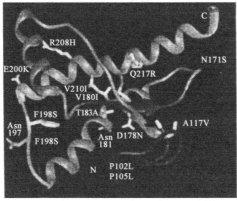

peptide

1. peptide	*n.* <生化>肽；缩氨酸
2. molecule	*n.* 分子
3. slightly	*adv.* 轻微地；稍稍
4. characteristic	*n.* 特性，特征，特色
5. resonance	*n.* 共鸣；回响；共振
6. oxygen	*n.* <化>氧，氧气
7. adjacent	*n.* 与…毗连的；邻近的
8. rigidity	*n.* 坚硬；严格；刚直；死板

Exercises

1. *Matching*

① peptide

② characteristic

③ globulin

④ antibody

⑤ carbohydrate

⑥ hemoglobin

（a）a family of proteins found in blood, milk, muscle and plant seed

（b）amide combining the amino group of one amino acid with the carboxyl group of another; usually obtained by partial hydrolysis of protein

（c）any of a large variety of proteins normally present in the body or produced in response to an antigen which it neutralizes, thus producing an immune response

（d）a prominent aspect of something

（e）a hemoprotein composed of globin and heme that gives red blood cells their characteristic color;

（f）an essential structural component of living cells and source of energy for animals; includes simple sugars with small molecules as well as macromolecular substances; are classified according to the number of monosaccharide groups they contain

2. *Fill in the blanks with the words or expressions given below, and change the form where necessary.*

peptide	characteristic	collagenous
kilogram	antibody	carbohydrate

① One thousand _____ go to the ton.

② A _____ that, on hydrolysis, yields two amino acid molecules.

③ Athletes usually eat a high _____ diet.

④ Generosity is one of his best _____.

⑤ An _____ agent that increases the antigenic response.

⑥ A strong liquid adhesive obtained by boiling _____ animal parts such as bones, hides, and hooves into hard gelatin and then adding water.

Translation

肽

当一个氨基酸分子的氨基与另一个氨基酸分子的羧基发生反应时，会形成一个肽键，同时释放出一分子水。这种 C—N 键把众多的氨基酸连接在一起形成蛋白质。

这种肽键比其它简单的 C—N 键略短。这说明由于肽键与羧基氧的共振稳定作用，使得肽键具有一定的双键特性。这样，紧邻肽键的基团就不能自由转动了。肽键的这种刚性使六个原子保

肽键

持在一个平面上。由于肽键的双键性质，亚氨基（—NH—）在 pH0～14 之间均不能离子化。此外，由于立体位阻现象，氨基酸残基上的 R 基团迫使肽键上的氧原子和氢原子只能以反式构型存在。因此，多肽和蛋白质的主链只可能在氨基酸之间的三个键中的两个键上做自由转动。

如果少数几个氨基酸以肽键连接起来，这样的化合物就称为"肽"。大多数天然肽是由蛋白质部分水解形成的。然而，有少数肽则是重要的代谢产物。鹅肌肽和肌肽是两种在动物肌肉中发现的组氨酸衍生物，这些肽的生物化学功能目前还不清楚。

谷胱甘肽存在于哺乳动物血液、酵母之中，特别是快速分化的细胞中。一般认为，这种肽具有参与氧化代谢和解毒作用的功能。氧化过程中，2 分子谷胱甘肽通过 2 个半胱氨酸残基之间的二硫键—S—S—连接起来。在蛋白质中未曾发现谷氨酸的 γ-羧基与半胱氨酸连成的肽键。

此外，还有具抗体和激素功能的肽。催产素和抗利尿素就是肽激素。

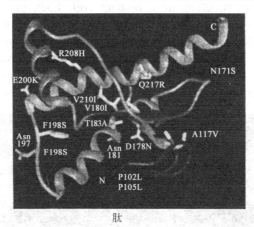

肽

练习参考答案 *(Reference answers of exercises)*

1. *配对（Matching）*
①—(b)；②—(d)；③—(a)；④—(c)；⑤—(f)；⑥—(e)

2. *用词或短语填空，根据需要变换形式（Fill in the blanks with the words or expressions given below, and change the form where necessary）*

① kilogram 　　　② peptide 　　　③ carbohydrate
④ characteristic 　② antibody 　　⑥ collagenous

Unit 5 Relationship between folding and amino acid sequence

Reading Material

Protein folding is the physical process by which a polypeptide folds into its characteristic and functional three-dimensional structure from random coil. Each protein exists as an unfolded polypeptide or random coil when translated from a sequence of mRNA to a linear chain of amino acids. This polypeptide lacks any developed three-dimensional structure (the left hand side of the neighboring figure 1). Amino acids interact with each other to produce a well-defined three dimensional structure, the folded protein (the right hand side of the figure 1), known as the native state. The resulting three-dimensional structure is determined by the amino acid sequence.

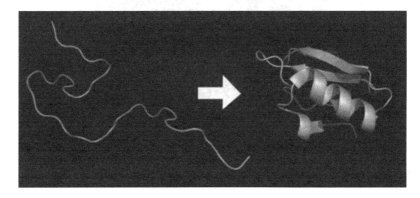

Figure 1　the unfold protein and folded protein

For many proteins the correct three dimensional structures is essential to function. Failure to fold into the intended shape usually produces inactive proteins with different properties including toxic prions. Several neurodegenerative and other diseases are believed to result from the accumulation of misfolded (incorrectly folded) proteins.

The amino-acid sequence (or primary structure) of a protein defines its native conformation. A protein molecule folds spontaneously during or after synthesis. While these macromolecules may be regarded as "folding themselves", the process also depends on the solvent (water or lipid bilayer), the concentration of salts, the temperature, and the presence of molecular chaperones.

Folded proteins usually have a hydrophobic core in which side chain packing stabilizes the folded state, and charged or polar side chains occupy the solvent- exposed surface where they interact with surrounding water. Minimizing the number of hydrophobic side-chains exposed to water is an important driving force behind the folding process(Figure 2). Formation of intramolecular hydrogen bonds provides another important contribution to protein stability. The strength of hydrogen bonds depends on their environment, thus H-bonds enveloped in a hydrophobic core

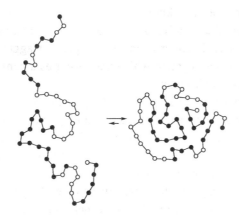

Figure 2   Illustration of the main driving force behind protein structure formation

In the compact fold, the hydrophobic amino acids (shown as black spheres) are in general shielded from the solvent.

contribute more than H-bonds exposed to the aqueous environment to the stability of the native state.

In the seminal research work published nearly four decades ago, C.B. Anfinsen hypothesized that "information dictating the native fold of protein domains is encoded in their amino acid sequence". However, with the explosive amount of protein sequence, structure, and fold data generated since the time of Anfinsen during the omics era, the emerging picture of the protein universe has challenged Anfinsen's dogma, for it has become evident that numerous protein folds have incredible sequence diversity with no consistent "fold code". In support of this observation, recent studies have shown that proteins with as low as 1-2% sequence identity may still adopt the same native fold, thus defying any tangible encoding of fold-dictating information into protein sequence . The pursuit of the elusive "fold code" has resulted in little more than patterns of amino acid sequence conservations specific to certain proteins, but no finding has been compelling enough to generalize universally or to utilize for biological applications .

In a recent study, scientists from Harvard-MIT have shown that, despite the enormous diversity within protein folds at the level of 1-dimensional amino acid sequence, nature has encoded fold-conserved information at higher dimensions of protein space such as the 2-D (protein contact maps) or 3-D (structure), that are known to be more intricately related to protein folding phenomena. The study published in PLoS ONE illuminated latent fold-conserved information from higher dimensional protein space using network theory approaches. By examining the entire protein universe on a fold-by-fold basis, the study revealed that atomic interaction networks in the solvent-unexposed core of protein domains are fold-conserved and unique to each protein's native fold, thus appearing to be the encoded "signature" of protein domains. This study hence uncovered that the protein fold code is a "network phenomena" in addition to a sequence and structural phenomena as commonly presumed. The discovery of such a protein folding code also confirms Anfinsens Dogma by proving that a significant portion of the fold-dictating information is encoded by the atomic interaction network in the solvent-unexposed core of protein domains.

The process of folding *in vivo* often begins co-translationally, so that the N-terminus of the protein begins to fold while the C-terminal portion of the protein is still being synthesized by the ribosome. Specialized proteins called chaperones assist in the folding of other proteins. A well studied example is the bacterial GroEL system, which assists in the folding of globular proteins. In eukaryotic organisms chaperones are known as heat shock proteins. Although most globular proteins are able to assume their native state unassisted, chaperone-assisted folding is often necessary in the crowded intracellular environment to prevent aggregation; chaperones are also used to prevent misfolding and aggregation which may occur as a consequence of exposure to heat or other changes in the cellular environment.

For the most part, scientists have been able to study many identical molecules folding together *en masse*. At the coarsest level, it appears that in transitioning to the native state, a given amino acid sequence takes on roughly the same route and proceeds through roughly the same intermediates and transition states. Often folding involves first the establishment of regular secondary and supersecondary structures, particularly alpha helices and beta sheets, and afterwards tertiary structure. Formation of quaternary structure usually involves the "assembly" or "coassembly" of subunits that have already folded. The regular alpha helix and beta sheet structures fold rapidly because they are stabilized by intramolecular hydrogen bonds, as was first characterized by Linus Pauling. Protein folding may involve covalent bonding in the form of disulfide bridges formed between two cysteine residues or the formation of metal clusters. Shortly before settling into their more energetically favourable native conformation, molecules may pass through an intermediate "molten globule" state.

The essential fact of folding, however, remains that the amino acid sequence of each protein contains the information that specifies both the native structure and the pathway to attain that state. This is not to say that nearly identical amino acid sequences always fold similarly. Conformations differ based on environmental factors as well; similar proteins fold differently based on where they are found. Folding is a spontaneous process independent of energy inputs from nucleoside triphosphates. The passage of the folded state is mainly guided by hydrophobic interactions, formation of intramolecular hydrogen bonds, and van der Waals forces, and it is opposed by conformational entropy.

Glossary

1. neurodegenerative	*adj.* 神经组织退化的
2. spontaneously	*adv.* 自然地;自发地;不由自主地
3. macromolecules	*n.* 大分子
4. chaperones	*n.* 分子伴侣
5. hydrophobic	*adj.* 狂犬病的,恐水病的,患恐水病的,不易被水沾湿的
6. charged	*adj.* 带电荷的
7. intramolecular	*adj.* 分子内的
8. seminal	*adj.* 繁殖的；开创性的
9. C.B. Anfinsen	〈人名〉安芬森❶，美国人
10. omics era	组学时代

---

❶ 1972 年诺贝尔化学奖得主，与莫尔(S. Moore，美国)、斯坦(W. H. Stein，美国) 共同研究核糖核酸酶的三维结构与功能的关系，以及蛋白质折叠链的自然现象。

11. tangible	*adj.* 明确的, 确凿的, 实际
12. elusive	*adj.* 难以捉摸的;难以找到的;不易记住的
13. enormous	*adj.* 巨大的, 极大的, 庞大的
14. intricately	*adv.* 杂乱地;复杂地; 难懂地
15. phenomena	*n.* 现象
16. PLoS ONE	国际学术刊物《公共科学图书馆•综合》
17. latent	*adj.* 1.潜伏的, 潜在的, 不易觉察的; 2. 隐藏的
18. in vivo	*n.* 在活的有机体内
19. GroEL	〈生物〉原核生物的一种分子伴侣
20. heat shock proteins	*n.* 热休克蛋白
21. entropy	*n.* 熵
22. enmasse	*v.* 全体地,一同地
23. Linus Pauling	〈人名〉莱纳斯鲍林❶（1901—1994）
24. covalent	*adj.* 共价的

Exercises

1. *Matching*

① nature state   （a）Specialized proteins which assist in the folding of other proteins

② primary structure   （b）A protein molecule folds spontaneously during or after synthesis.

③ hydro bonding   （c）The amino-acid sequence of a protein

④ self-folding   （d）Producibility of hydro electric power station

⑤ chaperones   （e）The state that protein has activity and do not denatured

2. *Fill in the blanks with the words or expressions given below, and change the form where necessary.*

spontaneously	secondary	seminal
co-translationally	environmental	tangible

① The process of folding *in vivo* often begins_____

② The amino-acid sequence (or primary structure) of a protein defines its native conformation. A protein molecule folds_____during or after synthesis.

③ Often folding involves first the establishment of regular_____and supersecondary structures, particularly alpha helices and beta sheets, and afterwards tertiary structure.

④ Conformations differ based on_____factors as well; similar proteins fold differently based on where they are found.

---

❶ 著名的量子化学家，曾两次荣获得诺贝尔奖（1954 年化学奖，1962 年和平奖）

⑤ A concretion of ＿＿＿＿＿＿＿＿ideas in her treatise.
⑥ This keeps everything open and ＿＿＿＿＿＿＿.

Translation

氨基酸序列和蛋白质折叠之间的关系

蛋白质折叠是一个物理过程，其中多肽通过无规则卷曲折叠成具有特定结构和功能的三维结构。当由 mRNA 翻译成氨基酸线性长链时，每个蛋白质都以未折叠的多肽或无规则卷曲形式存在。此多肽没有任何高级的三维结构（见图 1 的左侧）。氨基酸相互作用产生了特定的三维结构，即折叠的蛋白质（见图 1 的右侧），被认为是蛋白质的天然构象。由此产生的三维结构是由氨基酸序列决定的。

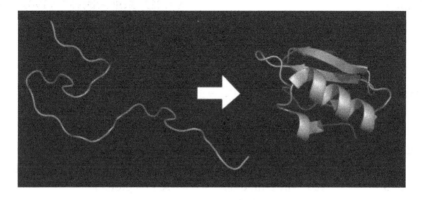

图 1　未折叠的蛋白质和折叠的蛋白质

对于许多蛋白质来说，正确的三维结构是其发挥生物活性必不可少的。未能折叠成特定的形态往往产生具有不同性质的无活性蛋白质，包括有毒的朊病毒。一些神经退行性疾病和其它一些疾病被认为是由于蛋白质错误折叠（不正确的折叠）的累积所造成的。

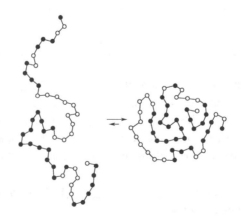

图 2　蛋白质结构形成的驱动力
在紧密折叠的形态中疏水性氨基酸（图中所示黑色球体）隐蔽起来远离溶剂

　　蛋白质的氨基酸序列（或一级结构）决定了它的天然构象。蛋白质分子在其合成的过程中或合成之后自发地进行折叠。虽然这些大分子可能被视为"自我折叠"，这一过程还决定于溶剂（水或脂双层）、盐类物质的浓度、温度，以及分子伴侣的存在。

　　折叠的蛋白质通常有一个侧链包装成的疏水中心以稳定蛋白质的构象，带电荷的和极性侧链位于溶剂暴露的表面，这也是其与环境水相互作用的位置。尽量减少疏水侧链暴露于水的数量是蛋白质折叠过程的一个重要驱动力（图2）。分子内氢键的形成为蛋白质的稳定提供另一重要作用。氢键强度依赖于他们所处的环境，疏水中心的氢键比暴露在水环境中的氢键对蛋白质天然构象的稳定作用要大。

　　在近40年前出版的开创性研究著作中，C.B.Anfinsen推测："蛋白质结构域的天然折叠信息是由其氨基酸序列编码的。"然而，在Anfinsen所处的蛋白质组学时代，随着蛋白质序列、结构和折叠信息的猛增，蛋白质界出现的问题向Anfinsen的推断提出了挑战，很显然，许多蛋白质折叠序列的多样性令人难以置信，而没有"折叠密码"可循。为了支持这些观察数据，最近的研究表明，至少有1%～2%的特征序列会折叠成相同的天然构象，这和蛋白质序列的折叠信息有明确的编码是截然相反的。为了寻找难以捉摸的"折叠密码"，人们对某些特定蛋白质氨基酸保守序列进行了研究，但至今仍没有发现具有普遍性或令人信服的应用到生物实践的规律。

　　在最近的研究中，哈佛大学、麻省理工学院的科学家发现，尽管蛋白质折叠在一维氨基酸序列水平上有巨大差异，但在蛋白质的多维空间中，例如二维（蛋白质联系地图）或三维（结构），天然构象有保守的折叠编码信息，它们被认为是与蛋白质折叠现象相关的更加错综复杂的信息。《公共科学图书馆·综合》出版的研究表明，可以利用网络方法研究蛋白质多维空间的保守折叠信息。通过在高度折叠的基础上考查所有蛋白质，研究显示未暴露于溶剂的蛋白质核心处原子相互作用而保守的折叠，并且只折叠成蛋白质的天然构象，因此表现出蛋白质结构的编码"特征"。该研究发现，蛋白质折叠密码不仅是一般推测的序列和结构现象，还是一个"网络现象"。这种蛋白质折叠密码的发现还证实了Anfinsens定律，证明了折叠指导信息的关键部分是通过蛋白质未暴露于溶剂的核心中原子间的相互作用编码的。

　　在生物体内，蛋白质的折叠与翻译过程往往是偶联的，当蛋白质的C-端仍在核糖体中合成时，N-端已经开始折叠了。有一种叫做分子伴侣的蛋白质协助其它蛋白质的折叠。细菌的GroEL系统是很好的研究例子，它协助球形蛋白质的折叠。在真核生物体内分子伴侣被称做热休克蛋白。虽然大多数球状蛋白质在没有分子伴侣的协助下能呈现出它们的天然构象，分子伴侣辅助折叠还是必要的，尤其是在拥挤的细胞环境内，以防止聚集；分子伴侣也被用来防止由于细胞内环境暴露于热或其它变动而引起的错误折叠和聚集。

　　在大多数情况下，科学家已经能够研究许多相同分子折叠的全部蛋白质。大体上看，蛋白质过渡到天然状态，给定的氨基酸序列通常沿着大致的路线和过程,经过相同的中间体和过渡态。一般折叠首先是建立规则的二级结构和超二级结构，特别是α-螺旋和β-折叠片，然后再形成三级结构。而四级结构的形成往往涉及已经折叠的亚基的"装配"和"联合装配"。通常α-螺旋和β-折叠片折叠非常迅速，因为它们是由分子内氢键稳定的，该理论最早由Linus Pauling证实。蛋白质的折叠可能涉及共价键，例如两个半胱氨酸残基间的二硫键或金属团簇形成的键。不久之前，通过研究更有利的天然构象，发现分子可以通过一个"融球"态的中间体进行折叠。

　　然而，折叠的重要事实，仍然是每个蛋白质氨基酸序列中都包含着指定的天然结构和形成天然构象途径的信息。这并不是说，几乎相同的氨基酸序列都会进行类似的折叠。构象的不同还决定于环境因素；在不同的位置发现，相似蛋白质具有不同的折叠。折叠是一个自发的过程，不依赖于核苷三磷酸的能量。蛋白质的折叠过程主要是通过疏水相互作用、分子间氢键和范德华力的驱动，而该观点与构象熵相对立。

练习参考答案 (Reference answers of exercises)

1. 配对（Matching）

　①—(e)；②—(c)；③—(d)；④—(b)；⑤—(a)

2. 用词或短语填空，根据需要变换形式（Fill in the blanks with the words or expressions given below, and change the form where necessary）

　① co-translationally　　② spontaneously　　③ secondary

　④ environmental　　　　⑤ seminal　　　　　⑥ tangible

Unit 6 Relationship between protein folding and disease

Reading Material

1. Disruption of the native state

Under some conditions proteins will not fold into their biochemically functional forms. Temperatures above or below the range that cells tend to live in will cause thermally unstable proteins to unfold or "denature" (this is why boiling makes an egg white turn opaque). High concentrations of solutes, extremes of pH, mechanical forces, and the presence of chemical denaturants can do the same. Protein thermal stability is far from constant, however. For example, hyperthermophilic bacteria have been found to grow at temperatures as high as 122°C, which of course requires that their full complement of vital proteins and protein assemblies be stable at that temperature or above.

A fully denatured protein lacks both tertiary and secondary structure, and exists as a so-called random coil. Under certain conditions some proteins can refold; however, in many cases denaturation is irreversible. Cells sometimes protect their proteins against the denaturing influence of heat with enzymes known as chaperones or heat shock proteins, which assist other proteins both in folding and in remaining folded. Some proteins never fold in cells at all except with the assistance of chaperone molecules, which either isolate individual proteins so that their folding is not interrupted by interactions with other proteins or help to unfold misfolded proteins, giving them a second chance to refold properly. This function is crucial to prevent the risk of precipitation into insoluble amorphous aggregates.

2. Incorrect protein folding and neurodegenerative disease

Aggregated proteins are associated with prion-related illnesses such as Creutzfeldt-Jakob disease, bovine spongiform encephalopathy (mad cow disease), amyloid-related illnesses such as Alzheimer's Disease and familial amyloid cardiomyopathy or polyneuropathy, as well as intracytoplasmic aggregation diseases such as Huntington's and Parkinson's disease. These age onset degenerative diseases are associated with the multimerization of misfolded proteins into insoluble, extracellular aggregates and/or intracellular inclusions including cross-beta sheet amyloid fibrils; it is not clear whether the aggregates are the cause or merely a reflection of the loss of protein homeostasis, the balance between synthesis, folding, aggregation and protein turnover. Misfolding and excessive degradation instead of folding and function leads to a number of proteopathy diseases such as antitrypsin-associated Emphysema, cystic fibrosis and the lysosomal storage diseases, where loss of function is the origin of the disorder. While protein replacement therapy has historically been used to correct the latter disorders, an emerging approach is to use pharmaceutical chaperones to fold mutated proteins to render them functional.

3. The Levinthal paradox and Kinetics

The Levinthal paradox observes that if a protein were to fold by sequentially sampling all possible conformations, it would take an astronomical amount of time to do so, even if the conformations were sampled at a rapid rate (on the nanosecond or picosecond scale). Based upon the observation that proteins fold much faster than this, Levinthal then proposed that a random conformational search does not occur, and the protein must, therefore, fold through a series of meta-stable intermediate states.

The duration of the folding process varies dramatically depending on the protein of interest. When studied outside the cell, the slowest folding proteins require many minutes or hours to fold primarily due to proline isomerization, and must pass through a number of intermediate states, like checkpoints, before the process is complete. On the other hand, very small single-domain proteins with lengths of up to a hundred amino acids typically fold in a single step. Time scales of milliseconds are the norm and the very fastest known protein folding reactions are complete within a few microseconds.

4. Energy landscape theory of protein folding

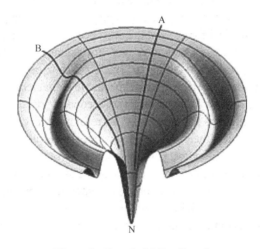

Figure 1   Protein folding funnel

In energy landscape, N is protein nature state which has the minimum energy, through path A protein will fold
to nature state without frustration, through path B protein will fold to nature state with some frustration

The protein folding phenomenon was largely an experimental endeavor until the formulation of an energy landscape theory of proteins by Joseph Bryngelson and Peter Wolynes, in the late 1980s and early 1990s. This approach introduced the *principle of minimal frustration*, which asserts that evolution has selected the amino acid sequences of natural proteins so that interactions between side chains largely favor the molecule's acquisition of the folded state. Interactions that do not favor folding are selected against, although some residual *frustration* is expected to exist. A consequence of these evolutionarily selected sequences is that proteins are generally thought to have globally "funneled energy landscapes" (coined by José Onuchic) that are largely directed towards the native state. This "folding funnel" landscape allows the protein to fold to the native state through any of a large number of pathways and intermediates, rather than being restricted to a single mechanism (Figure 1). The theory is supported by both computational simulations of model proteins and numerous experimental studies, and it has been used to improve methods for protein structure prediction and design. The description of protein folding by the leveling free-energy landscape is also consistent with the 2nd law of thermodynamics.

Glossary

1. hyperthermophilic	超嗜热菌
2. precipitation	*n*. 沉淀，沉降作用，沉淀物
3. neurodegenerative [ˌnjuərəudiˈdʒenərətiv]	*adj*. 神经组织退化的
4. prion	*n*. 朊病毒
5. Creutzfeldt-Jakob	*n*. 克雅病
6. bovine spongiform encephalopathy	*n*. 牛海绵状脑病
7. Alzheimer's Disease	*n*. 阿尔茨海默病
8. familial amyloid cardiomyopathy	*n*. 家族淀粉样心肌病
9. polyneuropathy	*n*. 神经病变
10. Parkinson's disease	*n*. 帕金森症
11. proteopathy	*n*. 蛋白质构象性疾病
12. antitrypsin	*n*. 抗胰蛋白酶
13. emphysema	*n*. 气肿;肺气肿
14. cystic fibrosis	*n*. 囊胞性纤维症
15. lysosomal storage diseases	*n*. 溶酶体贮积病
16. pharmaceutical	*adj*. 1. 药的; 2. 配药的; 3. 制药的
17. chaperones	*n*. 分子伴侣:抑制素
18. mutate	*vi*. 变化; 产生突变
	vt. 改变; 使突变

Exercises

1. *Matching*

① chaperones　　(a) modify (as a native protein) especially by heat, acid, alkali, or ultraviolet radiation so that all of the original properties are removed or diminished

② Alzheimer's Disease　　(b) is a mapping of all possible conformations of a molecular entity, or the spatial positions of interacting molecules in a system, and their corresponding energy levels

③ hyperthermophilic　　(c) an infectious protein particle similar to a virus but lacking nucleic acid; thought to be the agent responsible for scrapie and other degenerative diseases of the nervous system

④ prion　　(d) is a condition in which a person's brain gradually stops working properly.

⑤ energy landscapes　　(e) are proteins that assist the non-covalent folding or unfolding and the assembly or disassembly of other macromolecular structures

⑥ denature　　(f) is an organism that thrives in extremely hot environments

2. *Fill in the blanks with the words or expressions given below, and change the form where necessary.*

pharmaceutical	mutate	precipitation
misfolded	aggregate	degradation

① Antibiotics were of no use, neither were other _____.

② This function is crucial to prevent the risk of _____into insoluble amorphous aggregates.

③ Another pathway of organophosphate _____involves reduction.

④ The technique has been to _____the genes by irradiation or chemicals.

⑤ Like many other _____proteins identified in neurodegenerative disorders, abeta also accumulates inside the ad neurons.

⑥ We simulated the structure of reversible protein _____as a function of protein surface characteristics, protein-protein interaction energies, and the entropic penalty accompanying the immobilization of protein in a solid phase.

Translation

蛋白质折叠与疾病的关系

1. 天然态的破坏

在一些条件下蛋白质不会折叠成它们具有生化功能的形式。当温度高于或低于细胞生存的范围，将引起热不稳定蛋白质的去折叠或"变性"（这就是煮鸡蛋时蛋白会凝固的原因）。高浓度的溶质、极端 pH 值、机械力和化学变性剂的存也同样会使蛋白质变性。然而，蛋白质的热稳定性是并不是固定的。例如，嗜热细菌被发现生长于 122℃ 的高温下，这就要求它们所有重要蛋白质和蛋白质的装配在该温度下或高于该温度下应该是稳定的。

一个完全变性蛋白质缺乏二级和三级结构，以无规则卷曲形式存在。在一定条件下，一些蛋白质可以复性；但在很多情况下变性是不可逆的。有时细胞保护它们的蛋白质不被热变性，利用分子伴侣或热休克蛋白，可以辅助蛋白质折叠并保持折叠状态。一些蛋白质在所有细胞内都不折叠，除了有分子伴侣的协助，或把它们单独分离出来，以使它们的折叠不会因与其它蛋白质的相互作用而中断，或是帮助错误折叠的蛋白质去折叠，给它们第二次机会重新正确折叠。此功能是至关重要的，可防止发生沉淀而形成不溶性无定形聚集的风险。

2. 不正确蛋白质折叠与神经退行性疾病

聚集蛋白是与朊病毒相关的疾病，如克雅病、牛海绵状脑病（疯牛病）、淀粉样蛋白相关疾病（如阿尔茨海默病和家族性淀粉样心肌病或神经病变）以及胞浆内聚集的疾病（如亨廷顿病和帕金森症）。这些年龄退行性疾病均与错误折叠蛋白多聚化形成细胞外聚合物或细胞内含物有关，包括淀粉样纤维蛋白的交叉 β-折叠；目前并不清楚这种蛋白质聚集是否是疾病的根本原因，或仅仅是蛋白质动态失衡的一种反映，即有关蛋白质的合成、折叠、变性及其循环的平衡。错误的折叠和过度降解代替了折叠和功能活性，导致蛋白质构象性疾病的发生，例如抗胰蛋白酶相关肺气肿、囊肿性纤维化及溶酶体贮积病，这些部位的蛋白质功能丧失是紊乱的来源。然而蛋白替代疗法历来被用于纠正后者障碍，一个新兴的方法是使用药物分子伴侣折叠突变蛋白质，使它们能正常发挥功能。

3. 列文托悖论和动力学

列文托悖论指出，如果一个蛋白折叠按所有可能的构象顺序尝试，那么它将需要大量的时间，即使构象以很快的速度尝试（纳秒或皮秒级）。基于蛋白质折叠的观察发现，蛋白质的折叠比这快得多，列文托后来推测，并没有发生随机的构象搜索，蛋白质的折叠必须通过一个亚稳中间态。

折叠过程持续的时间依蛋白质不同有显著变化。当进行细胞外研究时表明，最慢的蛋白质折叠需要数分钟甚至是几小时才能完成，主要由于脯氨酸异构化，使蛋白质完成折叠之前，必须通过大量的中间状态，像检查站一样。另一方面，一些非常小的单结构域蛋白，只有100个氨基酸的长度，能够一步完成折叠。一般蛋白质折叠的时间是毫秒级，已知蛋白质折叠的反应最快的是几微秒内完成。

4. 蛋白质折叠的能量景观理论

这种蛋白质折叠现象一直处于实验探索阶段，直到蛋白质能量景观理论（energy landscape theory）的形成，它是由 Joseph Bryngelson 和 Peter Wolynes 在 20 世纪 80 年代末至 90 年代初提出的。这种理论阐述了最小失错原则，它认为进化已经选择了天然蛋白质的氨基酸序列，所以侧链间的相互作用主要是有利于分子的折叠状态的获得。不利于折叠的相互作用不被选择，尽管一些失错残基仍然存在。这种指定序列进化的结果是蛋白质通过全部"漏斗能量图景"（由 José Onuchic 提出），这对其形成天然态具有重要的指导意义。这种折叠漏斗图景允许蛋白质经过很多途径和中间体折叠成自然状态，而不是仅限于一种机制（图1）。该理论得到蛋白质模型的计算模拟和大量实验研究的证实，并已用于改进蛋白质结构预测和设计的方法。自由能测量对蛋白质折叠的描述也符合热力学第二定律。

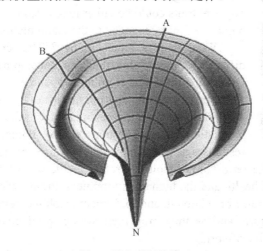

图 1　蛋白质折叠漏斗

考虑在能量的地形图中存在复杂的地形，除自然态（N）外可能存在多个极小值。不同的路径将不再是等概率的，除自然态外的能量极小值对应的是错误的折叠态（misfolding）。图中路径 A，无障碍地演化为自然态；路径 B，克服一个障碍才能演化为自然态

练习参考答案 *(Reference answers of exercise)*

1. 配对（*Matching*）

①—(e); ②—(d); ③—(f); ④—(c); ⑤—(b); ⑥—(a)

2. 用词或短语填空，根据需要变换形式（*Fill in the blanks with the words or expressions given below, and change the form where necessary*）

① pharmaceuticals　　② precipitation　　③ degradation
④ mutate　　　　　　⑤ misfolded　　　　⑥ aggregates

1. What is Biotechnology?

Biotechnology in one form or another has flourished since prehistoric times. When the first human beings realized that they could plant their own crops and breed their own animals, they learned to use biotechnology. The discovery that fruit juices fermented into wine, or that milk could be converted into cheese or yogurt, or that beer could be made by fermenting solutions of malt and hops began the study of biotechnology. When the first bakers found that they could make a soft, spongy bread rather than a firm, thin cracker, they were acting as fledgling biotechnologists. The first animal breeders, realizing that different physical traits could be either magnified or lost by mating appropriate pairs of animals, engaged in the manipulations of biotechnology.

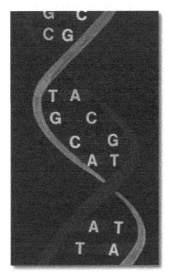

What then is biotechnology? The term brings to mind many different things. Some think of developing new types of animals. Others dream of almost unlimited sources of human therapeutic drugs. Still others envision the possibility of growing crops that are more nutritious and naturally pest-resistant to feed a rapidly growing world population. This question elicits almost as many first-thought responses as there are people to whom the question can be posed.

In its purest form, the term "biotechnology" refers to the use of living organisms or their products to modify human health and the human environment. Prehistoric biotechnologists did this as they used yeast cells to raise bread dough and to ferment alcoholic beverages, and bacterial cells to make cheeses and yogurts and as they bred their strong, productive animals to make even stronger and more productive offspring.

Throughout human history, we have learned a great deal about the different organisms that our ancestors used so effectively. The marked increase in our understanding of these organisms and their cell products gains us the ability to control the many functions of various cells and organisms. Using the techniques of gene splicing and recombinant DNA technology, we can now actually combine the genetic elements of two or more living cells. Functioning lengths of DNA can be taken from one organism and placed into the cells of another organism. As a result, for example, we can cause bacterial cells to produce human molecules. Cows can produce more milk for the same amount of feed. And we can synthesize therapeutic molecules that have never before existed.

2. Where Did Biotechnology Begin?

Certain practices that we would now classify as applications of biotechnology have been in use since man's earliest days. Nearly 10,000 years ago, our ancestors were producing wine, beer, and bread by using fermentation, a natural process in which the biological activity of one-celled organisms plays a critical role.

In fermentation, microorganisms such as bacteria, yeasts, and molds are mixed with ingredients that provide them with food. As they digest this food, the organisms produce two critical by-products, carbon dioxide gas and alcohol.

In beer making, yeast cells break down starch and sugar (present in cereal grains) to form alcohol; the froth, or head, of the beer results from the carbon dioxide gas that the cells produce. In simple terms, the living cells rearrange chemical elements to form new products that they need to live and reproduce. By happy coincidence, in the process of doing so they help make a popular beverage.

Bread baking is also dependent on the action of yeast cells. The bread dough contains nutrients that these cells digest for their own sustenance. The digestion process generates alcohol (which contributes to that wonderful aroma of baking bread) and carbon dioxide gas (which makes the dough rise and forms the honeycomb texture of the baked loaf).

Discovery of the fermentation process allowed early peoples to produce foods by allowing live organisms to act on other ingredients. But our ancestors also found that, by manipulating the conditions under which the fermentation took place, they could improve both the quality and the yield of the ingredients themselves.

Crop Improvement

Although plant science is a relatively modern discipline, its fundamental techniques have been applied throughout human history. When early man went through the crucial transition from nomadic hunter to settled farmer, cultivated crops became vital for survival. These primitive farmers, although ignorant of the natural principles at work, found that they could increase the yield and improve the taste of crops by selecting seeds from particularly desirable plants.

Farmers long ago noted that they could improve each succeeding year's harvest by using seed from only the best plants of the current crop. Plants that, for example, gave the highest yield, stayed the healthiest during periods of drought or disease, or were easiest to harvest tended to produce future generations with these same characteristics. Through several years of careful seed selection, farmers could maintain and strengthen such desirable traits.

The possibilities for improving plants expanded as a result of Gregor Mendel's investigations in the mid-1860s of hereditary traits in peas. Once the genetic basis of heredity was understood, the benefits of cross-breeding, or hybridization, became apparent: plants with different desirable traits could be used to cultivate a later generation that combined these characteristics.

An understanding of the scientific principles behind fermentation and crop improvement practices has come only in the last hundred years. But the early, crude techniques, even without the benefit of sophisticated laboratories and automated equipment, were a true practice of biotechnology guiding natural processes to improve man's physical and economic well-being.

Harnessing Microbes for Health

Every student of chemistry knows the shape of a Buchner funnel, but they may be unaware that the distinguished German scientist it was named after made the vital discovery (in 1897) that enzymes extracted from yeast are effective in converting sugar into alcohol. Major outbreaks of disease in overcrowded industrial cities led eventually to the introduction, in the early years of the present century, of large-scale sewage purification systems based on microbial activity. By this time it had proved possible to generate certain key industrial chemicals (glycerol, acetone, and butanol) using bacteria.

Another major beneficial legacy of early 20th century biotechnology was the discovery by Alexander Fleming (in 1928) of penicillin, an antibiotic derived from the mold Penicillium. Large-scale production of penicillin was achieved in the 1940s. However, the revolution in understanding the chemical basis of cell function that stemmed from the post-war emergence of molecular biology was still to come. It was this exciting phase of bioscience that led to the recent explosive development of biotechnology.

3. Overview and Brief History of Biotechnology

Biotechnology seems to be leading a sudden new biological revolution. It has brought us to the brink of a world of "engineered" products that are based in the natural world rather than on chemical and industrial processes.

Biotechnology has been described as "Janus-faced." This implies that there are two sides. On one, techniques allow DNA to be manipulated to move genes from one organism to another. On the other, it involves relatively new technologies whose consequences are untested and should be met with caution. The term "biotechnology" was coined in 1919 by Karl Ereky, an Hungarian engineer. At that time, the term meant all the lines of work by which products are produced from raw materials with the aid of living organisms. Ereky envisioned a biochemical age similar to the stone and iron ages.

A common misconception among teachers is the thought that biotechnology includes only DNA and genetic engineering. To keep students abreast of current knowledge, teachers sometimes have emphasized the techniques of DNA science as the "end-and-all" of biotechnology. This trend has also led to a misunderstanding in the general population. Biotechnology is NOT new. Man has been manipulating living things to solve problems and improve his way of life for millennia. Early agriculture concentrated on producing food. Plants and animals were selectively bred, and microorganisms were used to make food items such as beverages, cheese, and bread.

The late eighteenth century and the beginning of the nineteenth century saw the advent of vaccinations, crop rotation involving leguminous crops, and animal drawn machinery. The end of the nineteenth century was a milestone of biology. Microorganisms were discovered, Mendel's work on genetics was accomplished, and institutes for investigating fermentation and other microbial processes were established by Koch, Pasteur, and Lister.

Biotechnology at the beginning of the twentieth century began to bring industry and agriculture together. During World War I, fermentation processes were developed that produced acetone from starch and paint solvents for the rapidly growing automobile industry. Work in the 1930s was geared toward using surplus agricultural products to supply industry instead of imports or petrochemicals. The advent of World War II brought the manufacture of penicillin. The biotechnical focus moved to pharmaceuticals. The "cold war" years were dominated by work with microorganisms in preparation for biological warfare, as well as antibiotics and fermentation processes.

Biotechnology is currently being used in many areas including agriculture, bioremediation, food processing, and energy production. DNA fingerprinting is becoming a common practice in forensics. Similar techniques were used recently to identify the bones of the last Czar of Russia and several members of his family. Production of insulin and other medicines is accomplished through cloning of vectors that now carry the chosen gene. Immunoassays are used not only in medicine for drug level and pregnancy testing, but also by farmers to aid in detection of unsafe levels of pesticides, herbicides, and toxins on crops and in animal products. These assays also provide rapid field tests for industrial chemicals in ground water, sediment, and soil. In agriculture, genetic engineering is being used to produce plants that are resistant to insects, weeds, and plant diseases.

A current agricultural controversy involves the tomato. A recent article in the New Yorker magazine compared the discovery of the edible tomato that came about by early biotechnology with the new "Flavr-Savr" tomato brought about through modern techniques. In the very near future, you will be given the opportunity to bite into the Flavr-Savr tomato, the first food created by the use of recombinant DNA technology ever to go on sale.

What will you think as you raise the tomato to your mouth? Will you hesitate? This moment may be for you as it was for Robert Gibbon Johnson in 1820 on the steps of the courthouse in Salem, New Jersey. Prior to this moment, the tomato was widely believed to be poisonous. As a large crowd watched, Johnson consumed two tomatoes and changed forever the human-tomato relationship. Since that time, man has sought to produce the supermarket tomato with that "backyard flavor." Americans also want that tomato available year-round.

New biotechnological techniques have permitted scientists to manipulate desired traits. Prior to the advancement of the methods of recombinant DNA, scientists were limited to the techniques of their time-cross-pollination, selective breeding, pesticides, and herbicides. Today's biotechnology has its "roots" in chemistry, physics, and biology . The explosion in techniques has resulted in three major branches of biotechnology: genetic engineering, diagnostic techniques, and cell/tissue techniques.

4. Biotechnology on Agriculture – An Overview

Techniques aimed at crop improvement have been utilized for centuries. Today, applied plant science has three overall goals: increased crop yield, improved crop quality, and reduced production costs. Biotechnology is proving its value in meeting these goals. Progress has, however, been slower than with medical and other areas of research. Because plants are genetically and physiologically more complex than single-cell organisms such as bacteria and yeasts, the necessary technologies are developing more slowly.

Improvements in Crop Yield and Quality

In one active area of plant research, scientists are exploring ways to use genetic modification to confer desirable characteristics on food crops. Similarly, agronomists are looking for ways to harden plants against adverse environmental conditions such as soil salinity, drought, alkaline earth metals, and anaerobic (lacking air) soil conditions.

Genetic engineering methods to improve fruit and vegetable crop characteristics - such as taste, texture, size, color, acidity or sweetness, and ripening process, are being explored as a potentially superior strategy to the traditional method of cross-breeding.

Research in this area of agricultural biotechnology is complicated by the fact that many of a crop's traits are encoded not by one gene but by many genes working together. Therefore, one must first identify all of the genes that function as a set to express a particular property. This knowledge can then be applied to altering the germlines of commercially important food crops. For example, it will be possible to transfer the genes regulating nutrient content from one variety of tomatoes into a variety that naturally grows to a larger size. Similarly, by modifying the genes that control ripening, agronomists can provide supplies of seasonal fruits and vegetables for extended periods of time.

Biotechnological methods for improving field crops, such as wheat, corn and soybeans, are also being sought, since seeds serve both as a source of nutrition for people and animals and as the material for producing the next plant generation. By increasing the quality and quantity of protein or varying the types in these crops, we can improve their nutritional value. For example, a major protein of corn has very little of two amino acids, lysine and tryptophan, which are essential for human growth. Increased amounts of these amino acids could make corn products a source of improved protein.

Biopesticides and Biofertilizers

Biotechnology makes it possible to develop bacteria essential to herbicide and other pesticide compounds. Certain chemicals produced by these organisms are called allelopathic agents. These chemicals act as natural herbicides, preventing the growth of other plant species in the same geographic area. Black walnut trees, for example, release an allelopathic agent against tomato plants.

Modern high-yield agriculture entails consumption of vast amounts of chemicals for use as fertilizers and as agents to control pests and plant diseases, and any means that will permit the plant to do this work itself could result in significant savings for the farmer. For example, soybeans and certain other legumes produce their own source of usable nitrogen fertilizer by a process known as nitrogen fixation. This process is made possible by a bacterium that grows symbiotically on the plant's roots. (In a symbiotic relationship, dissimilar organisms live together in a mutually beneficial way.) In the nitrogen-fixing process, microbes capture atmospheric nitrogen and biochemically convert it into water-soluble nitrogen. This form of nitrogen is an essential nutrient for increasing the quantity and quality of plant yield.

This bacteria will not assist in the growth of other important crops, such as corn and cereal plants. But research on nitrogen-fixing bacteria and legumes may show how we can modify either the bacteria or non-leguminous plants, thereby making many crops more nearly self-sufficient in obtaining nitrogen.

Biotechnology is central to the search for effective, environmentally safe and economically sound alternatives to chemical pesticides. Biotechnology may be used to protect commercial crop plants from insect pests and promises to guard against further environmental deterioration and to provide a useful alternative to traditional methods of insect pest control.

Biopesticides degrade rapidly in the environment - a major environmental benefit. The active elements of bacterial pesticides are proteins that are fragile molecules. Once exposed to the sun and other natural elements, these proteins are quickly broken down, thereby prohibiting spread to groundwater and other animal and plant species. This will help keep our water supply safe to drink, our lakes and streams habitable for water life and recreation.

Unlike chemical pesticide technology, biopesticide technology is based on potent, naturally occurring proteins. These living particles are produced in nature by microorganisms such as Bacillus thuringiensis (B.t.). Discovered at the turn of the century, B.t. has been used without risk in the United States for almost three decades by home gardeners, farmers, and forestry officials. Its active component, a protein, specifically attacks the stomachs of target pests, disrupting their digestive tracks so thoroughly that the pests stop eating and eventually die of starvation. Higher organisms, such as mammals, fish, birds, and other non-target species remain unthreatened, however, because their stomach acid easily breaks down the protein toxin.

The delivery of these biopesticides varies in method and design. In one method, dormant spores of B.t. are dusted on crops. The spores then become active and multiply, covering plants with a bacteria poisonous to the target insects that feed on them. The B.t. toxin gene can also be inserted into the genetic makeup of crops, giving them a built-in resistance to insects. Similarly, the toxin gene can be put into a third party, such as a microorganism that lives within the plant's sap. These organisms - known as endophytes - multiply within the host plant and move throughout the plant's vascular system, forming a microscopic defense against feeding insects. This process resembles vaccines moving throughout a person's vascular system to defend against harmful disease.

Some of the concerns farmers raise about having to use increasingly dangerous pesticides to produce adequate crops may well be addressed by biotechnology. Further research in agricultural biotechnology and biopesticide development aims to provide attractive alternatives to the farmer that will lower overall unit cost of production and allow the farmer to be more competitive in the highly cost-sensitive world markets. While some uses of chemical pesticides will be necessary for decades to come, continued development by biotechnology companies of useful biological pesticides will offer farmers viable alternatives.

5. Biotechnology and industry

A Genentech-sponsored sign declaring South San Francisco to be "The Birthplace of Biotechnology."

With ancestral roots in industrial microbiology that date back centuries, the new biotechnology industry grew rapidly beginning in the mid-1970s. Each new scientific advance became a media event designed to capture investment confidence and public support. Although market expectations and social benefits of new products were frequently overstated, many people were prepared to see genetic engineering as the next great advance in technological progress. By the 1980s, biotechnology characterized a nascent real industry, providing titles for emerging trade organizations such as the Industrial Biotechnology Association.

The main focus of attention after insulin were the potential profit makers in the pharmaceutical industry: human growth hormone and what promised to be a miraculous cure for viral diseases, interferon. Cancer was a central target in the 1970s because increasingly the disease was linked to viruses. By 1980, a new company, Biogen, had produced interferon through recombinant DNA. The emergence of interferon and the possibility of curing cancer raised money in the community for research and increased the enthusiasm of an otherwise uncertain and tentative society. Moreover, to the 1970s plight of cancer was added AIDS in the 1980s, offering an enormous potential market for a successful therapy, and more immediately, a market for diagnostic tests based on monoclonal antibodies. By 1988, only five proteins from genetically engineered cells had been approved as drugs by the United States Food and Drug Administration (FDA): synthetic insulin, human growth hormone, hepatitis B vaccine, alpha-interferon, and tissue plasminogen activator (TPa), for lysis of blood clots. By the end of the 1990s, however, 125 more genetically engineered drugs would be approved.

Genetic engineering also reached the agricultural front as well. There was tremendous progress since the market introduction of the genetically engineered Flavr Savr tomato in 1994. Ernst and Young reported that in 1998, 30% of the U.S. soybean crop was expected to be from genetically engineered seeds. In 1998, about 30% of the US cotton and corn crops were also expected to be products of genetic engineering.

Genetic engineering in biotechnology stimulated hopes for both therapeutic proteins, drugs and biological organisms themselves, such as seeds, pesticides, engineered yeasts, and modified human cells for treating genetic diseases. From the perspective of its commercial promoters, scientific breakthroughs, industrial commitment, and official support were finally coming together, and biotechnology became a normal part of business. No longer were the proponents for the economic and technological significance of biotechnology the iconoclasts. Their message had finally become accepted and incorporated into the policies of governments and industry.

6. Yeast

1. General characteristics

Yeasts are one-celled fungi, 5-10μm in size. Yeast cells are usually spherical, cylindrical, or oval and are important for their ability to ferment the carbohydrates within various substances. They are widespread in nature, existing in soil and on plants. Yeasts have been used since prehistoric times in the making of breads and wines, but their cultivation and use in large quantities only started in the 19th century. Today, they are used industrially in a wide range of fermentation processes, as feeds and foodstuffs, as a source of vitamins, and to produce various antibiotics and steroid hormones. Yeasts can grow in a wide range of pH. For instance, *Candida* spp., *Torulopsis glabrata*, and *Yarrowia lipolytica* survive in the pH range from 3-8. Generally speaking, yeasts prefer to live at temperature between 25-35℃ under aerobic conditions. Pure yeast cultures are grown in a medium of sugars, nitrogen sources, minerals, and water. In anaerobic environments, yeast transforms simple sugars, such as glucose and sucrose, into ethanol and carbon dioxide.

Most cultivated yeasts belong to the genus *Saccharomyces*; those known as brewer's yeasts are strains of *S. cerevisiae*, which have been widely used for ethanol production. *S. cerevisiae* is the eukaryotic model organism in molecular and cell biology, similar to *E.coli* as the model prokaryote. Yeasts usually divide every few hours, though they have longer generation times than bacteria. Most yeasts are generally recognized as sage (GRAS), easy to be genetically modified, and easy to separate in downstream processing because of their relatively large size. *S. cerevisiae* is the most studied of simple eukaryotes. It is the first eukaryote with its genome completely sequenced and its genetics and physiology thoroughly characterized. The completion of the entire genome sequence of *S.cerevisiae* in 1996 was a milestone in the fundamental understanding of its physiology and will undoubtedly accelerate developments in the genetic improvement of *S.cerevisiae* and other yeasts.

Candida spp. Are methanol-utilizing yeasts. They produce lipases fo commercial interest, can grow on paraffin oil, fatty acids, triglycerides, and n-alkanes, and thus are widely used in bioprocessing and bioremediation. Kluyveromyces spp. can grow either as single cells or in filaments, which provide larger surface area and thus increase the product yield for industrial applications. *Pichia pastoris* can be used in the production of enzymes and recombinant proteins because it can grow on methanol to a high cell density. However, the heat generated from its fermentation must be removed due to the highly exothermic process. *Torulopsis glabrata* can decompose n-alkanes, polyols, and methanol. Its cells as well as *Candida* spp. are used for SCP production. *Yarrowia lipolytica* is well known for its ability to decompose fatty acids, hydrocarbons, and alcohols via the glyoxylate pathway. It has been considered as a preservative-resistant yeast with strong production fo extracellular lipases and proteases.

Yeasts have the advantages of rapid growth and ease of genetic manipulation. Other advantages of employing yeasts as hosts for fermentation are their abundance of metabolic activities and safety. These characteristics have brought yeasts many applications in chemical, food, and pharmaceutical industries.

2. Industrial applications

Yeasts have many industrial food and beverage production (the following table). Industrial yeasts are suppliers of enzymes, proteins, and chemicals. The commercial importance of yeasts extends to their application to the treatment of industrial wastes and effluents. For example, *Kluyveromyces marxianus* can remove heavy metals from waste stream; some *Candida* spp. can detoxify and remove pollutants from wastewater.

Industrial applications of yeasts

Applications	Examples
Baking and brewing	*Bread, beer, wine, spirits*
Bio-based fuels	*Bio-ethanol from sucrose, glucose, and xylose*
Bioremediation	*Heavy metal removal, wastewater treatment*
Chemicals	*Glycerol, bio-surfactants, enzymes, organic acids, and amino acids*
Health – care	*Human therapeutic proteins, steroid hormones*
Nutrition and animal feed	*Biomass, polysaccharides, vitamins, single cell proteins*

Alcoholic fermentation is the oldest known biological reaction. The German chemist Eduard Buchner (1897) discovered that a cell-free extract of yeast can induce alcoholic fermentation. Beer is an alcoholic beverage made from cereal grains, usually barley but also corn, rice, wheat, and oats, by yeast fermentation that consumes sugars in the grain and produces alcohol and CO_2. Two yeasts, *S. cerevisiae* and *S. bayanus*, are used to make wine by fermenting grapes. Yeast is responsible for the presence of both positive and negative odors in wine. For example, yeast may produce hydrogen sulfide when stressed. Adding nutrients to the fermentation tank can avoid this undesirable quality. The time of fermentation also determines wine character. Above all, subtle differences in ingredients determine the unique characteristics of each brewing process. Yeast fermentation is also used to make leavened breads. The main function for baker's yeast (*S. cerevisiae*) in bread dough is to produce CO_2 from sugars. The dough is placed in a warm and moist environment, enabling the yeast to multiply, and CO_2 produced during fermentation causes the dough to rise. Alcohol produced during fermentation contributes to the aroma of the bread. Secondary fermentation produces organic acids that also add to the flavor of the bread. In the making of wines, beers, spirits, and industrial alcohol, the fermented medium after separation and purification is the desired product, and the yeast itself is used in animal feeds. Yeast biomass is a rich source of proteins, nucleic acids, vitamins, and minerals.

Furthermore, yeasts contribute as hosts for expressing foreign genes not shared by prokaryotic cells in modern recombinant DNA technology. They are used to produce human proteins in spite of plasmid instability and the economic costs of providing growth medium. Gene expression is better in *S. cerevisiae* than in *E.coli* because *S.cerevisiae* is more capable of excreting and post-translationally modifying genetic products. *Pichia pastoris* has also been widely used with commercially available expression systems. Yeast RNA polymerase recognizes many animal promoters, and yeast utilizes inexpensive carbon sources. Recombinant yeasts take less time, reach higher yields, and are more genetically stable and cheaper than the insect and mammalian cell systems. Besides, yeast cultures are nonpathogenic, stable, and easy to operate and scale-up, in addition, stable mutants exist that enhance productivity.

7. Genetic engineering

The origins of biotechnology culminated with the birth of genetic engineering. There were two key events that have come to be seen as scientific breakthroughs beginning the era that would unite genetics with biotechnology. One was the 1953 discovery of the structure of DNA, by Watson and Crick, and the other was the 1973 discovery by Cohen and Boyer of a recombinant DNA technique by which a section of DNA was cut from the plasmid of an E. coli bacterium and transferred into the DNA of another. This approach could, in principle, enable bacteria to adopt the genes and produce proteins of other organisms, including humans. Popularly referred to as "genetic engineering," it came to be defined as the basis of new biotechnology.

Genetic engineering proved to be a topic that thrust biotechnology into the public scene, and the interaction between scientists, politicians, and the public defined the work that was accomplished in this area. Technical developments during this time were revolutionary and at times frightening. In December 1967, the first heart transplant by Christian Barnard reminded the public that the physical identity of a person was becoming increasingly problematic. While poetic imagination had always seen the heart at the center of the soul, now there was the prospect of individuals being defined by other people's hearts. During the same month, Arthur Kornberg announced that he had managed to biochemically replicate a viral gene. "Life had been synthesized," said the head of the National Institutes of Health. Genetic engineering was now on the scientific agenda, as it was becoming possible to identify genetic characteristics with diseases such as beta thalassemia and sickle-cell anemia.

Responses to scientific achievements were colored by cultural skepticism. Scientists and their expertise were looked upon with suspicion. In 1968, an immensely popular work, *The Biological Time Bomb*, was written by the British journalist Gordon Rattray Taylor. The author's preface saw Kornberg's discovery of replicating a viral gene as a route to lethal doomsday bugs. The publisher's blurb for the book warned that within ten years, "You may marry a semi-artificial man or woman...choose your children's sex...tune out pain...change your memories...and live to be 150 if the scientific revolution doesn't destroy us first." The book ended with a chapter called "The Future – If Any." While it is rare for current science to be represented in the movies, in this period of "Star Trek", science fiction and science fact seemed to be converging. "Cloning" became a popular word in the media. Woody Allen satirized the cloning of a person from a nose in his 1973 movie *Sleeper*, and cloning Adolf Hitler from surviving cells was the theme of the 1976 novel by Ira Levin, *The Boys from Brazil*.

In response to these public concerns, scientists, industry, and governments increasingly linked the power of recombinant DNA to the immensely practical functions that biotechnology promised. One of the key scientific figures that attempted to highlight the promising aspects of genetic engineering was Joshua Lederberg, a Stanford professor and Nobel laureate. While in the 1960s "genetic engineering" described eugenics and work involving the manipulation of the human genome, Lederberg stressed research that would involve microbes instead. Lederberg emphasized the importance of focusing on curing living people.   Lederberg's 1963 paper, "Biological Future of Man" suggested that, while molecular biology might one day make it possible to change the human genotype, "what we have overlooked is euphenics, the engineering of human development." Lederberg constructed the word "euphenics" to emphasize changing the phenotype after conception rather than the genotype which would affect future generations.

With the discovery of recombinant DNA by Cohen and Boyer in 1973, the idea that genetic engineering would have major human and societal consequences was born. In July 1974, a group of eminent molecular biologists headed by Paul Berg wrote to *Science* suggesting that the consequences of this work were so potentially destructive that there should be a pause until its implications had been thought through. This suggestion was explored at a meeting in February 1975 at California's Monterey Peninsula, forever immortalized by the location, Asilomar. Its historic outcome was an unprecedented call for a halt in research until it could be regulated in such a way that the public need not be anxious, and it led to a 16-month moratorium until National Institutes of Health (NIH) guidelines were established.

Synthetic insulin crystals synthesized using recombinant DNA technology

Joshua Lederberg was the leading exception in emphasizing, as he had for years, the potential benefits. At Asilomar, in an atmosphere favoring control and regulation, he circulated a paper countering the pessimism and fears of misuses with the benefits conferred by successful use. He described "an early chance for a technology of untold importance for diagnostic and therapeutic medicine: the ready production of an unlimited variety of human proteins. Analogous applications may be foreseen in fermentation process for cheaply manufacturing essential nutrients, and in the improvement of microbes for the production of antibiotics and of special industrial chemicals." In June 1976, the 16-month moratorium on research expired with the Director's Advisory Committee (DAC) publication of the NIH guidelines of good practice. They defined the risks of certain kinds of experiments and the appropriate physical conditions for their pursuit, as well as a list of things too dangerous to perform at all. Moreover, modified organisms were not to be tested outside the confines of a laboratory or allowed into the environment.

Atypical as Lederberg was at Asilomar, his optimistic vision of genetic engineering would soon lead to the development of the biotechnology industry. Over the next two years, as public concern over the dangers of recombinant DNA research grew, so too did interest in its technical and practical applications. Curing genetic diseases remained in the realms of science fiction, but it appeared that producing human simple proteins could be good business. Insulin, one of the smaller, best characterized and understood proteins, had been used in treating type 1 diabetes for a half century. It had been extracted from animals in a chemically slightly different form from the human product. Yet, if one could produce synthetic human insulin, one could meet an existing demand with a product whose approval would be relatively easy to obtain from regulators. In the period 1975 to 1977, synthetic "human" insulin represented the aspirations for new products that could be made with the new biotechnology. Microbial production of synthetic human insulin was finally announced in September 1978 and was produced by a startup company, Genentech., although that company did not commercialize the product themselves, instead, it licensed the production method to Eli Lilly and Company.

The radical shift in the connotation of "genetic engineering" from an emphasis on the inherited characteristics of people to the commercial production of proteins and therapeutic drugs was nurtured by Joshua Lederberg. His broad concerns since the 1960s had been stimulated by enthusiasm for science and its potential medical benefits. Countering calls for strict regulation, he expressed a vision of potential utility. Against a belief that new techniques would entail unmentionable and uncontrollable consequences for humanity and the environment, a growing consensus on the economic value of recombinant DNA emerged.

8. Single-cell protein and gasohol projects

Even greater expectations of biotechnology were raised during the 1960s by a process that grew single-cell protein. When the so-called protein gap threatened world hunger, producing food locally by growing it from waste seemed to offer a solution. It was the possibilities of growing microorganisms on oil that captured the imagination of scientists, policy makers, and commerce. Major companies such as British Petroleum (BP) staked their futures on it. In 1962, BP built a pilot plant at Cap de Lavera in Southern France to publicize its product, Toprina. Initial research work at Lavera was done by Alfred Champagnat, In 1963, construction started on BP's second pilot plant at Grangemouth Oil Refinery in Britain.

As there was no well-accepted term to describe the new foods, in 1966 the term "single-cell protein" (SCP) was coined at MIT to provide an acceptable and exciting new title, avoiding the unpleasant connotations of microbial or bacterial.

The "food from oil" idea became quite popular by the 1970s, when facilities for growing yeast fed by n-paraffins were built in a number of countries. The Soviets were particularly enthusiastic, opening large "BVK" (*belkovo-vitaminny kontsentrat*, i.e., "protein-vitamin concentrate") plants next to their oil refineries in Kstovo (1973) and Kirishi (1974).

By the late 1970s, however, the cultural climate had completely changed, as the growth in SCP interest had taken place against a shifting economic and cultural scene (136). First, the price of oil rose catastrophically in 1974, so that its cost per barrel was five times greater than it had been two years earlier. Second, despite continuing hunger around the world, anticipated demand also began to shift from humans to animals. The program had begun with the vision of growing food for Third World people, yet the product was instead launched as an animal food for the developed world. The rapidly rising demand for animal feed made that market appear economically more attractive. The ultimate downfall of the SCP project, however, came from public resistance.

This was particularly vocal in Japan, where production came closest to fruition. For all their enthusiasm for innovation and traditional interest in microbiologically produced foods, the Japanese were the first to ban the production of single-cell proteins. The Japanese ultimately were unable to separate the idea of their new "natural" foods from the far from natural connotation of oil. These arguments were made against a background of suspicion of heavy industry in which anxiety over minute traces of petroleum was expressed. Thus, public resistance to an unnatural product led to the end of the SCP project as an attempt to solve world hunger.

Also, in 1989 in the USSR, the public environmental concerns made the government decide to close down (or convert to different technologies) all 8 paraffin-fed-yeast plants that the Soviet Ministry of Microbiological Industry had by that time.

In the late 1970s, biotechnology offered another possible solution to a societal crisis. The escalation in the price of oil in 1974 increased the cost of the Western world's energy tenfold. In response, the U.S. government promoted the production of gasohol, gasoline with 10 percent alcohol added, as an answer to the energy crisis. In 1979, when the Soviet Union sent troops to Afghanistan, the Carter administration cut off its supplies to agricultural produce in retaliation, creating a surplus of agriculture in the U.S. As a result, fermenting the agricultural surpluses to synthesize fuel seemed to be an economical solution to the shortage of oil threatened by the Iran-Iraq war. Before the new direction could be taken, however, the political wind changed again: the Reagan administration came to power in January 1981 and, with the declining oil prices of the 1980s, ended support for the gasohol industry before it was born.

Biotechnology seemed to be the solution for major social problems, including world hunger and energy crises. In the 1960s, radical measures would be needed to meet world starvation, and biotechnology seemed to provide an answer. However, the solutions proved to be too expensive and socially unacceptable, and solving world hunger through SCP food was dismissed. In the 1970s, the food crisis was succeeded by the energy crisis, and here too, biotechnology seemed to provide an answer. But once again, costs proved prohibitive as oil prices slumped in the 1980s. Thus, in practice, the implications of biotechnology were not fully realized in these situations. But this would soon change with the rise of genetic engineering.

9. Introduction to Nucleic Acids and Application to Infectious Disease Detection

Advances in technology in the last 30 years have driven changes and advancements in how the

hospital clinical or medical laboratory analyzes specimens to provide useful data to physicians for patient diagnosis, monitoring or treatment of disease states or disorders. Prior to the 1970s most tests that a physician ordered on his or her patients were analyzed in the hospital clinical laboratory using manual methods which involved careful pipetting of reagents and patient samples, mixing in test tubes and using a spectrophotometer to measure; performing blood cell counts using a specially designed slide (hemacytometer) and microscope; or streaking specimens for culture growth and performing a number of biochemical tests manually on the organism to determine its identity.

In the 1970s automated testing for analysis of blood samples (e.g. glucose, cholesterol) was introduced that allowed the clinical laboratorian to perform more tests more quickly. In the 1980s enzyme immunoassay allowed the introduction of more efficient testing methods for hormones, drugs of abuse, and therapeutic drug monitoring.

In the late 1980s and 1990s further miniaturization of electronics brought the

advance of Point of Care technology that increased testing at the patients bedside or in the physicians office. The advancing technology of today is DNA or Molecular Technology. Molecular technology is at the threshold of many possibilities for use in the clinical or hospital laboratory. Currently, molecular technology is used to identify disease causing organisms, genetic disorders or tumors.

10. Use of DNA in Identification

How much spelling difference is there? Well, there is almost complete identity between any two human beings. Look at the neighbor to your left and to your right. You're 99.9% identical. That should make you feel very common, part of a common species. But of course, in a genome of three billion letters, even a tenth of a percent difference translates into three million separate spelling differences. And so I invite you again to look to the left and look to the right and notice how unique you are. There is no one in this audience who has the same DNA sequence as anyone else.

And indeed, your DNA sequence is unique amongst all DNA sequences of any human that has ever lived and will live for quite some time to come. Unless you have an identical twin, in which case you do have someone who has the same DNA sequence. But apart from that, your DNA sequence is yours and yours alone. Should you choose to leave your DNA sequence behind here in some form in some biological tissue, in principle, I ought to be able to look at it and by its uniqueness know whose it is.

Thus is born the notion of DNA identification. And it was quickly realized that this DNA identification would be especially useful in legal cases, in the criminal courts. Of course, law enforcement officials over the course of many years have looked for things that uniquely identify individuals, so as to find evidence that links a criminal to the scene of a crime. In fact, 1992 was the 100th anniversary of the use of fingerprints as an identifier.

They're uniquely powerful. They are essentially unique, and there are computer databases for fingerprints that are online across the country and are used. They're great, except that for many crimes, no fingerprints are left behind. A very common example, and an important example, is rape. For property crimes you may find fingerprints, but for many violent crimes it's harder sometimes to find fingerprints. So scientists look for other markers, biological markers, for example, as you might find in a semen sample from a rape. There has been success looking for protein differences, cell surface differences, things like the HLA complex and blood groups. But in fact, the variation is nowhere near as spectacular as in fingerprints - that is, until it was possible to read DNA.

DNA gives us rich results, and just as detailed as a fingerprint, in principle. You might think what we do is to take a sample and just read out a DNA text in its entirety. It would be a wonderful thing if we could get that from a sample, but that is the business of the Human Genome Project, not the business of the local constabulary yet. So when we do DNA comparisons, we can't read all three billion letters. What is done instead is that a very small handful of sites of variation are examined. Sites of variation here on this chromosome, perhaps, or one here, or one here, and one picks enough sites of variation to be able to have enough markers of difference.

At least in the forensic applications commonly done today, people don't actually read out the sequence. For economic reasons, for being able to do this more quickly and more cheaply, they look instead at regions that have spelling differences that are due to repetitions of some sequence. There are repeat sequences all over the genome and, in any particular region, let's pretend this is chromosome #1, you may have three copies. I might have four copies, someone else five copies, someone else one copy - typically, an unimportant repeat that has no biological function, but we all might differ.

By taking that DNA and cutting it with an enzyme that recognizes a distinctive site here, running it out by electrophoresis to be able to separate these fragments by size, and probing it with a piece of radioactive DNA from this region, one can visualize bands corresponding to the lengths of these fragments. And each of these different chromosome configurations, each of these different spellings due to different numbers of repeats, can be visualized as different-sized bands on a ladder, much like a bar code. And so a forensics scientist, examining an evidence sample E here, might probe it first with Probe #1 for the first site of variation and see the pattern. Then he or she might probe it for the next site, the next site, and the next site, and compare it to the DNA patterns taken from two suspects, Suspect #1 and Suspect #2.

If Suspect #1 has a different DNA pattern than the evidence, the suspect is excluded from having committed - well, more exactly - from having left this evidence. It's another question of how the evidence relates to the crime. But that evidence sample of DNA cannot possibly be Suspect #1's.

Suspect #2's DNA corresponds perfectly at each of the four places of variation on the human chromosomes examined. Does this mean that Suspect #2 is indeed the person who left that evidence sample? What does it mean, to say Suspect #2 is included amongst those who left it? Of course, to know how strongly we should take this evidence, we need to know how rare that pattern would be - if it's a question of population genetics - and for that purpose databases have been assembled of how frequent these patterns are in the population. These are tricky questions, and we'll return to them very briefly.

Those are simply the ideas underlying DNA fingerprinting, as it's popularly called, or DNA typing or DNA identification, as we prefer to call it. Within five years of the notion of DNA spelling differences being used for medical purposes, there were already private companies, Selmar, Lifecodes, and others, which grew up to provide DNA typing services to law enforcement officials, and by 1989 the FBI had its own DNA typing lab in the Hoover Building in Washington. There were dramatic ads in the appropriate press, such as this one here from Selmar (showing ad). "DNA Fingerprinting Links the Criminal to the Crime," with the handcuffs here being a double helix.

For the most part, this has been a dramatic and broad success. Increasingly, in rape cases, there is no need for a victim to testify about whether a sexual act took place. There's no question, typically, about mistaken identity being the problem, because DNA from a semen sample can be used to link a suspect to that semen sample. In fact, it has been useful for excluding innocent people. The FBI says that, of many test results, that they could never exclude with standard blood markers, nearly a third of those people are exonerated immediately upon DNA testing. Many rapists, because of this, now plead guilty.

In essence, DNA evidence is rapidly becoming, in principle, an irrefutable proof of identification. But of course, nothing is ever so simple. Scientists are a demanding lot, a skeptical lot, a rigorous lot. It's not enough to say it's okay in principle - it must be okay in practice as well. And although everyone agrees that this is a spectacular technology, controversies have erupted in the scientific community from time to time over whether it's really being done right. Fights erupt over DNA fingerprinting because it's such an important technology.

What have these fights been about? They have not been about how to do it in principle. They have been about how to do it in practice, and how well-regulated the practice is. For example, DNA fingerprints should look like bar codes. (Showing a slide) Here is a not-very-good example of a DNA fingerprint, which was used in a criminal case in New York. It's one I know well, because it was one where I was asked to serve as an expert witness, which is how, from my medical genetics background, I got deeply involved in this.

It was an interesting case, because it showed what scientists can do when they put their heads together. Halfway through this case, when all the evidence was being considered, all the scientists who had testified as witnesses for the prosecution, and all the scientists who had testified for the defense, met outside the courtroom without the lawyers present and talked about the evidence. And at the end of the day we agreed the evidence was terrible, and we went back to court with a joint statement for the witnesses on both sides, saying the evidence was no good. It was the first case in which DNA fingerprinting was actually thrown out because of the way it was practiced. It was also an example, I think, to the legal community, that scientists are not necessarily hired guns to say whatever you tell them to say.

The other controversy that has arisen is about how to interpret a match. What frequency should you put on it? How rare is a pattern? How odd is a match? And for this, the controversy is a technical one and a complex one, but it has to do with the fact that the frequency of the different DNA patterns of different genes vary across the population. This is actually a blood group frequency distribution. Similar things are known for other types of DNA differences. And so there has been active controversy about exactly what weight we should put on samples. Are the odds being quoted one hundred-fold too high? Are they exactly right? Maybe they're one thousand-fold too high. Scientists are arguing actively about this.

There is a good mechanism in the scientific community for focusing on such arguments. It is the National Research Council Committee from the National Academy of Sciences. For my own sins in that New York case, I served on this Committee for a period of three years, which finally culminated in the production, after a very, very long gestation, of an NRC report called, "DNA Technology in Forensic Science."

The really important thing the committee has done is calling for defined standards for laboratory work. For new standards of statistical calculations. And most importantly to my mind, it called for a mandatory proficiency test - that the laboratories that are doing this work should be subjected regularly to blind proficiency testing, to insure that they did the work well on a regular basis. It is in some sense appalling that there are no mandatory standards for something as important as forensic testing. There are higher standards, indeed for the laboratory practices of someone who will diagnose strep throat than for the laboratory practice of someone who will create a DNA fingerprint that could be used to send someone to Death Row.

Another point to mention is databases. There has been discussion about creating national databases of everyone's DNA type. That way, when a rape is committed, there's no need to find a suspect. You take the segment sample and get its DNA pattern, and compare it to a database of everyone's DNA pattern and find out whose it was. There are many people who feel understandably uncomfortable about such a national database. So legislatures have instead decided in some states to set these up, not for all citizens, but for only those convicted of, say, sex offenses, and other states for those convicted of any felony.

There is a lively controversy over what sorts of databases should be set up and there are those who say - why should it matter? Why should you care if you're in a database? After all, if you're innocent, there's no chance the technology will do you any harm. Well, even if standards are being discussed and looked at, and I'm an optimist, I feel that the standards are being worked out well. I think the Academy's report and many other steps are doing a great job of putting this on the most rigorous footing possible.

PCR is a marvelous technology to amplify DNA. It allows you to take a specific region of DNA on the chromosome, and by using little black primers here and copying back and forth, back and forth, just the particular region you want to copy, making two, then four, then eight, then sixteen, up to millions of copies of a particular region, and so in principle it is possible to start from the DNA of a single cell and get enough DNA to analyze it. That makes it possible not just to analyze blood stains of the sort that were seen before in which you could get one microgram, one millionth of a microgram of DNA, or semen swabs from a rape, some of which give you enough to analyze by standard techniques, but in fact even shed hair has enough DNA at its root. A urine sample, saliva sample, will have enough DNA in most cases. It's possible that by licking an envelope you deposit enough DNA to trace from the seal of the envelope.

Obviously, a technology that is so powerful and that is that sensitive must be used even more carefully, since you can imagine that if I sneeze on something, my DNA is there, too. And so there is tremendous need to avoid contamination. Whether laboratory practice is up to that - the proficiency tests have to be put in place to guarantee that they're up to that. These are questions under debate.

In 1975, the military in Argentina overthrew the government of Isabel Peron, and this was a very rigid ideological military. It was a military which said such things as the following quote from the military governor of Buenos Aires, a direct quote from a speech to the public: "First, we will kill all the subversives, then we will kill their collaborators, then their sympathizers, then those who remain indifferent, and finally, we will kill the timid."

They had a lot of enemies indeed (showing a slide) as shown in this "tree of subversion." This is all the subversive groups, based on a similar drawing that was made in Germany for the SS during the Nazi Regime.

I note for you just briefly, because I can't read everything, the roots of the tree of subversion are Marxism, Zionism, and Free Masonry. But other important branches include the liberals, evangelicals, the Anglicans, and the Rotary Club. It's on there.

The military junta set out in a systematic fashion to eradicate the opposition and to terrorize society, and did so with sweeps through neighborhoods, picking up subversives and non-subversives, rather indiscriminately, taking whole families at times, young families. Many people disappeared, and no one knew because of the lack of coverage, the actual scope of what was going on. They only knew their own children had disappeared.

Eventually, after the fall of the government, the Commission on the Disappearances of Persons found 9,000 documented cases of disappearances. Correcting for underreporting and the lack of documentation, it's estimated that about 15,000 persons were "disappeared." Well, as these cases began to build up, older women, grandmothers, typically, of young men and women in their 20s and 30s began to get together in the main square, the Placo de Mayo in Buenos Aires, and began to talk, as support groups for one another, looking for their lost children. They began to talk, and they began to march, and they began to protest.

And as they protested, people came to the square and shared with them stories and the stories said, we've heard of cases of children appearing in military families that were previously childless, and the wife wasn't pregnant. They would occasionally have stories from people released from prison saying that their friend had been seen alive in prison and had given birth. Midwives and obstetricians were at times kidnapped and blindfolded from the streets of Buenos Aires, taken to military prisons, forced to help in the delivery of children, then blindfolded and put back on the streets. Sometimes during the delivery, a woman might say to such a midwife or obstetrician, "My name is so-and-so. Please tell my mother." And in once case that has been documented, the midwife did this favor, and she was later killed for it.

Phony birth certificates began showing up at the schools a few years later, and registrars quietly told the grandmothers at the Placo de Mayo - or told someone who told the grandmothers - and the grandmothers took notes. By 1983, when the Falklands war led to the fall of the military junta, the grandmothers contacted the AAAS, the American Association for the Advancement of Science, and asked for help in identifying and proving that these were their children, and they demanded that genetics be used to do it. They got in touch with Mary Clair King, a professor at the University of California Berkeley - a true hero to me - a friend and colleague, whose work I am describing.

Mary Claire King went and worked with the grandmothers of the Placo de Mayo to begin, as they say, "searching for two generations." She began to try to get court orders for some of the children taken into military families, to do some sort of genetic typing and show that, indeed, they belonged to these biological grandparents, rather than to the alleged adoptive parents.

Originally, simple HLA typing was used, typing of cell surface markers, but this was not terribly powerful in these cases. DNA fingerprinting of the sort I described before was used, but for technical reasons I won't go into, was not as powerful. More powerful, unique sequences of DNA would be needed. And so Dr. King's group turned to looking at a particular bit of DNA called the mitochondria DNA. It exists in a little organelle - a little package outside the nucleus of the cell. It's a small bit of DNA, and what's important about it is that you get it from your mother. It's only passed on in the egg, not the sperm. And so mom passes it on to all her kids and every female passes it on to all of her kids. If I can read snippets of unique, variable sequence mitochondrial

DNA, I can trace maternal lineage.

The older woman at the top is Heidi Llemos, and these are two of her grandchildren. She and her adult daughter and her son-in-law were all kidnapped by the military. She was tortured and eventually released. Her adult daughter and her son-in-law were eventually killed. But the daughter was two months pregnant when she was picked up, and a prisoner told Heidi that her daughter had been kept alive and had given birth in prison.

Heidi spent ten years looking for that grandchild of hers. She eventually found a child living with a woman who had been the military guard in charge of female prisoners at the prison and, it was quite plausible that this child was her daughter's, and she demanded that the courts do DNA testing. Mitochondrial DNA sequences were obtained under court order, and were found to match perfectly between this girl and Heidi. She went to court and demanded the return of the granddaughter.

The military family made the argument, "How can you return this grandchild to a family she's never known?" claiming it wasn't in the child's best interests. The girl didn't even know Heidi Llemos. The grandmothers of the Placo de Mayo said that when the society knows that these people murdered her parents, how can you not release her, because when she becomes an adult she'll find out. Is it worse to move families now, or to find out when she's an adult that she's been raised all of her life by her parents' murderers? The Supreme Court of Argentina agreed. . . . . Overall, about 51 living children have been identified, and most of these have been restored to their natural biological families.

Let me also mention to you two other applications of DNA identification technology. It turns out to be useful in identifying not only humans, but plants as well. One of the great uses of DNA fingerprinting turns out not just to be in the criminal courts but in the civil courts - for corn and tomato cases. People spend a tremendous amount of time developing strains of corn by old breeding techniques, and they can never gain intellectual property protection for it, never get patent protection on it, because there's no way to prove this corn plant was theirs. So they put all this work into developing the strain, and someone steals the strain, and they can't prove anything about it. Well in fact, now you can do DNA fingerprinting on corn plants, and many large seed companies routinely maintain databases of the DNA fingerprints of all their important varieties, so they can go to court and prove their ownership. It creates economic protection, and it gives people an incentive to develop things.

And then, very briefly, the ultimate in DNA paternity testing. As I was getting on the plane yesterday to come here, I found in the New York Times a story about DNA taken from a 40-million-year-old termite, preserved in amber. And DNA sequencing by PCR has been done on this termite to answer questions about who is the parent of the modern-day cockroach - was it really the termite? They are comparing and finding all sorts of novel things out as to whether the termite really was or wasn't the evolutionary ancestor of the cockroach. Indeed, if we take DNA paternity testing way back, it brings us to our common origins as a species, and to the common unity of life.

Basic science. It leads us in unexpected directions that have social consequences. No one sets out to develop DNA identification, the looking at DNA spelling differences for the purpose of criminology applications. The research was driven by a whole different set of challenges and questions, and yet the capability to read and interpret DNA spelling differences has had consequences in all of these areas.

As a society, we can be pleased and proud that our technology, that our science, has had social applications, but what we must do together as scientists and as a society is to make sure that we apply these technologies with the highest of standards. We must strive to apply them - as with Argentina - to the highest of purposes.

11. "Mad Cow" Disease

As of 2001, the spread of mad cow disease in Europe-including, Great Britain, Ireland, The Netherlands, France, Spain, Germany, Belgium, Demark and Portugal and the appearance of the variant form of Creutzfeldt — Jakob disease (vCJD) in humans in many of these nations, is continuing to cause great concern among officials in Europe and in the United States. A couple of years ago the United States, in order to protect blood supply, banned blood obtained from any donor who lived in Great Britain or Ireland for six months between 1980 and 1996. these individuals are not allowed to be blood donors to the United States blood supply, for life. The issue has become even more of a concern as the spread of this disease occurs in Europe. As a consequence, the United States is considering extending the ban of donation of blood from individuals who may have lived for a time in other European countries.

Reports of diseased cattle in the British Isles and in many nations of Europe has again raised concern about the possible transmission between species of a yet-to-be clearly identified infectious agent. The syndrome presently affecting many of the cattle in the British Isles, "Mad Cow" disease, is a normally extremely rare neurological disorder that affects the central nervous system of the animal. The brain of the animal is slowly, progressively, severely damaged. It is a kind of disease which falls into the category of disease known as spongiform encephalopathy. In this particular case the disease would be known as bovine spongiform encephalopathy (BSE. An encephalopathic condition means that the brain is pathologically damaged, and spongiform means that if one examines the diseased brain tissue, the diseased tissue is spongy – porous – no longer intact.

The first reports of bovine spongiform encephalopathy (BSE) surfaced in Great Britain in 1986, and were thought to be linked to the recent practice of supplementing cattle food with bone meal prepared from slaughtered sheep. The reason for the linkage is that the disease the cattle were diagnosed as having appeared strikingly similar to that of the disease in sheep known as scrapie. Sheep with scrapie rub their bodies against walls and fences until the skin is completely raw. Eventually, the animal succumb to the degeneration of the brain. Similarly, cattle become more and more unmanageable and eventually must be destroyed. When the brains of these cattle were examined, there was clear evidence of spongiform encephalopathy.

While cattle had not before been observed with this disorder – at leat to the extent of such numbers within a herd which would lead to such investigation or reporting of symptoms – sheep had long been know to somehow acquire this disease –even though the disease is extremely rare among sheep. Consequently, as a precaution the health authorities began to operate under the supposition that this disease might have been passed from one species to another by some unidentified infectious agent. Subsequently, at least as far as I am aware, the supplementing of cattle food with sheep bone meal was halted in an attempt to stop whatever might be occurring. I am not aware of a reported case of "Mad Cow" disease occurring in the British Isles prior to 1986.

Unfortunately, there are several human diseases which fall into this category of spongiform encephalopathies, and include: kuru, Creutzfeldt – Jakob (pronounced: Kroytzfelt - Yakobe) disease, and Gerstmann – Str? Ussler – Scheinker syndrome of humans. All of these diseases result in eventual spongiform encephalopathy, and like scrapie, and now "Mad Cow" disease, are possibly transmitted by a relatively new kind of suspected infectious agent called a prion – the term prion is an acronym coined several years ago by the scientist, Stanley Prusiner. The acronym stands for: proteinaceous infectious particle – Prusiner just changed the letters around a bit. Prusiner studied the best – documented spongiform encephalopathy, sheep scrapei, and determined that the only identifiable thing which could transmit this disease from animal to animal was unlike any other infectious agent before identified – the disease appeared to be transmitted by pure protein, alone. In October, 1997, Stanley Prusner was awarded the Nobel Prize in Medicine for his identification and characterization of the Prion and the association of this protein with neurological disorders.

Now, certain extraordinarily small disease – causing infectious agents called viruses have been known for a long, long time – these infectious agents may infect for example, bacteria (know as bacteriophage), plants (plant viruses like tobacco mosaic virus), and animals (poliovirus, HIV, influenza virus, to name only a few). However, without a single exception every virus identified to date has been found to contain a genome (genetic material) comprised of nucleic acid (either RNA or DNA), which contains all of the information (genes) for the formation of virus progeny (offspring). No form of existing life ever identified on the earth – (or semi- life form like a virus which requires a host cell in order to make more virus) which can propagate its own form has ever been found to be devoid of either DNA or RNA. Only viruses have RNA as a possible genome – all other known life forms have only DNA as their central genetic information. Therefore, an infectious agent which consists of protein alone, is extremely difficult to yet comprehend, e.g., how can copies of itself be made? How can a protein cause an on – going, progressive disease and the disease be transmissible?

There is no known mechanism which accounts for protein alone serving as a template for making many copies of the same protein, or for a protein alone to cause infection (an infection is the invasion of a host by a microorganism which results in the presence and growth of the microorganism – an infection may not lead to disease – a disease is any deviation from the normal function of the body that is characterized by a defined set of symptoms – an infectious disease is there fore a disease caused by the establishment and growth of any infectious organism which results in defined dysfunction as a result of the presence of the organism or product of the organism). Although protein toxins are well –known (such as botulism toxin; tetanus toxin) – these proteins are not infectious – the organism which produces the toxin is the infectious agent and the cause of the disease – which may result from release fo the toxin from the living organism (like Clostridium botulism – botulism; or, *Clostridium tetanii - tetanus*). Yet, Prusiner and by now many other investigators have failed to identify anything but protein in these infectious particles known as prions.

As it turns out, the protein in question (prion) is also present in a normal form in all animal – it is called PrP. As far as I know, the actual function of this protein is not known. The gene which encodes this protein is found on chromosome number 20 in humans (humans have 23 pairs of different chromosomes – for a total of 46 – one of the chromosomes within each numbered pair comes from your mother, and the other from your father). The PrP protein is abnormal (structurally different in sheep with scrapie – is called PrP – c). It is this altered form of PrP (PrP-sc) which is apparently infectious. If PrP- sc is given to healthy sheep, the normal PrP is either over- produced and somehow altered to PrP- sc; the information form the normal gene (called messenger RNA) is possibly altered in the presence of PrP- sc, or, the injected PrP- sc reproduces. Reproduction may occur in the following way: altered PrP –sc proteins interact with normal PrP and this interaction causes a change in the folding pattern of the normal protein. This now abnormally folded, and therefore now abnormally shaped protein can then interact with other, normal PrP protein molecules. Consequently, over time there is an exponential increase in the number of dysfunctional PrP proteins within the cell. Thus, one would naturally interpret the appearance of more and more abnormally shaped PrP within a cell as a result of an "infection" – a result of a reproductive event that leads to a continuous increase in the number of abnormal particles inside the cell. Why this alteration of normal PrP protein to an abnormal shape results in brain damage is not yet understood. Too, how the original, altered form (disease form) of PrP enters the bloodstream and eventually enters the cells of the brain is also unknown. In this regard, a possible receptor in the membrane of cells that line the intestine may have been found that could bind and transport PrP- Sc into the cell that bound it – and therefore eventually allow the protein to enter the bloodstream.

Whatever their makeup, prions are clearly infectious; when brain tissue from infected animals is treated to isolate the protein thought to cause scrapie, and the altered form of the protein alone (prion – PrP - sc) is injected into healthy animals, spongiform encephalopathy eventually results. The transmission of disease can be accomplished by injection fo prion preparations from diseased sheep into mice – and the subsequent transmission of the disease from mouse to mouse by purification of prions from a diseased mouse and subsequent injection of healthy mice with these prion preparations.

In addition to these experimental results, the disease known as kuru (another human spongiform encephalopathy) has long been recognized and was first diagnosed among certain issue of the tribe's member who had died onto their body as a way to receive the life "power" of the victim- and later within this tribe, women who participated in these rituals acquired the disease (possibly through cuts in the skin). As cannibalism has decreased, so too, has kuru. There are other examples of a connection between an infectious agent of some kind and spongiform encephalopathies among humans – one important possible connection which has ominous association with the recent outbreak of "mad cow" disease. This connection is to the human spongiform encephalopathy known as Creutzfeldt – Jakob disease (CJD).

This human disease is extremely rare –but- there are cases of acquisition of this disease through organ transplantation (donor later found to have CJD), and receipt of human blood products (donor later found to have CJD). And, these patients have, just as the donor, the altered form of PrP, e.g., PrP-sc, present within their brain tissue. Persons receiving human blood products will be informed if the "batch" of blood product from which their material was supplied is later found to contain donor material from a person who developed CJD after donating the blood product(s) – there is no simple test for this disease. Further, Creutzfeldt – Jakob disease appears to run in families. It is not known, however, whether there is direct transmission of the disease (via an infectious agent) within the family, or whether there is transmission of genetic susceptibility to the disease, the disease CJD, is normally observed ed in humans of 50 years of age, or older.

Also, here is a site which has been established as a CJD information tracking site as well as a discussion/ support group site for those with friends or family members thought to have or known to have been diagnosed with CJD. The site is: CJD Watch.

The association of Creutzfeldt – Jakob disease (CJD) with 'Mad Cow' disease has only recently been suspected (1996 or so) – a group of younger – aged people (a cluster) within Great Brain were diagnosed with a variant of Creutzfeldt – Jakob disease – an unheard of circumstance a the time. Since then, numerous cases of vCJD have appeared in Europe and the number of cases is expected to increase. Indeed, as of January, 2001, there are approximately ninety cases reported.

These people in Great Britain and elsewhere in Europe who were diagnosed with CJD, are mostly very young – usually in their 20's. the condition CJD has before been observed only in humans older than 50 years of age. And, the lesions in the brains of these recent patients are atypical of the standard CJD symptoms- in that there are what are called "plaques" within the tissue – rather   than the predominant spongiform characteristic. These plaques are areas of pathology in the brain tissue which contain a tangled mass of a protein known as amyloid protein- this appearance of "plaugues" containing a tangled web of amyloid protein are normally found in patients who suffered from Alzheimer's disease – not CJD. Additionally, the PrP (prion protein) found within the brain tissue of these patients is indeed altered – therefore- the sum of these data is one of the connections which made health authorities suspicious that BSE had perhaps been transmitted to humans.

As said before, this disease is very rare –maybe less than two – hundred out of 270,000, 000 people per year in the United States (about one person per million people) – thus, to find a number of individuals with this disease – and in particular to find the disease among the young- and to date, only within Great Britain; the in-common consumption of beef or beef products; their relative youth; and, their similar symptomology (outward characteristic of CJD –but – all symptoms of which were atypical CJD symptoms – Alzheimer's disease – like amyloid protein plaques in the brain, prion protein in the brain tissue, all less than 50 years-old; and, rapid onset of brain degeneration once symptoms appeared). There were no apparent associations among any of the patients with potential sources of CJD – none had received any human blood products; none had received human organ transplants; and, there was no history of CJD in any of the families.

Thus, with the known outbreak of bovine spongiform encephalopathy in 1986, and more recently, it is suspected that an infectious agent – if it is an infectious agent- may have been transmitted first from diseased sheep to cattle, and now from cattle to humans. There have been a limited number of investigations since 1986 which have examined the possibility that BSE could be transmitted to humans. In one of these studies, there appears to be a species barrier which prevents such transmission.

Unfortunately, one cannot know whether or not a cow (or a person for that matter) is infected – there are no obvious symptoms of disease until the animal is significantly affected; and presently, there is an absence of methodology which could detect the disease – can't test for an altered form of PrP (PrP-sc) – found only in brain tissue (not in the blood). The symptoms in cattle appear a long time after apparent infection –early symptoms might not even be noticeable. And, there is no absolute evidence yet that this disease can or cannot be transmitted from cattle to humans. Consequently, there is currently significant debate as to the procedure to be used by the health authorities in Great Britain. One sad but possibly necessary thing to do will be to slaughter every single cow in the British Isles- a procedure with obvious devastating effects on those who depend upon the beef industry for their livelihood.

Imagine the devastating effect on the United States, if every member of every cattle herd in the nation had to be killed- as only a precautionary measure! Imagine the lengthy debates which would include testimony from scientist after scientist after scientist – virologists, neurologists, microbiologists, immunologists, biochemists; from others with knowledge of such diseases- veterinarians, physicians, statisticians; epidemiologists; from still others – economists, historians, beef industry representatives, lawyers; governmental organizations- U.S. Department of Agriculture, National Institutes of health, Centers for Disease Control, Congress, the President –every single knowledgeable person would be asked to help to decide what to do. For your information, since 1989 all imports of beef, beef products or live cattle from Great Britain into the United States have been banned.

Since 1989 the National Institutes of Health, Centers for Disease Control, and the United States Department of Agriculture have established an on-going coordinated inspection fo all cattle herds within the U.S. To date, (January, 2001) no cases of BSE have been publicly reported in the United States.

There are now confirmed reports of BES (Mad Cow Disease) appearing in cattle in other European countries; approx, 200 cases in Switzerland, 100 in the Republic of Ireland, 30 in Portugal and possibly 80 in France and Germany. Cases are also now present in Lichtenstein, Belgium and Spain.

There have been several gatherings of scientists from across the world-to aid in investigation of this possible disease transmission from cattle to humans.

These recent events provide powerful examples of how much we do not understand – and the need to support efforts to investigate such things –such as the transmission of disease among species- investigation of the biochemical mechanism of such transfer-investigation of a possible association of infectious agents (no matte what these agents might be) with neurological and other disorders –rare though they may presently be, investigation of the causes of diseases in general- among all living things. We should support genetic work which allows production of life –giving human substances in bacteria (cloning) – would prevent the exposure of humans who need human substances to sustain life, but who must presently obtain such substances from human donors.

In order to perform this work, science needs popular support- which can lead to monetary governmental support of basic research – popular support which can lead to an understanding of what science is about- the search for the truth. Science deserves an understanding by everyone for the necessity to investigate difficult, and what might initially appear to eclectic things. For such understanding, one needs education. Scientists must make this education possible, available to everyone – no matter the person's science background. To make wise but difficult decisions, one needs education. To avoid the pitfalls of panic and lack of an informed, reasoned attack on any problem – one needs education. It is hoped that the situation in Great Britain and Europe will be soon resolved without further damage.

12. Future Fuel

According to the Volkswagen Corporation, automobile fuels by the year 2000 are likely to consist of gasoline, methanol from coal, diesel oil, and liquefied petroleum gas, with only a small percentage of ethanol derived from biomass. "Gasohol," used widely during the energy crisis of the 1970s in the United States, is a blend of 10 percent ethanol with 90 percent gasoline. The alcohol production process involves three steps: reduction of the material to water-soluble sugars, fermentation to produce alcohol, and distillation by boiling to separate the alcohol from the water.

Considerable applied science and social science research went into alcohol development as an alternative source of energy. Brazil and other countries actually became committed to full-scale production, with mixed results. For a number of reasons, the energy crisis abated by the 1980s, and the avenue of alternative fuels was de-emphasized in the U.S. Nevertheless, certain discoveries were made. Alcon Biotechnology, a joint venture between John Brown Engineers and Allied Breweries, developed a continuous-fermentation process that could be housed in a standard shipping container. The process appealed to and gained approval in countries such as the

Philippines, which had been trying to produce more fuel alcohol to offset growing oil import bills. Although significant sales of the new process did not materialize, the process may revive if oil prices rise significantly.

Fermented fuel from biomass has made headway in a few parts of the world, and other processes, such as production from waste products, are being investigated by biotechnology companies. Biomechanics, Inc., for example, was one of the first companies to become involved in anerobic waste treatment technology. Anaerobic digestion of wastes takes place in the absence of air and results in the conversion of organic matter, by bacterial action, into a useful mixture of methane and carbon dioxide. In this process, over 93 percent of the effluent is converted into gas, leaving 3 percent as sludge, which is more efficient than the comparable biomass conversion into alcohol.

The first commercial bioenergy plant was built in Ashford, Kent, England, by RHM, and was followed by a second facility in Bordeaux, France. As part of a continuing development program, five mobile plants have been sited at industrial locations in the United Kingdom. They were used to treat effluents from dairy, cider, pectin, confectionary, yeast, brewing, distilling, and chemical plants. In Italy, the process was used to treat effluents from cheese and ham processing, and in Spain, in slaughterhouse operations. Savings on water charges for effluent treatment and energy savings derived from use of the methane show that a bioenergy plant can make a financial profit not realized through aerobic treatment, as well as satisfy statutory requirements for disposal of waste.

In the U.S., firms like BioTechnica have been examining methods in which landfill waste-disposal sites can be converted into "bioreactors" for methane production. Many landfills take in 5,000 tons of refuse every day. One percent of the national energy need could be satisfied by this type of process. The new concept envisions designing the landfill site from scratch as a giant bioreactor, with gas production as the basic objective. Although the overall energy contribution is likely to be small, the magnitude of the national requirement makes the technology important.

Another viable route for energy production appears to be in developing enzymes, like cellulase, which break down cellulose. An estimated billion tons of cellulose that could be converted into chemical energy goes to waste in the U.S. each year. The gene that codes for cellulase has been isolated by scientists at Cornell University and grown in large quantities by E. coli. Although still in the development stages, the finding shows how rDNA technology can eventually transform biofuel production.

The energy crisis of the 1970s produced many new ideas about energy generation, one example being photobiological generation, the production of hydrogen by whole microorganisms. Before support for this approach was reduced by the Reagan administration in the 1980s, a number of photosynthetic bacteria, nonphotosynthetic bacteria, cyanobacteria, and green, red, and brown algae were discovered. These organisms produced the enzyme hydrogenase, which is necessary to make hydrogen. Professor David Hall of King's College, London, believes that such a system could supply the world's current energy needs using 0.5 million square kilometers (0.1 percent of the earth's surface, an area about the size of France). If fossil fuel reserves become depleted, these energy alternatives may become future realities. Whether the farmer or rural areas will benefit by this possibility depends on the methods actually employed and their location.

参考文献

[1] 包怡红. 食品科学与技术专业英语. 哈尔滨：哈尔滨工业大学出版社，2007.

[2] 贾洪波，孙兴参. 生物技术英语. 哈尔滨：哈尔滨工业大学出版社，2003.

[3] 刘彩云，赵光强，常志隆. 生物学专业英语教程. 北京：科学出版社，2007.

[4] 邬行彦，储炬，宫衡. 生物工程生物技术专业英语. 北京：化学工业出版社，2006.

[5] 杨尚天. 可再生资源增值产品的生物加工：新技术及其应用. 北京：科学出版社，2007.